The ~~ROBOT~~
Who BECAME
A **HUMAN**

10 Wisdom Lessons to Become a Free
Human and Live on Your Own Terms

ANTON BROERS

BALBOA.PRESS

A DIVISION OF HAY HOUSE

Balboa Press books may be ordered through booksellers or by contacting:

Balboa Press
A Division of Hay House
1663 Liberty Drive
Bloomington, IN 47403
www.balboapress.com
844-682-1282

Cover Art by Rick van Staten

Print information available on the last page.

ISBN: 979-8-7652-3143-2 (sc)
ISBN: 979-8-7652-3144-9 (hc)
ISBN: 979-8-7652-3145-6 (e)

Library of Congress Control Number: 2022913138

Balboa Press rev. date: 09/26/2022

To Vikas Malkani,
my guru, mentor, and coach.
Thank you for lighting my path with wisdom.

Praise for Anton and his work

Having had the privilege and joy to know Anton over the years, it is lovely to see him coaching a wider audience with his powerful perspective and insights through his book.

Anton's sincere commitment to helping others is inspiring and I believe many will benefit from the principles and concepts he brings to life in this book.

Jessica Uhl
ex-CFO and Board Member, Shell

Every once in a while, a rare book comes along that has the power to change lives.
This is such a book.

A blockbuster of wisdom, this book shows you the way to live a life of happiness, success, fulfilment and freedom.

If there was just one book I had to read this year, it would be this one.
Anton has written a masterpiece.

Vikas Malkani
The Wisdom Coach

Anton has the special gift to be able to translate the concept of mindfulness in meaningful lessons and practices that I have used for some years now and that keep me balanced, considered and ultimately more happy. Many times he shares the inspiring lessons in the form of a story or a parable which makes them easier to remember and better to understand.

I am sure this book will therefore offer you practical wisdom and serve as a navigation guide to improve the rest of your life.

Johan Atema
CEO NAM B.V.

Anton is an accomplished storyteller whose beautiful book is a much-needed parable for our modern times. It is a heartfelt account of his transformation journey told through the prism of wisdom in clear and simple but compelling language.

I am transported back to the days when I met him in our meditation course years ago. He was meticulous in note-taking, diligent in practice, and deeply curious about life, purpose, joy and freedom. And on the days when I could not attend our classes, he kindly shared his notes and generously recounted the valuable life lessons taught in the session.

These priceless life lessons shine through in this narrative, which is profound yet pragmatic. Anton weaves the stories brilliantly, inviting us to shift our minds from that which keeps us bound to smallness and limitation to that which opens us to possibility and fulfilment. In an approach that blends inspiration and instruction, he imparts wisdom that illuminates, truths that liberate, and insights that empower. The call to awaken to our fullest potential is, indeed, one we should heed -- lest we sleepwalk through life.

Yvonne Corpuz
Global Executive

I have had the pleasure to experience Anton as he is in business and real life and I have seen and learned a great deal from him as a meditation teacher. He is an authentic and wise person who practices what he teaches.

I have had the privilege to preview this book. What a wonderful inspiring book! Reading the book was very special to me because I feel like I was part of his journey. I did not want to stop reading. The book is full of practical wisdom and I am already putting some of the lessons to use in my own life and my relationships. I know the inspiration in this book will positively change me and I can't wait to share the book and its content with others, including my children.

I highly recommend this book. Read it, enjoy it, keep it close to you, and use it to make your life more enjoyable, happy and successful!

Monte Fisher
Financial Controller / Consultant

A brilliant first book by Anton Broers, a company executive turned life wisdom coach.

It is an easy and engaging read and full of invaluable lessons from a first-hand journey of self-discovery and transformation.

I highly recommend this book to anyone who wants to explore how to live purposefully and fully!

Yong Shen
ex-CEO Swiss Education Group
International Business Leader / Executive

Many of us have experienced times in which we feel somehow unfamiliar with life - we're a bit lost, or have the feeling we're not doing the right thing, or life feels like a struggle. In these instances we want to take charge, course correct, and make life flow (again).

If you recognize this and want practical guidance on how to do this - read this book!

Anton has been, and still is, a great source of inspiration for me. He is a textbook example of 'practice what you preach'. Putting his wisdom lessons into practice over the past few years has absolutely made me happier, healthier and more free.

Paul Lemmens
Stay-at-home Dad

A wonderful book with valuable wisdom and empowering life lessons that can transform one's life for the better.

In *The Robot who became a Human,* Anton explains in a fun and clear manner how to reprogram our mind for a life of freedom and contentment.

It's a delightful read! I highly recommend it.

Dr. Narjes Gorjizadeh
Bestselling author of *Grow Your Mind, Grow Your Life*

Wisdom is the key to unlock life's greatest potential, bringing peace, joy, success, and happiness in the way we live, work and play. Anton Broers as a meditation and life coach brings this gift of wisdom to everyone who engages with him.

I am very glad that he has finally decided to write this gem of a book to optimize the lives of people around the world. If you want the best of what life has to offer, do yourself a favour, read this book today!

Tony Tan
CEO Imperium / Airdigital.AI
Host of the Tony Tan Show and Podcast

I would like to warmly recommend this special book.

It takes the reader on a journey of self-discovery through the eyes of main character Dax who is living his life based on patterns and fixed ideas and slowly uncovers what life has to offer when you free your mind and start living on your own terms. Each chapter provides new levels of depth and input for your own personal development toward your best life.

The book is based on Anton's own life, his experiences, learning and growth. He and I worked together as leaders in the corporate world and I find the book and the way it is written very relatable. I would like to therefore especially recommend it to anyone in a corporate (leadership) role.

Dagmar Mekking
Director of the Shell Alumni Network (www.shellalumni.org)

I have had the privilege of knowing Anton and his family for nearly 15 years, first through work and now as friends.

From the moment I met him, he has shown his passion for people and that we, through our self-control, are in charge of our personal well-being and happiness.

He has further honed his personal growth in this area since then and is now a maestro in positive self-reinforcement and a maintaining of a healthy mind and disposition.

I'm looking forward to his book and to practice the vital skills and wisdom he imparts.

Malcolm Chapman
Internal Audit practitioner

When Anton and I met in our university years we had three simple mantras for life: Set Priorities, Be Positive and Organize Yourself. Thirty years fast forward, the school of life and Anton's passion and dedication to unravel the secrets of it, have accumulated in this book.

An inspiring book worth reading for everyone who is searching for greatness and is willing to put the helm of life in their own hands. The story of Dax makes you stop in your tracks, reflect and enriches your backpack of life-skills that is relevant to your situation.

Aart-Jan van Triest
CEO Fitchannel.com

I highly recommend *The Robot who became a Human* by Anton Broers. A fascinating story packed with wisdom and life lessons that will stay with you forever.

Anton is passionate about sharing wisdom with the world and this book is a fabulous read for anyone seeking life changing wisdom.

Sally Forrest
Author – Speaker – Coach

Our life is shaped by our mind, for we become what we think.
—Buddha

Contents

Preface..xvii

Chapter 1   The Robot...1
             Know Thyself

Chapter 2   Power..17
             Citizen of Two Worlds

Chapter 3   Responsibility..37
             Stop Driving the BMW

Chapter 4   Promise...57
             Set Sail on Your Own Star

Chapter 5   Passion..77
             Follow Your Heart

Chapter 6   Priority..99
             The Most Important Person

Chapter 7   Self-Belief...121
             The Secret Ingredient

Chapter 8   Perspective 145
             Trip to the Moon

Chapter 9   Lifetime 173
             Did You Have Fun?

Chapter 10   Change 197
             You Better Dance

Chapter 11   Contribution 219
             Empty Your Pockets

Chapter 12   The Human (Freedom) 243
             Kill the Cow (or Bear)

Acknowledgments 269
About the Author 271

Preface

Life is a gift that we must celebrate, and
wisdom gives us the way to do this.
—Vikas Malkani

This is the story of Dax and his journey toward his best life. It is a journey that I wish for everybody to make in their lifetime. It is a journey that sets you up to live the life of your dreams, to live a life of meaning, to live life on your own terms, to live life in freedom. It is a journey that results in a life full of happiness, joy, inner peace and calm, contentment, abundance, achievement.

The story of Dax is based on my own personal story. It describes my learning and growth in life under the loving guidance of my wisdom teacher, Vikas Malkani. Just like Dax finds Rama to open his eyes and take his life in his own hands, I found Vikas as my guide to enter and walk the path of self-realization toward my best life.

True success in life is not only about material, outer possessions. First and foremost, it is about creating inner riches. A life without love and celebration on the inside is not a successful life.

It was Vikas who taught me that life is an inside job, that my best life starts in myself, and that when we create a rich inner foundation, our life in the external world will be similarly plentiful.

I want to share my story with you, dear reader, because it is a story that can make your life bigger, better, and brighter, just like my life expanded in all of its aspects.

I also want to share it because it is a story about essential life lessons that are not part of our standard education and learning. We are taught a lot in our lifetimes. But it is all external knowledge that we are acquiring—facts and figures that might make us understand the external world but that do not give us insight in who we are as human beings.

We don't learn about ourselves. We don't learn about our innate power and how we can take our lives in our own hands. We don't learn about our biggest treasure—the power of our mind and how to unlock it.

I know from experience how beneficial the essential learning of your inner self is.

My wife, Cate, and I found Vikas soon after we moved to Singapore, back in 2007.

Vikas has been my guru, my mentor, and my coach ever since. He has lighted my path by making ancient wisdom practical and simple. He has shown me how to live my best life through his example. He has advised and inspired me on my life's journey. My learning with Vikas has been of immense value. It has been the best investment I have made in my life.

This book is about my life, my quest, my journey, my path, my lessons, my learning, my experiences.

It is written for people like the Cate and Anton we were back in 2007: human beings who want personal growth; human beings who want to understand life better; human beings who want to unlock their unlimited inner power; human beings who want to remain calm in the storms of life; human beings who want to build a stable inner foundation; human beings who want to find more happiness and meaning; human beings who want to make the most of the gift of life.

If you, dear reader, also desire to live life to the max, you have chosen the right book.

I wish you an inspiring and enjoyable read. I wish you the materialization of your best life!

Sending you my love and gratitude,
Anton

The Robot

Know Thyself

Although we think that we think, most of the time we
are being thought by the hypnosis of conditioning.
—Deepak Chopra

Man lives like a robot. Mechanical.
Efficient. But with no Awareness.
—Osho

We all have these moments in our lives that will always be vivid memories. It just takes a small reminder or a similar situation, and our mind swirls back to the occasion or the person; the birth of our child or the day we met our loved one; 9/11 or the final of the football world championship. There are moments that are as alive to us many years later as they were at the time they happened.

I still remember the day that marked the beginning of the significant transformation of my life. My life was already good back then, but since that day I have been enjoying my life more. I am happier, I am calmer, I am healthier, I am more successful, I am on purpose, and I am more contented. Since that day, my life has become bigger, better, brighter, and braver. It was the day I met Rama in Singapore, and I would love to share my story with you.

We had lived in Singapore for a few years when I came home one night and asked Jane, my darling best friend and partner, how her day had been. She looked excited and told me about the social event she had been to and where *this guy* came to speak. *This guy* turned out to be Rama, and that morning, he had spoken about wisdom and the power of the mind and how, by deliberately choosing your mindset, you can turn your mind into your best friend and ally for life. Jane told me she felt truly inspired and that she had decided she wanted to learn from this gentleman. She said to me, "Rama will give another talk next week. Dax, you have to go. You will love it."

And so I ended up sitting in a small room with twenty other people a week later, listening to Rama and feeling energized and enthusiastic as he shared some of his wisdom inspiration. It felt like some little lights were switched on in me. The practical, insightful things he spoke about seemed to make sense and were addressing questions I had been carrying in my mind ever since I started my search for a better understanding of life many years before.

All the self-help books I had read and tapes I had listened to had given me good vibes and a bit of clarity, but not much had changed in my life. Life had continued to be quite a mystery to me, and my longing for greater appreciation and awareness had only been growing. Why was it that apparently my thoughts were so important? "As I think, so I shall be" was a line I had come across in all the wisdom books I had read, a line that still left me intrigued. Where does my thinking come from anyway? What is the purpose of life? Is it performance at school and in a professional career, creating a comfortable life with material pleasures, growing a family and a social network, and slowly but steadily getting older? Or is there more to life? Why is it that some people seem to cruise through life while others struggle every day? Is life just a random event where one needs luck, or is it possible to be the master of one's own destiny?

Over the years, I had developed an enormous longing to learn about life and how to live it, and I immediately felt that Rama might have many answers to quench my thirst. My silent thoughts reminded me of my good friend Hank. Once he had asked, while looking at my bookcase and noticing the many books about personal growth, whether these books were self-help or just *shelf*-help books. *Would it be possible to turn the self-help inspiration into real benefit for our lives?* I wondered.

As my mind was busy, I heard Rama say, "Any questions?" I woke up from my inner reflections and raised my hand. "Yes, sir," Rama said, and he signaled that I could speak.

I asked him two questions. "What would be the right training to start with?" Rama answered that learning about your mind through meditation is the basis for understanding yourself and life and thus the right start. Then I challenged him with the question of whether taking inspiration would be all worth it because, "Is change and growth possible at all? Am I not just the way I am?"

Rama smiled and kindly said to me, "Well, sir, I can certainly give you wisdom insight and share life lessons with you that have worked for many, including for myself. But you will only know whether such guidance is valuable and beneficial based on your own experience. So if you want to know, step forward, take action, learn and practice, and see for yourself."

I went home that evening feeling energized, curious, and convinced that I would like to start learning with Rama. Little did I know what a fantastic ride it would become—a ride that would easily exceed any expectations I might have had about my own power and freedom. Jane was not surprised to welcome me home in such an exuberant state. "My gutfeel tells me," she said, "that learning from Rama is exactly what you have been yearning for ever since we met, Dax. I am ready to be inspired as well. We are in this together."

Basic mind training with Rama started a few weeks later. Although I was excited, I also felt a sense of hesitation when I was on my way to the classroom. Doubts were roaming my mind. What if the lessons made you feel good in the moment of hearing them but did not do anything for your life thereafter? What if, after all, it was just impossible to change? What if, as human beings, we were just wired in a certain way, and our destiny in life was just a given? I had heard stories of motivational speakers who were hired for amazing sums of money by companies to imbibe a change spirit in their employees but without lasting success. A few days after the high-energy, almost hysterical, speaker engagement, where the people seemed to be ready for anything, nothing was left of the apparent change spirit. People were as adamantly against the change as before. They were also wondering why they had allowed themselves to be seduced into making all kinds of commitments because of the external excitement, while on the inside they had never been convinced. Would this be one of those events?

The atmosphere in the room was relaxed and welcoming when I arrived. There were various other students who were quietly chatting with each other or calmly waiting for the class the start. Soft music was being played in the background, which had a soothing effect on me. I was walking around, taking in the place, and looking at some of the products that were offered for sale. I saw books and tapes and all kinds of bracelets, chains, and stones, the purpose of which I was not familiar with at the time. While I was getting settled, suddenly someone tapped on my shoulder, and when I turned around, I looked into the happy and gentle face of Rama. He said, "Welcome, Dax. Very good you have come. It looks like you have stepped forward despite your doubts and questions." Rama supposedly could read my mind.

I responded, "Thank you, Rama, and yes, my curiosity won the battle over my doubts, so here I am. Still, I am not sure whether I am able to change. I am not sure that it is possible. I have seen so many people around me wanting to change, but they never did."

Rama listened calmly and said, "As human beings, we always have a choice. You have decided to attend this basic mind training. Did somebody else make the choice for you, Dax? No. You did, right? This is one of the fundamental lessons of life. You always have a choice. It is your birthright. Cannot be taken away from you. When you get to know your mind and start to train it, you will learn about your inherent power and how you can make your choices in the most optimal way. It is great you have taken the action to be here. We can all change, but without action, no results." Rama laughed graciously, nodded his head, and went on to welcome other people. I felt a bit more confident about my choice to start my mind-training journey.

Everybody sat down when it was time to start. Rama was standing in front of the group of students and watching silently. I noticed the serenity, stability, and strength that he exuded. He was clearly enjoying himself in a calm and peaceful way. At exactly 7:00 p.m., Rama began the training.

"Welcome to the day that your life will change. Your training with me is about inner transformation. It will be all about you. Change does not result from outer injection. External advice or external knowledge at best leads to temporary change. Structural change requires inner change. You change when you change your inside, when you change your inner system. The masters say, 'As within, so without,' so here is my promise to you: when you work on your inner self, change in your outer reality *will* happen. Guaranteed. You have a challenge to overcome though. Without you knowing and through your external training and upbringing, you have forgotten what it is to be a human being. You are all *robots!*"

I still remember Rama's opening sentences, and I will probably never forget them. They hit me, they impacted me, and they were a wake-up call. I listened intently to the rest of the insights and stories that Rama shared that evening, but my mind had gotten stuck on these questions: *Am I a robot? How? What does it mean?*

I drove home. Jane was still awake, and so was I. I felt more awake than ever. We sat down and talked for the next two hours about Rama's words. They somehow resonated at an intuitive level, but I found them difficult to understand. My idea about robots was quite different from what Rama had suggested. In my mind, a robot was like a tool that can be programmed to execute certain actions. A robot acts automatically. With a robot, you know what you can expect. That's why in industries, more and more, people are replaced by robots for standard labor activities. As a company, you know what you are going to get, and besides, robots never complain. How was I a robot?

I had a good night of sleep in which I dreamt about robots. They all had different human faces. It was clear that my mind was actively overthinking what I had heard the evening before. I woke up feeling curious and alive. Under the shower, I remembered an inspirational line that I had come across many times in my self-learning: when the student is ready, the master appears. I couldn't help thinking that I was the student and that the moment had come to meet Rama, the master, and to really learn about life. At breakfast, I picked up my phone and wrote the following WhatsApp message:

> Dear Rama,
> Your inspiration last night has been a big eye-opener for me.
> I feel more interested than ever and don't want to wait to hear more till the second training session.
> Can we meet earlier please?
> Thank you, Dax

Later that morning, I received a response with an invite to meet Rama that same evening. I could not think of anything else the rest of the day.

I entered the place where we were meeting with a slight feeling of nervousness. I could detect both a feeling of positive anticipation, an eagerness to learn more, as well as a negative disbelief, a fear that my hopes were still way too high. *Apparently, our mind is capable of having a positive and a negative perspective on the same thing,* I thought.

Rama was already there and welcomed me with his calm and kind demeanor. "Sit down, Dax. Let's chat," he said. "I believe you enjoyed last night. Is that right?" I nodded. "And you were very intrigued but also challenged with my statement that you are not a human being but a robot. Correct?" Again, I nodded.

"Let me explain, Dax. This might give you the clarity that you have always wanted to have. You *are* a robot! In fact, almost all people are robots. You are robots living according to the standards of society; living according to the ideas and convictions of other people; living according to the rituals and practices of the tribes you are part of.

"You are not born robots. You are born utterly free, full of potential and ready to live and enjoy the life of your dreams. But then, as you grow up and without knowing or realizing it, slowly but steadily, you are molded into carbon copies of the world and the people around you. I am not talking here about your physical appearance. Many people believe these days that beauty through plastic surgery brings happiness, which, by the way, is a very wrong belief. No, I am talking about the molding of the mind. We are all born with a mind. We are not born with a mind*set*. Our mindset consists of our ideas, our beliefs, our convictions, our expectations, our conditioning. While you grow up, your mind gets set on the basis of what you hear and see and feel and observe around you. In short, your mindset develops based on the examples of your surrounding environment and the people you interact with. Most of you are not aware of this, and you never question your mindset.

"The first really important thing you need to understand, Dax, is that your thoughts create your reality. Masters throughout the ages have said, 'As you think, so you shall be.'"

Wow! There was the sentence that had intrigued me for so long, and now, without asking, Rama had brought it up. This was not a coincidence. I knew I was in the right place at the right time and I was on the verge of getting answers to questions that had kept my mind busy for a long time. I couldn't contain my enthusiasm. I was moving around on my chair.

Rama continued. "Your mindset is the basis for your life. You can choose how you set your mind, but usually people don't do this deliberately. Unconsciously, we develop a mindset based on the mindset of other people. The right mindset can truly help you in your life. But unfortunately, most of us do not develop a supportive and empowering mindset. Let me share with you examples of ideas that people learn in their childhood that can become part of their mindset:

"I have to comply with the rules.

"I have to get good grades at school.

"I have to compete and win.

"I have to make sure other people like me.

"I have to look like Kim Kardashian.

"I have to gather and own material stuff.

"I have to listen to my parents and teachers.

"I have to be nice and well behaved.

"I have to help others; I cannot say no.

"I have to be realistic in life; big dreams only result in disappointment.

"I have to adjust myself to the group.

"I have to contain my emotions.

"There are many *I have to* instructions branded in our mind. Many times we think, *Only if I comply with these instructions am I good. If I do differently or behave differently, I am not good.* It is wise to understand, Dax, that these are rules that have been defined by others and that you have unconsciously accepted and adopted. Your mind has been programmed by others, and these rules impact how you live your day-to-day life, silently and automatically. That is why you are a robot. Without being aware, you live according to preprogrammed ideas and expectations."

I was listening intently. This made good sense. I was going over my inherited ideas about life, and I had to agree with Rama that much of what I was thinking was not necessarily of my own deliberate choosing. Why was I pursuing the professional career I was in? Why did I think that Ralph Lauren clothes were so cool? Why did I frequently not speak my mind but instead chose to keep my thoughts inside? Why did I not like confrontations with other people? Many questions about choices I had made appeared in my mind. And at the same time, I was thinking, *Is it possible to get a different programming of my mind? How do I change my mindset if I want to? What is a mindset that would truly help me in my life? How do I find out better what I think myself?*

Rama noticed my mind at work and asked me how I was doing. "Feeling good, Rama. I am chewing on the things you are sharing with me. Triggers many questions."

"That is very good, Dax," Rama said. "You can only start to think for yourself if you learn to consciously connect with your own thoughts. You are on your way!" he said with a smile. "Not all inherited mindsets are bad, you know. If your robotic mindset serves you in life, great! The thought *I am good, no matter what*, for example, is a powerful mindset to have and will help you in many challenging situations that you might encounter in your life. But much of the ideas that have become part of your robot mind are not helpful to you. They do not support you in living life on your own terms. They block you, they keep you small, they guide you toward wrong decisions, and they hinder you from being authentic and real and true to yourself. I love to tell stories to illustrate the point I am trying to make. Let me tell you about a little eagle.

"An egg fell down from an eagle nest high up on a cliff. It landed next to a little pond where a duck was swimming around. The duck noticed the egg, swam toward it, picked it up, and brought it to the nest that she and her lovely partner had built a week ago. The duck put the eagle egg next to her own eggs, and from that moment on, the duck couple took care of the egg. A few weeks later, little duckies and a little eagle were born. They left their eggs, looked around in excited anticipation, and started living. The little birds all grew up as one happy duck family. They swam in the pond, walked on the land, flew a bit to bridge small distances, and ate grass, weeds, small insects, berries, and nuts. They quacked and splashed the water together, and they made sure that they were not grabbed by dogs and cats and pikes and rats. Mum and dad duck and all the other members from the large duck tribe in the meantime were continuously cheering the little children on their progress and telling them they were growing up nicely. The little ones became fine adult ducks.

"One day, a wise old eagle flying high up in the air was scanning her surroundings. When she looked down and spotted the pond, for a moment she thought she saw an adult eagle among ducks. She flew down to confirm her impression, and yes, there was a healthy, strong eagle swimming around in the pond, following a group of ducks. She did not understand what she was seeing. She sat down on the side of the pond, whistled toward the eagle, and shouted, 'Hey, my friend, come over here.' The eagle's reaction was a reluctant one. Could he trust this large prey bird? But the wise old eagle immediately said, 'Don't worry. I just want to ask you a question. I am not here to hurt you.' After a while, the eagle in the pond found the courage to swim toward the visiting eagle and looked at her. She said, 'What are you doing here? Do you know that you are an eagle who is supposed to fly high up in the skies?' The duck eagle looked in amazement and said, 'What do you mean? I am a duck!'"

Rama took a deep breath and then asked, "How do you like that story, Dax? Does it somehow sound familiar?"

Yes, the story certainly hit home for me. It instantaneously brought back memories from my own life where I had not pursued my dreams or followed my gutfeel because I believed I couldn't. I shared the example of me really liking this girl but never finding the courage to tell her. She loved dancing, and one time at a party, she was on the dance floor all alone. My friends, who knew I liked her, tried to coax me to join her, as this was my chance. I told my friends, "I am not a dancer," and I did not. After the school year, she and her family moved to the other side of the country, and I never saw her again.

"Typical example," Rama retorted. "We all have unlimited potential, but we keep ourselves small through our thinking. The thought *I am not a dancer* kept you from taking action. Never mind though, Dax. Life always presents you with second chances. It looks to me like you found your best friend and partner in Jane. Am I right?"

I smiled and said, "Yes, Rama, you are very right!"

Rama proceeded. "When you grow up with the wrong ideas, you will just grow old. When, on the other hand, you develop the right mindset, you possess all that you need to live a great life. Nothing will stop you from growing to be who you want to be. It is all about getting to know yourself. Have you ever heard of the Oracle of Delphi, Dax?"

"Yes, but what about it?" I said.

"People from Athens, Greece, used to visit the wise men and women at the Oracle of Delphi to seek their counsel and advice on life's problems. The oracle was located on a mountain, so people had to climb many stairs to get there. Any advice they received from the sages on the mountain was similar: look at yourself. They did not even have to climb all the stairs to get this wise counsel. On the first step of the stairs, carved out by craftsman, the following inscription could be found: *Know thyself.*

"You see, Dax, the resolution to any problem you think you have in your life lies in you. The masters would say that it is just a matter of getting to know yourself. And do you know how you can do this? You get to know yourself through getting to know your mind. Mind training, also called meditation, introduces you to yourself, and that is the only way to become human and take life in your own hands."

"Rama, can you please elaborate?"

"Let me give you an example, Dax, to illustrate how you can make your own decision with mind awareness. Somebody does something, and you react as if a button has been pushed. Your inner software, your robotic programming, makes you react in an automated way. Before you know it, you have unconsciously created a problem with this other person.

"Let's say somebody insults you, and you become angry. This has happened before. You have learned to become angry in case somebody offends you. You think, *Why does this person do this? Who does he think he is? It is right to be angry with the other when he hurts me like this. It is right to show the other person that I am strong, and I have to exercise my strength through fighting back.* And after these preprogrammed, split-second considerations, you reach out aggressively to the one who insulted you. Your learning from the past has resulted in your unconsidered reaction in the moment.

"So here it is, the robotic behavior: somebody pushes your button, and you become angry.

"The robot does not take a moment to observe the situation and assess the circumstances. The person who is insulting you may be right. Or the person may be a fool and completely wrong in his remarks. Or the person may just be a nasty person, someone who enjoys throwing insults at other people. If the person happens to be right, your response could be one of gratefulness. Feedback that is true and that can help you develop and grow is a good thing. So rather than getting angry back, you could thank the person for his helpful suggestions. If the person is just stupid and knows nothing about you but still throws negative things at you, why would you react? There is no need. The other is just plain wrong. Why would you be concerned with things that you know are just wrong? It is ridiculous to get excited about such remarks. If the person is just a bad person who takes pleasure in throwing insults at others, there is nothing you need to do. You can simply realize that this is who this person is, and therefore the remark is not personal, and you can leave it.

"You live in a mechanical, robot-like way. You have been programmed by the past, and just the push of one of your buttons is enough to throw out your standard emotions and reactions. This does not serve you. It basically means that the people around you, the circumstances happening to you, and the situations you are in lead your life. You have given your control away. Something happens, and you react automatically. You are not leading your own life. You are not the boss. Circumstances and other people are."

"I understand what you are saying, Rama."

"When you get to know the software of your mind, Dax, you will get to know yourself. You will find out what part of the robotic programming serves you in life and which elements do not. Through mind training, you can reprogram yourself, and you can start taking back control over your life. It does require effort, Dax, but the good thing is that everybody can do this."

I took a deep breath. I was taking in everything that Rama was so graciously sharing with me. I watched the clock and saw that three hours had passed seamlessly. I had hung on Rama's every word and lost track of time. I realized I was learning more about myself and about life in a matter of hours than in all my twenty-plus educational years together. Jane and I had been good students during our school and university days. We had both proven that we were very capable of taking in information and reproducing it effectively when taking exams. It had gained us well-recognized diplomas and job opportunities in the labor market. But all that external knowledge had not helped us to understand ourselves. It had not taught us about our inner mind power. And I now realized it had set us up to live ordinary lives in many ways.

I remembered the story of the American company Invisible Fence. This company developed an inventive solution for keeping dogs on the owner's non-gated premises. Invisible Fence places a simple, easily removable fence around the property and puts a small receiving device around the neck of the dog. Whenever the newly arrived puppy is outside the house and gets too close to the fence, it gets a small electrical shock. In a number of weeks, the little dog learns where it can go without getting the unpleasant little shock. Then the company comes back and removes the temporary fence because it is no longer needed. The result is that the dog will never leave the premise on his own again.

I relayed the story to Rama.

"I like it," he said. "Good example of how we all get conditioned and how it impacts our lives. Although the threat of the electrical shock is no longer there, the dog will never leave the premise on its own because it believes it will get hurt when it moves beyond the property boundaries."

Rama paused.

"You are also conditioned, Dax. Do you know that? Everybody has a conditioned mind. You get conditioned to accept certain circumstances even if they are detrimental to you. You get conditioned to behave in a certain way even if the results from such behavior are not in your favor. You get conditioned to unconsciously react to situations, just because that is what you have learned, even if the reaction does not serve you. Conditioning is the thing that turns people into robots. Just like the little puppy dogs, you learn it without realizing it, and you never ever question until you become aware of it."

The clock indicated it was past midnight. Rama did not show any trace of fatigue, but I started to feel tired. Much of my doubt had been replaced by the *I want more* sensation. I felt inspired, but I also observed that my mind was working overtime. I was not able to take in a lot more lessons from Rama. I *wanted* more, but I first needed a rest.

Rama looked at me and said, "This is probably enough for tonight, Dax. You already knew to some extent how important your thinking is: as you think, so you shall be. Much of your thinking is fixed in your mindset. It is wise to realize that your thinking is the basis for your whole life. I always say you can reconcile your life with your mindset. That is why your mindset and thoughts are so important. You now know that much of your mindset has been imprinted by others. You have adopted other people's perspectives and ideas of life without ever asking whether that is what you want. You don't adopt a puppy without getting to know the puppy, do you? You should also not adopt the ideas of others without validating them. But it happens. It happens unconsciously. You don't realize it. But now you have become aware. Awareness is the first step toward change."

"You have given me much food for thought, Rama, Thank you!"

"When aware, Dax, you can ask yourself, 'What mindset would I like to have?' The right mindset sets you up for your biggest, brightest, and best life. We can all develop it. It does require time, energy, and effort, but it is all well worth it. Who does not want to live life to the max?"

"I want to!" I responded.

"I can be your guide on this journey, Dax. I can show you the path. That is what I do. So the question is, are you interested in going on this wonderful quest toward your best life?"

The Robot—Learning Box

Wisdom	As I think, so I shall be (in other words, my thoughts create my reality). Structural change requires inner change. As I change my inside, my outside experience of life will change. As within, so without. Only in that order. I have unlimited potential, but I keep myself small through my (conditioned) thinking. Awareness is the first step toward change.
Awareness	You are a *robot*! Your *mind* has been largely *set* (mindset) by others, not by you. You are conditioned. Your mindset is the basis for your life. Your mindset (invisibly) guides your life. You always have a choice. It is your birthright. You can learn to choose your thoughts and set your mind. When you live in a mechanical, robot-like way, you are not the boss over your life. You are being led by other people, situations, and circumstances. When you get to know your mind and train it, you can start to reclaim control over your life.
Story	The eagle who thinks he is a duck. *(You are an eagle!)* Invisible Fence
Practice	Get to know your mind. Watch your thoughts. Become aware of how you think.

2

Power

Citizen of Two Worlds

You are the author of your own life story.
—Vikas Malkani

A man is but the product of his thoughts.
What he thinks, he becomes.
—Mahatma Gandhi

I woke up early the next morning. I had slept well and dreamt of some kind of adventure into the unknown. I thought back to last night. "Inspiration can truly give a boost," I reflected. The night had ended with a big hug between Rama and me. Rama had explained that hugging is a very powerful and healthy habit. A hug fulfils our inner longing for affection and attention, and our body benefits from physical touch. "A loving hug charges your inner system," Rama had said. Although I did not fully understand what he meant with the inner system, I had felt the positive energy from our goodbye hug. Rama's last words, just before I jumped in my car to go home, had been "Enjoy your night, Dax, and let me know if you are ready to embark on the odyssey of your lifetime!"

At breakfast, I shared last night's events with Jane. I must have beamed with joy and passion because she said, "Wow, it is clear that you are super excited. Your enthusiasm is contagious!" She smiled, looked at me, and asked whether I thought I was ready for the next step. Jane said, "If you ask me, this is an opportunity not to be missed, Dax. I support you all the way!"

I gave her a big hug. "You are the best, Jane. Thank you for your gracious and selfless support."

My self-help study had taught me an important lesson: life presents us with opportunities. Many people do not believe this to be true. They look at their lives and conclude that they are the unlucky ones who simply don't get any chances. They think, *I just have to live with it; it is not my fault.* I had had some of that fatalistic thinking going on in my life. I remembered the time when I had been really jealous of the colleague who had gotten an early promotion at work. I was of the opinion that I should have been selected, and I felt sorry for myself: *I never get these kind of opportunities.* After learning the lesson, I became more actively focused on finding the opportunities. It worked. I started spotting more opportunities in my life, including this fantastic one to live and work in Singapore. Working and living abroad had been one of my childhood dreams. There are always opportunities, but you might miss them, I had learned. Based on the conversation with Rama, I now understood this better. "My mindset and my thoughts must have an impact on spotting opportunities," I reflected.

Rama's offer to guide me to develop the best possible mindset for life certainly was a great opportunity. Jane had immediately confirmed this. She was much more sensitive to whatever life was offering than I was, and I had learned over the years that her gutfeel usually was spot-on. When life presents you with an opportunity and you recognize it, there are only two options: you can step forward and say yes or you can step back and say no. People many times choose the no option, sometimes for good reasons but many times for the wrong reasons of fear and doubt. Fear and doubt keep us small in life.

They make us step away from the good things that are available to us. I caught myself getting trapped in exactly these kinds of limiting thoughts. My mind had unconsciously already started looking for reasons why I should not pursue the possibility that Rama had given to me. *Will I have the time? What will it cost? Is this really something for me? What to do with the appointments in my calendar? Can I do this? Is my excitement just a thrill of the moment? What if the wisdom inspiration is not true?* My mind was busy validating the no option, and I was aware of it. My doubting mind had gotten hold of me again. Jane was clear in her advice: "Share your concerns with Rama and ask for his guidance."

Rama was available for a short coffee a few days later. "Welcome to your robotic mind, Dax!" he started off, saying with a smile. "As we grow up, many of us are taught to think in problems, to focus on what might go wrong or what is missing. This perspective of the mind becomes a habit, and whenever an opportunity occurs, automatically the mind starts looking at it from the *why not* angle. The mind is a powerful tool, Dax. Never underestimate its force. You give your mind a task, and it will deliver. Unconsciously, you have given your mind the assignment to find issues and reasons to say no. Believe me, your mind will find them. You will find what you seek is age-old wisdom. It is therefore wise to become aware of the exact instruction you give to your mind. Your mind will help, but if you give it the wrong instruction, the result might not be what you really want. You get what I am saying?"

I did. I nodded. Then I asked, "So now what, Rama?"

"I don't have a lot of time this morning, Dax, so I only have a few things to share with you. Firstly, it is *your* decision. You owe it to yourself to take your own decisions in life. Especially when it is a big decision. It is your life, not the life of somebody else. Secondly, ask your mind why a yes might be the right answer. See what positive arguments your imaginary mind comes up with. You with me so far?"

"Definitely!"

"Excellent. Thirdly, when you were young, you learned to swim, right? Do you think you would have learned to swim if you had never jumped in the pool? Here is the thing, Dax: sometimes in life, the right answer is yes, and you will have to leap despite all the fearful thoughts in your mind. The only reason you learned to swim is the fact that you jumped in the water and got started."

"True."

"Fourthly, let me give you an ancient wisdom lesson for life. This one has been shared by masters throughout history because they knew how cunning the mind can be. Most people live with a mindset that says, 'I will believe it when I see it.' This is a mindset that holds you back; it stops you in your life. The mindset of the wise is *I will see it when I believe it.* The wise master keeps an open mind to life, believing in the impossible. This mindset helps to live a bigger life with better results. It helps to take action and leap. Check your mind, Dax. See what you think, and choose what you want to think!"

Rama looked at me. "I hope this helps. It is now over to you, my friend. I will patiently await your response." He gave me a big hug, and with that, Rama was gone.

I used the days thereafter to make up my mind. As Rama had instructed, I assigned my mind to help me find reasons to say yes. Although the occasional no thought still appeared, I found that his advice worked. I started seeing many reasons why yes would be the right answer. These reasons gave me a sense of liberation, a feeling that I could be free to live life on my own terms, whatever exactly those were. Also the wisdom line on first believing, then seeing did its work. I remembered moments in my life where, despite uncertainty, my belief had been strong and had helped to create the experiences I wanted. It had taken quite a while for me to say, "I love you," to Jane for the first time. My belief that it was the right thing to do had only been getting stronger, but still I delayed speaking the words for a long time. When I finally jumped, I gained the loving, joyful, and supportive relationship I had always hoped for.

As I changed the way I was looking at the opportunity provided by Rama, I found that my perspective on it changed. A week after he had told me that we are all robots and had invited me on the journey to become human again, I sent him a brief message:

Dear Rama,
I am ready to jump!
Dax

Jane and I were having dinner two days later when our doorbell rang. I stood up, walked to the front door, and opened it. A young girl from the mail delivery service looked at me with a friendly face. "Mr. Dax?" she asked. "Yes," I said, and she handed me a package. "This is for you." I thanked her, closed the door, and went inside. We did not have any pending purchase orders. Surprise packages always give me the Santa experience, a pleasant curiosity about the inside. Although we were still eating, I could not contain myself, and with Jane's nonverbal approval, I opened the parcel. I found a small, handwritten letter and a closed envelope. I first picked up the letter and read the following.

Dear Dax,
Congratulations on your decision to jump toward your best life!
I am very happy for you.
Your first stop: New Delhi, India.
I have made an appointment for you with my good friend Master Amir.
Flight tickets and hotel reservation in the envelope.
Keep your mind open and enjoy!
Sending you my love and a big hug,
Rama

I was perplexed. When I looked at the tickets, I noted a travel time coinciding with the public holiday a week later. *Impeccable planning, Rama,* I thought.

Jane was as amazed as I was. "I guess off you go," she muttered. We finished our dinner in silence, overthinking the big surprise.

It was an early-morning flight to India. The sun was still rising, and the sky was a beautiful blue-orange with a few mysterious dark gray clouds. I did not know what to expect. I was on my way to the hotel that was mentioned on the reservation, but I had no idea how and where I would be meeting with Master Amir. I was consciously practicing Rama's guidance to believe in order to see, and I was pretty confident that it would all work out fine. The flight landed on time, embarkation was efficient, and soon enough I was in line to catch a taxi to my hotel.

I had never been to India. I knew the country via Mahatma Gandhi's story and legacy. I felt a bond with the country through my connection with various masters of life whose wisdom and lessons were a daily inspiration for me. I had learned in school and via the news about the sheer amount of people living in India and the fast economic growth the country was realizing. So I knew a bit about India but not really, because to know, you have to have experienced. My India experience started in the taxi. My respect for the taxi driver grew by the minute. The way he was navigating through traffic was simply impressive. Nice roads but too many cars. It was the first time in my life that I saw six rows of cars in only three lanes, all going in the same direction. No spot on the highway was left empty. Whenever one car gave some way, another car filled the gap. I was watching in astonishment and was glad that I was not sitting behind the steering wheel. When we left the highway, the many cars were supplemented with large crowds of people. The driver woke me up from my bewilderment when he suddenly said, "Sir, we have arrived at your hotel." We drove through a gated entrance, and from one second to the next, we had moved from truly busy land to a place of serenity and quiet. I thanked the taxi driver wholeheartedly for getting me safely to my hotel.

I checked in at the front desk, and with the card key in my hand, I started walking toward the elevator when the hotel clerk shouted, "Sir,

sir! Sorry, I forgot. There is a message for you." I turned around and looked at the courteous girl behind the counter. "This morning, an advanced master honored us with a visit to the hotel. When he walked in, the lobby fell silent. People felt the presence of an enlightened being. He informed our concierge, Mr. Dax, that you would be arriving at lunchtime and asked him to tell you to be in front of this coffee shop at three p.m. today." She handed me a little piece of paper with the name and address of a coffee shop. "He thanked the concierge, and then he left as graciously as he had arrived."

"Thank you," I said. I now knew where to meet Master Amir. This gave me one hour to freshen up. I took a shower in my beautiful hotel room on the third floor, put on comfortable clothes, called for a taxi, and asked the taxi driver to bring me to the address on the note.

Although traffic was hectic, I arrived at the indicated address thirty minutes early. I was in a little park with trees, nicely mowed lawns, and benches everywhere. Surrounding the park were all kinds of stores, mainly shops selling food and beverages. Kids were playing, and everywhere I looked, I saw local people relaxing, chatting, or waiting in line at one of the shops to get a consumption. There were hardly any other tourists. I noted the coffee place, and I decided to just wait and enjoy the livelihood of the surroundings. "Master Amir will probably be able to find me," I guessed.

He did. Out of the bustling crowd, exactly on time, a youthful-looking man suddenly appeared. He walked straight up to me and said, without hesitation: "Hi, Dax. Nice to meet you. I am Amir." I must have looked surprised because the man immediately added, "You are kind of the only Westerner here at the moment, Dax. So I figured it must be you. Right?" I looked at Master Amir. He was elegantly dressed in khaki pants with a nice light blue jacket and comfortable Nike sneakers. The master exuded a stable and peaceful yet powerful energy. He looked at me with a kind and patient expression, with the brightest eyes I had ever seen. "Dax?" he repeated.

"Uh, yes, Master Amir, it is me. Dax. I am so glad and honored to meet you. Thank you very much for having me."

"Nice to meet you too, Dax, and please call me Amir. I know Rama introduced me as Master Amir to indicate that maybe I can teach you things that are beneficial for you. But we are all potential masters. We all have things to teach to other people. Unless you prefer to go with Master Amir and Master Dax, let's just use Amir and Dax. All right?" Master Amir had a big smile on his calm face.

We bought a coffee and set out for a stroll.

"You have arrived in India for the first time, and you have come here to learn a bit. Right, Dax? Learning requires an open and observant mind that is available in the moment to learn from anybody and anything. Many people have closed minds because they think they know everything. They believe that their opinions and ideas are the best, and they are in a constant fight to convince others to accept the viewpoints they have. An open mind requires space. If your mind is full—that is, full of yourself—nothing can be added. With a full mind, you miss what life has to offer and teach you. The ignorant people think they know it all; the wise realize that they hardly know anything. It is reported that the Oracle of Delphi declared Socrates the wisest man of the world on the same day that Socrates declared, 'I know nothing,' to some of his students. People were puzzled and went to confront the oracle. 'You must be wrong this time.' The oracle laughed and said, 'Only the wisest person in the world has the courage, the innocence, and the humbleness to declare, "I know nothing."' If you want to learn, Dax, open your mind and create some space. That way, you truly have the opportunity to grow from your life experiences. Are you ready to learn, my friend?"

I nodded. Yes, I was eager to learn!

"We will go for a walk, Dax. I want to show you daily life in Delhi. Be an observer. Keep your eyes open. Keep your other senses open and learn."

With that, Amir set out to walk. I had no idea how old Amir was. He looked young, and he certainly was full of energy. He walked briskly, and during the afternoon, he showed no sign of fatigue. I followed him through the streets of New Delhi. We came to an open area, and I noticed a large crowd on the street. People were holding up boards with statements, and they were shouting slogans. Thousands of people had gathered to protest against something. I could not make out what the protest was about because the signs and the yelling were all in Hindi. People were very emotional. I saw people crying, I saw people being outraged, and I saw people making throwaway gestures. The group got angrier by the minute.

"Rama told me that you have been intrigued by the wisdom line *as you think, so you shall be* for a long time, Dax. I can congratulate you. You have been inspired by the right line. It is one of my favorites! If you truly understand the content of this wisdom, you have found your power. You have found a power that will always be yours. That power is what I would love to share with you this afternoon. How does that sound?"

"Sounds like a great plan, Amir!"

"Excellent, Dax. I have a question for you: in how many worlds do you think you live?"

What a strange question, I thought, and I answered hesitatingly, "One, I guess."

"Most people have never wondered about this question and will give the same answer as you: 'I live in one world, the world that I see when I look around me.' The first thing that I would like you to understand is that you are a citizen of *two* worlds! The one world that everybody is familiar with is the external world. It is the world around us, the world that we experience through our five senses. It is the places and the people we are visiting this afternoon. It is your family, your colleagues, the news, the weather, your bank account, the stock exchange, the governments, the planet's energy sources, the flora and the fauna. In short, it is everything apart from yourself. This external world keeps you so busy and occupied the whole day that it makes you forget about the second world you live in: your internal world. Are you following, Dax?"

"Yes, I am, Amir, but what is this inner world of mine?"

"Good question, Dax. Pretty much all that we learn in our lives, at schools, at work, and via the news is about the external world. You don't learn a lot about yourself, who you are as a human being and how you function. Your inner world is the world of your human trinity: your mind, your heart, and your body. Understanding your human trinity is the most valuable insight you can acquire in your life. Leveraging the insights will help to significantly improve your life experience."

Amir paused for a moment. Then he continued. "The three components of your inner system all have an important function. The function of the mind is to think. All your thoughts arise from the mind, either consciously or unconsciously. Your heart you know as the organ that continuously pumps blood around, sending oxygen and nutrients to all parts of the body and removing carbon dioxide and waste products. In the human trinity though, the heart is the place where you feel. It is the place where you experience emotions. When you put your hand on your heart when you feel highly emotional, you physically connect with your feelings. The function of the body is to take action. You use your body for all that you do, like speaking, playing, traveling, listening, eating, engaging.

"So you live in two worlds, Dax, just like everybody else. You are a citizen of two worlds: the external world and your internal world. You know why everybody should learn about the inner world of the human trinity at a young age? Because that is where your power is!"

Amir had started walking again. "Do you realize, Dax, that there is a continuous interaction between the two worlds? Just now, when we watched the protest, you saw a good example of this. When I say that your power is in your inner world, I implicitly also say that your power is *not* in the external world. Let's take the protest as an example. A protest is like a fight. You don't like something; you want the thing to be different. Your robotic mind wants to control the external world. You are taught that life ought to be your way. If things don't go to your liking, your automated response is to fight. You strive to change things. You strive to convince people to think and act like you. This will not work. There will always be things that you do not agree with, things that are not in line with your views, preferences, and ideas. You can spend your life fighting the externals, but you will never win. I want you to be aware, Dax, that your power is *not* in controlling the external world."

I was listening intently. "I think I understand that my power is not in the external world, Amir, but what is this power of mine in my internal world? Can you please explain?"

"Very good question, Dax. Coming to it. Let me first ask you another question: do you know a shop or a website where you can buy happiness or where you can buy stress?"

"No I don't, Amir. Why are you asking?"

"No shops for happiness or stress, right?" Amir grinned as he continued. "Here is the thing, Dax: your emotions are not caused by the things happening around you, and you cannot buy them. No, your emotions are caused by your thoughts! The first powerful lesson of the human trinity is this: as you think, so you shall feel!"

Rama looked at me, and then he moved on. "You grow up believing that your emotions are caused by people or events or circumstances in the external world. This is what your robotic mind thinks: *I am happy because of my beautiful partner; I am concerned because of the deteriorating economy; I am stressed because of my job; I am contented because of my new house; I am overjoyed because of my new Prada dress; I am afraid because of the increase in street violence.* But this is just not true. Your *mind* is creating your experience. Your *mind* is creating your feelings. Shakespeare said it very well in *Hamlet*: 'Nothing is either good or bad; thinking makes it so.' Your thoughts about things are the real reason for your feelings. Remember the following, Dax: thoughts, not things, create your emotions. You can't buy happiness or stress in the outside world. You don't get your feelings from the outside. Your emotions are self-generated. They are an inside job."

"Let me stop you right there, Amir. I would like to ask you a question," I said.

"Great, Dax. A questioning mind is an effective tool to get to a real understanding of things. Understanding your human trinity is fundamental for your life. Please ask anything you like because I really want you to get this."

"You say that all my emotions are caused by the way I think. But what about the next reorganization at my company? What about the health issues that my mum is experiencing? What about the nuclear threats in the world? What about a global virus spreading around? What about the killing of yet another black man by cops? You must agree with me that these are all things that drive emotions. People get worried. People get fearful. People get angry and upset. How can these things *not* be the cause for how I feel?"

Amir smiled. "Great question, Dax, and very important we bottom this out. When you use your mind consciously, you will come to realize that you always have a choice. You can choose how you think about the person or about the situation. You can choose what you focus on. You can choose your perspective. Do you realize, Dax, that in any situation that you consider good, there is also bad? And similarly, in any situation you label as bad, there is also good. You have way more control over how you feel than you ever imagined. If you learn to exercise your inborn ability of choice, you acquire a handle to manage your emotions. As you choose your thoughts, so you can choose your emotions. Isn't that great?"

I was reflecting on what Amir was sharing with me. It did make a lot of sense. I was thinking back to situations in my life where I had observed different people reacting differently to the same things. The last reorganization at work had outraged some colleagues. Yet others felt glad because, in their view, it brought the much-needed change. And there were fellow workers who had reported ill because of feelings of depression and anxiety. I recounted the event with Amir and said, "It is true: same situation, very different feelings." I also mentioned the recent breakup of a befriended couple where various friends had opposing perspectives on the situation. Some, like me, felt happy and relieved because a split allowed both of them to be free and happy again, something they both had not been for a long time. Others felt sad and reached out to bring the pair together again. There were also people who felt disappointed and resentful because "you don't split up when you have kids." Same situation, very different feelings. I said to Amir, "There appears to be a role for the person in assessing circumstances. There must be something in between the event and the feeling. Otherwise everyone would feel the same. I think I'm starting to get it, Amir!"

"Spot-on, Dax. That in-between thing, as you call it, is your mind and how you are using it. You can always decide what to think. Your power is in choosing the focus of your thoughts!" Amir looked cheerful.

In the meantime, we had arrived at a huge outdoor food market. Amir stopped and signaled for me to have a walk around. I smelled the most wonderful flavors and aromas. There was an amazing amount of food stalls with a variety of food choices I had never seen before. People were enjoying an early dinner or standing in line to make a purchase. Stall owners were shouting to promote their dishes, and there was a pleasant buzz coming from the social interaction between customers.

"Too bad it is not dinnertime yet," Amir said with a mischievous smile. "But don't worry. We will also have a fantastic Indian dinner tonight!

"You see the marketplace, Dax? Why is it that some people are having a mouthwatering biryani while others are enjoying an enticing butter chicken? Why do some people have plain white rice while others are eating a delicious garlic naan? Why are some people having a cold glass of refreshing Kingfisher beer while others are drinking a wonderful mango lassi?"

Finally a simple question, I thought. "Easy one this time, Amir. People are having different dishes and complements and drinks because they have different likes and thus have made different choices."

"Very true, Dax. When you go to a food market, it would be stupid to not make your own choices. When you go out to eat to a heavenly

29

place like this, it is wise to choose what you like. I trust you agree with me on this one."

I certainly did. I loved Indian food and was already looking forward to the evening dinner.

"Making your own food choices is so obvious," Amir continued. "Making your own thought choices is more important but not obvious at all. Everyone has the power to choose their thoughts, yet so few people deliberately use their power. When you choose your thoughts, you claim power over how you feel. But you don't learn to do this because you learn from people who don't know. You also don't learn it at your schools. You *allow* your emotions to be driven by the ever-changing events in the external world. You see something that you have been taught is good, and you feel well. You see something you have been taught is bad, and you feel bad. You do not choose your focus. That is why the world seems an emotional roller coaster to you. Your emotions go up and down and up and down dependent on what is happening in the external world. When you claim your power to choose your thoughts, you claim control over how you feel. As you take control over how you feel, you take control over you. Dax, your power over your emotions and hence yourself is in your inner world."

"I get it, Amir. I get it."

He indicated it was time to reconvene our tour. We left the food market and walked through a residential area. People were coming home from their day's activities. Behind a green fence, I could see a large playground with toys like little bikes, manual go-karts, cricket gear, footballs, and Hula-Hoops. A signpost showed the name of a day care center for children. Parents were standing outside the fence, waiting to pick up their children. Amir indicated for us to hold. I looked around. There was hardly any social interaction among the adults. Most people were looking at their smartphones, swiping or typing frantically. Some were talking through their phone. At that moment, the building opened, and hundreds of enthusiastically cheering children came out running. The parents' faces lit up, phones were put away, and their attention shifted to the lively youngsters.

"When you train your mind, Dax, you will learn to choose your thoughts consciously. That is a key skill for your life, believe me. An untrained mind is like a drunken monkey, always distracted and always led by the external world. Did you see the parents? They were all fully occupied by their smartphones. When you allow your mind to always be distracted, you miss what life offers you in the moment. The people you saw missed the opportunity for interpersonal connection. When the kids came, there was again distraction but this time a good one. It is beneficial to learn to consciously choose the distractions you want!"

"That makes good sense to me, Amir."

Amir smiled and said, "What about some great Indian food distraction?"

It was time for dinner. Amir took me to a small, local restaurant where everybody seemed to know him. He was welcomed by the chef as if he was his best friend. Without ordering, we were served the most exquisite Indian food I had ever tasted.

"How are you enjoying dinner from my good friend Raj? He is famous here, Dax. You can probably understand why. Great food here and now. Great learning this afternoon. You have power over your emotions. That is lesson one of the human trinity. I think you got it, right?"

With my mouth busy tasting the delicious food, I only nodded.

"There is another big human trinity lesson that you should be aware of. As you think, so you shall feel was step one. The second step of the trinity is: as you feel, so you take action. You can probably imagine that the actions you take in your life are different when you feel good versus when you feel bad. Which actions do you think are more effective in creating the life that you want, Dax? That must be the positive-feeling actions. Agree? Do you know why this is important? Well, step three of the trinity says, as you take action, so you create your life! Your life is simply the result of all the actions you have taken up to now and the actions you will take from now on. Your life is built upon your actions. When you start to manage your mind to be positive, you will create positive feelings, and consequently, you will take positive actions. These positive, conscious actions help to build the life that you want. Choosing your thoughts can thus make you the deliberate creator of your own positive life. As you think so you shall be. And also, as you think so your life shall be. Dax, there you have it: the secret explanation why your thoughts define you and your life. You are your thoughts and emotions and your life is created by your actions that are rooted in your thoughts. Amazing, right? And quite simple. Your whole experience of life starts in your mind!"

I was listening.

"Reality is always created twice, Dax: first in your mind, then in the material world. So you better make sure that what you imagine and think of in your mind is the reality you want to create!"

"Wow." I had stopped eating. I remained silent for a number of minutes and then said, "Amir, thank you so much. This has been the best learning experience of my life. My power is in my inner system, in how I set my mind. My power is in choosing the focus of my thoughts deliberately. It helps me to learn, it helps to manage how I feel, it thus helps me to manage myself, it helps me to take deliberate action, and, by doing so, it helps me to create the life that I want. Wow, this is fantastic and practical insight in my own power. My power starts in my mind! How can I ever thank you?"

"No worries," Amir responded. "There is no greater pleasure than introducing people to their own inner power. Know that your life starts in your mind. Your thinking is the basis for everything in your life. Rama explained to you how you are a robot. You have developed a mindset and a way of thinking that is largely not yours and is not always beneficial for your life. You have adopted it from the people around you, and it does not always give you the results for your life that you want. Rama wanted you to meet me first, Dax, because he wanted to ensure you understand that your power is in your thinking. Rama also wanted to make sure that you understand why. The human trinity makes this very clear. If you really want to thank me, Dax, then go and exercise your power to live the life that you want. That is the best thank you I can dream of. It is quite late in the meantime, my friend. Time to wrap up, unless you have a final question."

"Thank you, Amir. Truly amazing how your guidance in just a few hours has made things so clear. No further questions on your wisdom sharing, Master," I said, smiling. "It is very clear where my power is! If I may, I do have two other questions."

"Please," Amir kindly responded.

"Nothing to do with my inner power, but I am curious about your clothes. I have been thinking about it the whole afternoon. You are very stylishly dressed, Amir. But isn't it common for a master to walk in like an orange coat?"

Amir was laughing. "Hahaha, nice one, Dax. What about your second question?"

"My other question is about the Himalayas. I read in so many books that masters live and teach in the Himalayas. Isn't that the place where you would like to be?"

Amir looked at me with a kind and calm expression. "Nice wrapping-up questions, Dax. I can keep it short. I choose my own clothes, just like I consciously choose my thoughts. Sometimes I also wear this orange coat you have heard of. Sometimes I wear shorts and a polo shirt, sometimes a suit and tie. The thing about the orange cloak is that it is just a robotic idea of the mind. Life is not fixed. So no, it is not the standard, but people do wear orange cloaks. Remember, Dax, your power is on the inside, not in what you wear on the outside."

Now I was smiling. "I like it how you link my question with the key lesson for today, Amir!"

"About the Himalayas, Dax. It is true that masters live there. People also visit the mountains for practice and training. That is perfectly fine. A period in solitude can help you to strengthen your inside and grow your inner power. But my advice would never be to stay there. Life happens in the interaction between your inner world and the external world. So if you want a true test of your inner foundation, go and experience everything that the external world has to offer. The outside world will test and challenge you, and this way

Anton Broers

you have the opportunity to truly become the master of your inner power."

That made a lot sense. The external world as my natural training and learning ground. My visit with Master Amir was coming to a close. The dinner had been superb, the lessons about my power in the inner world even better. My stomach felt contented, and my soul felt blissful. We left the restaurant, and it was time to say goodbye. Amir gave me a big, loving hug. "Go claim your inner power, Dax. Take control over your mind to manage your emotions and to create the life that you want," he whispered in my ear. I felt emotional from the love and inspiration.

"Thank you, Master Amir. Thank you so much."

Back in my hotel room, I found a little note.

Dear Dax,
You are your thoughts becoming real. Never forget that, my friend.
Thank you for traveling to New Delhi. It was a pleasure to meet you.
Now go and exercise your inner power to benefit your life.
Sending you love and hugs,
Amir
By the way, Rama asked me to tell you that your next appointment is in two days with Mrs. Christine Yeo in Singapore. A taxi will pick you up at your home that day at 10:15 a.m.

Power—Learning Box

Wisdom	I am a citizen of two worlds: my outer world and my inner world. My power is not in controlling the outer world. I will never win. My power is in my inner world, the world of the human trinity. My power is in my thinking. When I choose my thoughts deliberately, I can manage my emotions, and I become the conscious creator of my life. I will see it when I believe it.
Awareness	Life presents you with opportunities. It depends on your mindset whether you see them (or not). Whatever task you give to your mind, it will help you to deliver it. Be conscious of the tasks you give. You will have to experience before you know. Experience only comes from saying yes to opportunities and leaping despite fearful thoughts in your mind. You will miss what life has to offer and teach when your mind is full. Learning requires an open and observant mind. Just as you make your own food choices, it is wise to make your own thought choices.

Story/ Model	Human trinity (mind, heart, body). As I think, so I shall feel. Not things but thoughts create my emotions. As I feel, so I shall take action. My emotional state defines my type of action. As I take action, so I shall create my life. My life is built on the actions I take.
Practice	Observe the human trinity at work in you. Observe how your thoughts cause your emotions. Observe how your emotions trigger your actions. When feeling emotional, check in with your mind. What thoughts are causing the negative emotion? Replace these thoughts with a good-feeling thought and focus on in for thirty seconds. Instruct your mind consciously. Be clear on what you are looking for.

3

Responsibility

Stop Driving the BMW

The moment you accept total responsibility for
everything in your life is the moment you claim
the power to change anything in your life.
—Hal Elrod

Let go of blaming. Blaming solves nothing. There is
nothing in your life that is not your choice, your doing,
your karma. Take responsibility for your own life.
—Swami Rama

My mind was actively thinking about the lessons of Master Amir.
Way past midnight, I fell asleep, but I woke up early. My flight back
to Singapore was not before the afternoon. I had decided to make
one touristic stop and to visit the Qutub Mina, India's tallest minaret
and a UNESCO World Heritage Site. After a taxi dropped me off, I
climbed to the top and stood there, taking in the breathtaking views
of the surroundings. *The external world, beautiful, full of history, but
there will be people who think nothing of this place,* I thought. "My outer
world experience is defined in my inner world." The taxi ride to the
airport was hectic, just like my first encounter with Indian traffic

the day before. But my perspective had changed. Rather than an unorganized chaos, I observed an invisible ordering mechanism that made everything go well. I did not spot any car accidents on the road. "The power of choosing the focus of my thoughts," I reflected with a smile.

I wish I had known my inner power when I was a child on the sports field, I thought as I was waiting to board my plane. I had always been a sore loser in the various sports I had practiced. I had always had a more than average talent for sports, but I had never truly enjoyed being out there on the pitch and competing. The risk of losing had always held me back from throwing myself fully in the practice. With Master Amir's guidance, I could now see how my focus on the possibility of losing had never resulted in great sporting experiences. I was still a frequent tennis player, and there and then I resolved to change my focus. Next time on the court, I would direct my mind to focus on the benefits from the physical exercise. I would focus on all the shots that worked out well. I would focus on the personal connection with my opponent. As I was overthinking, I could already feel the joy of my next tennis game.

The plane flight was efficient and on time. I was home before midnight, and Jane was still awake, awaiting my return. I gave her a big hug, and we talked for more than an hour. She loved the stories. "Tomorrow is already your next appointment?" she said. "Rama knows how to keep the momentum! Sounds great, Dax. Let's use the rest of the night to get a good rest so that you are ready to meet Mrs. Christine."

After breakfast the next morning, I searched on Google for Christine Yeo—a common name because I got many hits, but one Christine Yeo stood out clearly. Many references to a very successful business lady in Singapore appeared on my screen. This Christine Yeo had made a fortune from building her own business from scratch. A lady in her midforties, she was also spending a lot of her time making the world a better place through her charity foundation and her board membership in various nongovernmental organizations. *Maybe this is her*, I thought. At exactly 10:15, an impressive limousine parked in front of our house. A smartly dressed driver got out and rang my doorbell to indicate he had come to pick me up. I gave Jane a kiss, and off I went to my second learning appointment orchestrated by Rama.

Singapore is small, and traffic is efficient, so within fifteen minutes, we were at the entrance of the Botanic Gardens. The driver stopped the car. When I got out, he told me that Mrs. Yeo would be meeting me at the little café in the middle of the gardens. I walked into the park and followed the signs to the café. I liked the gardens. Singapore's tropical climate provides for a lush green experience all year-round. The gardens seemed to be always blooming, exuding a lively natural energy. The plants and the trees do not mind what season it is or the state of the economy. They give their best to the world every day. Whenever I went for a walk in the Botanic Gardens, I came out feeling energized and peaceful. This time though, my mind was not really connected with the beautiful nature. I was thinking about my imminent get-together with Mrs. Yeo, and I was wondering what our engagement would be all about. Collected in my thoughts, I arrived at the café. It was still early, so there were not too many people. A father was playing hide-and-seek with his two young daughters. An elderly lady was having a coffee while reading a book. Two youngsters were in line to pick up a drink, busy talking. A woman standing next to the café was finishing a phone call, saying: "My appointment has arrived. I got to go. Take good care. You owe it to yourself." She put her phone in her expensive handbag, walked over to me, and said gently, "Hi, Dax. I am Christine. Nice to meet you!"

A charming lady stood in front of me. Not a tall lady—her length must have been around five four—but she radiated a power that gave her a big presence. "Hi, Christine. I am Dax indeed. I am very pleased to meet you. Thank you very much for the opportunity."

Christine looked at me. "Rama's friends are my friends. It is my pleasure. Always good to share my experiences and contribute to another person's growth and happiness." She looked delighted. "What would you like to drink, Dax? I can recommend the decaf herbal infusion hot tea or one of the cold sparkling teas." Christine bought us two drinks to go, and we went for a stroll in the garden.

"How was your trip to Master Amir?"

I shared my amazing experience with Christine. It was only two days ago that Amir had introduced me in my inner power. It felt ages ago, maybe because Amir's lesson had reconnected me with what I had always known deep down inside but had forgotten a long time ago.

"Sounds great, Dax. I still remember my visit to Amir, an enlightening encounter. Understanding where my power is has been of tremendous help in my life. Since I met Amir, I have been more watchful of my mind, and I have made efforts to ensure I choose my thoughts consciously every day. It does not mean everything always goes exactly as I wish it to go. But through managing my mind, I have found that I am able to manage myself much better, whatever the situation. Managing myself has helped me to manage my life into the direction that I dreamt of since I was a little girl."

"So you also had the opportunity to learn from Amir!" I did not wait for Christine to answer. I was intrigued by her little-girl dream remark. It sounded like she had been able to realize her dreams, and I was eager to learn more about that. Who would not want to live their childhood dreams? "What dreams did you have when you were a little girl, Christine? How did you turn them into a reality?" I was wondering whether Rama had sent me to Christine to learn about living your dreams.

"Great bridge to what I would like to share with you today, Dax. It is good to have dreams for your life. When you know what you want, you are more likely to succeed. How can you achieve if you don't know what you want to achieve? As a little girl, I saw so many people who were not happy. I saw miserable people every day, and I said to myself, 'That is not what I want.' I resolved to live a life of enjoyment, a life of happiness, although I was not at all clear how. As a young girl, I was already sensitive to the needs of helpless little children. I grew up in a middle-class family. All my basic requirements were met. Traveling through Asia, though, made me realize that this is not the case for every child. I decided I wanted to make a positive contribution to the well-being of children in my life. I dreamt about being a hero who would improve the lives of thousands of little, innocent kids.

"You know what happens with dreams, Dax? Most of them get forgotten when we grow up. So it happened to me. Slowly but steadily, my noble childhood hopes for my life disappeared to the background as life started taking over. More and more, I was led by my external environment rather than my own inner guidance. You recognize some of this, Dax?"

I nodded.

"The good thing is that you can always reconnect with your aspirations. It is never too late to reopen your box of dreams. Sometimes you need help in your life. I needed a wake-up call to get back to the pursuit of my dreams. I was seventeen, and I would like to share my story with you. How is the cold tea by the way?"

"I love the refreshing, sparkling tea. And I would love to hear your story, Christine."

"That's good, Dax. You might wonder why Rama sent you to me. But bear with me. The story I am about to share with you has been the game changer for my life. At seventeen, I learned one of the most important skills for success in life. I want to instill in you the words of wisdom that I received from my favorite college teacher. Are you ready?"

"I am, Christine. Normally when walking here, I am all eyes for nature's beautiful flora and fauna. Not today. Today, I am all ears to hear your story," I said with a grateful expression on my face.

"Great, Dax. Let me start my story at primary school. If I may say, I was a smart little girl. I loved going to school for two reasons. I loved learning new things. My favorite subject was mathematics. The challenge to solve the little calculus puzzles was always a joyful experience. I also liked history and biology. Learning about past events and especially the lessons therefrom and learning about the wonders of nature gave me practical lessons for life. The other reason why I loved it so much was the daily opportunity to play with my friends. I had many friends, both girls and boys, and together we ensured we had a fun time every day. Primary school was pure joy for me. I still remember the headteacher saying at our graduation, 'Your primary school years come to an end here. When at an older age you reflect on your life, you might conclude that these years have been the best of your life.' I was eleven at the time, and although I did register her remarks, I did not fully appreciate the truth in her statement. I came to understand at a later stage.

"At twelve, I started secondary schooling, and all went well the first three years. My academic performance was good, except for the odd subject that I just did not like. I still had many friends. But then things at home started changing. My mum and dad were no longer happy with each other. Incomprehension between them turned into frustration. Frustration turned into anger. Anger turned into regular fights. Regular fights drove them apart and brought sadness to all of us. At that moment in my life, I was not yet aware of the human trinity, Dax. The situation had a big bearing on me. I could not handle it. I became negative, recalcitrant, and unpleasant. I started to revolt against everything and everybody. Let me spare you the details, but the bottom line is that I changed. I changed from a joyful, fun-loving, determined girl into a cynical, troubled, lazy girl. I no longer took an interest in my friends and hobbies, and my performance at school seriously deteriorated.

"Then one day, while at school, my physical education teacher asked me to hang around for a while after class. I really liked her. She still is my favorite teacher of all my years in school. When the other children had left, she told me about a recent meeting where teachers met to discuss pupils with apparent problems. There was widespread concern about me. Teachers not only mentioned my worsening results; they also referenced various situations where I had been in fights with other kids or had been aggressive toward teachers. There had not been sufficient time to discuss a possible solution. The discussion about me had ended with a collective 'let's keep an eye on Christine' agreement.

"My PE teacher had been astonished. In her classes, she had not noticed many of the changes in my behavior. The physical exercise probably gave me sufficient opportunity to get rid of my frustrations and anger. Besides, I really liked her, as I already said. My teacher was not the kind of person who liked wait-and-see solutions. She was more the action-oriented individual, and that is why she had pulled me aside. 'What is going on, Christine?' she asked me with a concerned look. 'Do you recognize what these teachers are saying?' And that is where I started explaining what was all wrong in my life. First and foremost, my parents. It was my parents. Their selfishness and inability was the big reason for all of this. If only they had spent some serious effort resolving their problems. But there was more. The family of my best friend had moved to a foreign country a year ago. We had only kept in touch for a few months, but then she had stopped replying. This year's school schedule was terrible, and some of the teachers I had for the first time were just very bad teachers. I must have gone on blaming and accusing other people and all kinds of situations for my misery.

"With hindsight, I have to say how impressed I am with the patience of my PE teacher. She listened and took in everything with the kindness she always offered to everybody. When I was finally done talking, she said, 'Wow, Christine, a lot has happened in your life. Still I have a question. I only hear other people and external circumstances as reasons for your situation. Where are *you* in the explanation?' You can probably imagine, Dax, that her question left me dead silent for a while. My teacher spoke to me about *my* responsibility. That is a sensitive topic for many people, and it certainly was for me at the time. Do you know why responsibility comes with a negative connotation for people, Dax?"

"I think I do, Christine. When things don't go your way and you realize it is your own responsibility, your mind can start blaming you. Telling yourself, 'It is my fault,' can be painful. It makes you realize that you are not infallible. It means that you have to admit to yourself that you made a mistake. People don't like this usually. I certainly don't. I find it difficult to confront myself with my errors. It hurts on the inside. Is that why people think negatively about responsibility?"

"You are right, Dax. The pain you describe is exactly what I felt when my teacher asked me that question. She brought my issues back to *me*. In life, it is so easy to find excuses and play the victim. Excuses why things don't work out without looking at your own role. Reasons outside of yourself that are the cause for your problems and troubles. 'It is my mum,' 'It is my boss,' 'It is the government,' 'It is the global virus'; people are good at finding fault elsewhere, but they forget to look in the mirror. That is exactly what I used to do. The question of my teacher was the biggest wake-up call of my life. It taught me that my life is *my* responsibility. I learned that if I want things in my life, it is up to *me* to make it happen. That day at school, I discovered the power of responsibility. Taking responsibility for your life is the second superpower that Rama wants you to imprint in your mindset, Dax. Your human trinity inner power is the first. When you use your mind power and you take responsibility, nothing can stop you in life."

I had been listening with full attention. It was becoming clear why Rama had organized for me to first meet Master Amir and Mrs. Christine Yeo. He wanted me to acquire the two superpowers for life.

"That sounds empowering, Christine. Your story reminds me of something I read a few years back. In his book, an Indian master talked about the two biggest diseases in the world. They are victim-ites and excuse-ites, just as you described. These diseases are widespread and are like viruses. If you don't kill them, the negative impact from them on your life will get bigger. If you surround yourself with people who suffer from these illnesses, there is a good chance you'll get infected. Ever since I read about those diseases, I have watched my own behaviors. Can't say I have fully contained them, but I have gotten better in not letting my life be ruled by them. The wisdom of that master has made me look more frequently into my own mirror and to query about *my* role. I know I can still do a lot better. I am very curious about your story. What happened after your teacher introduced you to the power of responsibility?"

"I thanked my PE teacher for her personal care and interest. I told her that her question made sense and that I would take some time to reflect on my own role in the misery. When I started contemplating my part in the state of affairs of my life, I quickly came to the conclusion that *I* was the main character. This sounds so obvious. I mean, how can you *not* be the lead role in your life? But if you have made a habit of finding fault outside of yourself, it is not so clear at all. When I gained this insight, I decided there and then to stop driving the BMW!"

"Huh, what? Were you driving a BMW when you were seventeen?"

"Hahaha, no, Dax. This is not about the car. I actually love BMW cars. I have driven many throughout the years. With the BMW that I determined to stop driving, I mean I stopped *bitching, moaning, winching.* That BMW gives you some satisfactory feeling in the short run, but it will not get you anywhere in your life. I resolved to take full responsibility for my life!"

"Got it. Nice expression, Christine. I like it. I will remember this BMW. It would be good for me to stop driving it. Hahaha. Then what happened?"

"I can't say I immediately got good at it, Dax. I had allowed quite a lot of victim behavior in my system, and habits are not killed overnight. I was serious about my undertaking though. Every time I slipped back and started finding fault in others, I reminded myself of the choice I had made. You know what I did, Dax? I put up a yellow stickie with the words 'I am responsible' on various spots in my room. I could not miss these notices. So even if my mind was busy finding excuses, I knew that on the same day, I would bump into one of these written messages. Slowly but steadily, taking responsibility became my natural way of dealing with things. In order to change, you first need to make a decision. Then you need to take actions that are in alignment with your goal. If you find yourself going back to old behaviors, do not punish yourself for it. Be aware of it, for example with the help of some yellow notes, and if you are, correct the situation. Over time, you will find that you can change the way you act and go about life. It certainly worked for me.

"My first priority was to turn around my quite dramatic performance at school. The good thing at school is that there is always a next test, so the opportunities to take responsibility automatically arrived. This is actually the same in life, as I have learned. Life will always give you new possibilities to practice what it is you want to do. You just have to keep your eyes open. Long story short, I managed to pass the school year and graduated with honors the year after. And I learned some very important life lessons. I trust Amir shared with you how you are the creator of your own life—right, Dax?"

I confirmed.

"I did not know this at the time, but implicitly I learned this very powerful lesson by doing. Your life is the result of all the actions you have taken in the past and will take in the future. You should realize that you are participating in all of these actions. Have you ever heard that not taking action is also taking action? That is how the masters explain that you are a participant in *all* of your life. You can either participate actively, or you can participate passively. You know what I found? I found that if you accept responsibility for your actions, you can become the owner of your life. This is the principle of ownership and responsibility. I came to realize that my life is my creation, that I am responsible for it. I learned that taking responsibility is not something you should be scared of because it might hurt. It is something you should embrace and cherish because it gives you the power to create what it is you want to create and to change what it is you want to change. Who wouldn't want to have such power? You tell me, Dax!"

"Can't argue with that, Christine. Your explanation of responsibility is very clear. This way, responsibility truly is a superpower. Now please continue. What happened after your graduation?"

"Coming to that, Dax. But first you might have wondered why we are meeting in these magnificent Botanic Gardens. Nature nourishes, and it has a calming influence. It is great to connect with nature just for the enjoyment of it. But there is more: nature has so many lessons to teach us. I would like to present you to a very dear friend of mine."

We were now on the rain forest walking trail of the park. Christine pointed me toward a peculiar-looking tree consisting of a trunk in the center, surrounded by what appeared to be many lianas.

"Any idea what kind of tree this is, Dax?"

I love nature, and I love to be in nature, but my factual knowledge about nature is very limited. I shook my head. No, I did not have any idea.

"This is a strangling fig, Dax. This tree is a great friend of mine. I regularly visit here to just sit down and be here in silence. It feels as if we are enjoying each other's company. The fig has a very important lesson on responsibility to teach us all. It is not the strangling bit; don't you worry. Hahaha. The lesson is about taking responsibility in a situation where finding excuses not to live and grow is so much easier than to take life in your own hands. You might not be a nature expert, Dax, but you do know that usually the growth of a tree starts at the roots in the ground, right?"

Yes, I did.

"Not this tree, Dax. This fig starts its life up in the canopy of another tree. Fruit-eating birds and bats disperse its seeds on the branches of rain forest trees. When these seeds germinate, they send numerous aerial roots to the ground. As they get anchored into the forest floor, the roots thicken. More and more roots are being produced, and together they engulf the host. Eventually, the strangling fig takes over from the host tree that dies from strangulation. Imagine, Dax, you are a tree without a root. In such a case, it is not too difficult to find excuses for not living the life that you want. No foundation, no nourishment from the ground, no direct access to water, not much sunlight. The basic ingredients for the life of a tree are missing. What do you think happens if the fig's life is led by these types of excuses? Not much tree will grow! But that is not what this tree does. The strangling fig remembers its purpose, and it finds ways to grow and become the tree it is destined to be. Isn't that amazing? I call this taking responsibility. You know now how important this lesson is for me, so you can understand why I love this tree so much."

"Great story, Christine. The fig clearly does not care about all its problems and challenges. It takes responsibility to grow and thrive without playing the victim. I can see why the two of you like each other. You both like to take your life in your own hands!"

"That's right. Let me come back to your question what happened after my graduation. No excuses and no victim behavior became my driving force in life. My *I am responsible* mindset made me consciously reconnect with my dreams and hopes for life. I realized that if I wanted to turn my dreams into reality, I would have to make choices and take actions that were in alignment with my personal objectives. Ever since I was a child, I had loved food. I had also been concerned about the large number of people in Asia who do not have sufficient food every day. After graduating from university, I decided to start my own agriculture business, with two primary objectives. Firstly, I wanted to purchase food produced by local farmers across Asia. Secondly, I wanted to use part of the revenues I would be generating to give back and distribute food to the underprivileged in the region. The early part of my business journey was a typical one—full of challenges and disappointments and only some minor successes. I had the occasional moments where I earnestly doubted my business and myself, but I refused to give in to finding fault. The development path of my business was a great test for me of how serious I truly was about taking responsibility.

"After some five years, I realized a breakthrough when I found a group of investors with a similar passion for nutritious food and sharing. Shortly after, a second breakthrough happened when I concluded my first pan-regional contract with a large customer. Finding eager and immensely committed suppliers had not been an issue from almost day one. To cut a long story short, together with many other great people, we built the largest agricultural food-supply company of Asia in almost twelve years. In all these years, I had managed to stick to the two founding objectives regarding food supplies and food sharing. I added a third for my staff, my suppliers, and even for my customers: taking responsibility. Everybody makes mistakes, and everybody sometimes makes the wrong choices, but everybody has the power to take responsibility. It has meant that certain staff, suppliers, and customers are no longer part of our business. But it has helped to promote the *I am responsible* mindset among thousands and thousands of people across Asia. You can imagine that I have promoted this mindset on numerous occasions, like in interviews for newspapers or magazines or when speaking at symposia. One journalist once referred to me as 'Mrs. Responsible,' and since then, that has become more or less my nickname. Five years ago, I sold my business to a group of buyers under the proviso that my three business principles were kept alive. Until today, they have stuck to their word. Since then, I have spent my time managing my two charities. One is about educational and training programs for children across Asia on the topic of—you must have guessed it—responsibility. The other is providing food supplies to poor communities in many Asian countries."

I had been listening to Christine's story with growing admiration. *A lady on a mission,* I thought. Clear about her life's objectives and armed with a growing conviction of responsibility, she had achieved massive business success. But not only that. She had made sharing and contributing to society a key target for her business at a young age. She had learned and grown in life. And she came across as a kind, humble, and happy human being. "Wow, Christine, phenomenal story. Can you share more of your lessons from life?"

Christine smiled.

"Rama asked me to introduce the power of responsibility to you, Dax. Of course there are many more lessons about creating happiness and success. I learned these from Rama after I met him volunteering at an event of one of my foundations. Soon I realized that I had met a wise man from whom I wanted to learn. Rama has been my wisdom coach ever since. He has taught me so much, but never has he suggested that he can fix my life. Rama is very clear in his guidance: *my* life is *my* responsibility. Wisdom helps to optimize my life, but *I* have to create my life myself. Nobody else will do this. A teacher or a coach who suggests that he can heal your life is not the right person to learn from. It is simply a false promise. I am sure that Rama will ensure that the key lessons for life will all be coming your way, Dax. Be patient. You will get everything you need to know to live your best life. I would like to stick to my favorite topic, if you don't mind."

"You take your responsibility in a very responsible way," I replied jokingly.

"There is another thing about responsibility that I want to share with you. Have you ever wondered about the word *responsibility* and what it actually means? The word is made up of two words: response and ability. Using these two roots, it becomes clear that responsibility means *the ability to respond*. I know that Master Amir has introduced you to the concept of the two worlds. You are a citizen of both your outer world and your inner world. You remember, right?"

"I sure do!" I said.

"Great! It is good to realize that your inner and outer world are in continuous interaction with each other. Your outer world produces stimuli, and these stimuli hit your inner world. For example, your partner tells you that she loves you; or you are fired by your employer; or the stock market shoots up. The outer world is moving, and you are constantly being touched by it. You then touch back. This endless touching from one world to the other and back again is a good definition of life. The way you process the external stimuli through your human trinity has a big impact on your life, Dax. It is valuable to understand how your inner system processes the stimuli. Do you have an idea how the stimulus usually enters your human trinity?"

I had to think about this question for a while. Christine was patient. After some time, I said, "I think at feeling level. Is that right?"

"Correct. Most of the time, you first experience an external stimulus at feeling level. You know that each feeling is superseded by a thought from Master Amir's lessons. But the thing is that you connect faster with how you feel than with how you think. Can you follow me?"

"Yes, I can, Christine."

"When the stimulus is a positive one, all is OK. Jane says she loves you. You feel good about it and probably reach out to give her a hug. The stock exchange has gone up. You look at your portfolio and are happy with the gains. Agree, right? Negative stimuli are the more problematic ones. Let me explain how. Your boss tells you that you are fired. This hits you. In the moment, you start to feel sad, confused, angry, frustrated. You feel a whole bag of negative emotions. Now think of the human trinity: as you feel, so you take action. You feel bad, and without thinking, you move into action. Negative feeling, negative action. Let's say you start to shout at your boss. You start to swear, and you vent all your negative emotion toward the person. You *re-act* in emotion. This will not make the situation any better normally. You with me?"

I was listening attentively and nodded.

"Reacting out of emotion does not result in the best possible action. Emotional reactions do not create outcomes to your liking. They are the kinds of actions you later regret. We all know these in our lives. When you move from emotion to action, you do not trigger your innate power. You do not leverage the power of your mind, the power of your thinking. Here is the secret for always taking the best possible action, whatever the circumstance. Listen carefully because this is valuable for your life, Dax. When a negative stimulus hits you, become aware of your negative emotional feeling. Do not take action yet. First, connect with your mind. Instead of moving from emotion to action, move from emotion to thinking. Claim your mind power. At thinking level, assess the situation and consider your options. Then make a decision about which option is the best course of action. From there, you move to taking action. This way, your action has become a conscious action, a deliberate action. Dax, do you know the name of such an action? It is a *response*! The difference between a reaction and a response is the awareness you bring to your action. When you react, you act without awareness. You act out of emotion triggered by the external stimulus. You allow the external world to lead your action. You have given your power away. When, on the other hand, you respond, you act deliberately. You take control over the external stimulus, you make up your mind, and decide on the action you want to take. When you take responsibility for your life, you develop the *ability to respond*. You become a responder to life. Responses create far better outcomes than reactions. With reactions, you will often feel victim to external circumstances. With responses, you become the master over your life. This is the wisdom principle of responsibility and responses. Responsibility is a super skill that allows you to create the best possible results for your life."

I really liked Christine's practical perspective on responsibility. The way she explained this was simple and practical. I could see how it was possible that different people got different outcomes from similar situations. This had nothing to do with the situation; it had everything to do with the reaction or the response. The people who created better results basically were the better responders. I thought about challenging situations in my life. My reaction to the recruiter who had once told me I had not been hired for a university student traineeship. I felt so offended and had gotten so angry that I made things worse. At the end of our conversation, the man had said, "See, that is why we think you can be a bit arrogant." It had been a great lesson and allowed me to deal with another rejection shortly after in a much more positive way. Upon receiving the negative message, I consciously managed my thoughts and asked the lady whether she had some advice for me that would help me to improve my application effectiveness. The input I received from her had been very useful, and hence, that time I gained from a similar situation. Wow. Christine was making things very clear. I felt inspired and happy with the insights I was receiving. A happy, contented smile formed on my face.

"I love it, Christine. This is very powerful indeed. And easy to understand. It reminds me of events in my own life. I do have a question though. If this is so simple, why are so few people responders? Why does almost everybody seem to always react out of emotion, even though it only gives you suboptimal results?"

"Good question, Dax, and a good opportunity to connect some dots of the things you have learned so far. My friend the fig takes responsibility for his life. A tree does this instinctively. The fig follows its instincts, and out of this natural process, it becomes an impressive tree. Nothing can come in between; it happens. Human beings also have an inner guidance system. It is called intuition, or inner tuition. Intuition is part of your consciousness. Following your intuition provides you with an effective guide for life. Your intuition goes beyond your emotions and will guide you toward your power. It will guide you toward taking conscious action. You have a problem though. Your intuition has become diffused. Your intuition is not naturally accessible anymore. You know why? Your intuition gets blocked by your mind. Your robotic mind comes in between your intuition and your action. Your robotic mind has grown to believe that finding fault on the outside is a good thing. Then at least you are not to blame. The robotic, untrained mind is one that loves finding excuses. It is one that feels comfortable thinking you are a victim, because that is much better than thinking it is you. Your automated mind also has all kinds of preprogrammed reactions to certain instances in life. When somebody gets angry with me, I have to be angry in return. When I lose, I have to be sad and disappointed. When I don't get what I want, I have to be annoyed and frustrated. Our robotic mind thinks it knows it all and is a subconscious guide for our reactions in life. So here you are, Dax, disconnected from your intuition and guided by your inner programming of ideas and beliefs that might not serve you. You have forgotten about your inner mind power. When you get to know your mind, you will come to realize this. A mind that is fueled with the belief *I have to find fault* keeps you away from following your gutfeel. A mind that is full of preconceived ideas will make you react in a predefined yet unconscious way to situations. A mind, on the other hand, that is fueled with the belief *I am responsible* sets you up to connect with your intuition, to think and to become a conscious responder. This is the way of the master. This is the way to create your best life."

We had come to the exit of the Botanic Gardens. The hours with Christine had flown by. I felt blessed and grateful for the time I had spent with her. She had enriched my life with her story and her lessons on taking responsibility. At the entrance, a beautiful BMW was parked. As we approached, a driver stepped out and opened the door for Christine to step in. She saw the grin on my face.

"Yes, Dax, I told you. This BMW I love very much! It has been a good couple of hours together. Thank you for your time and interest. I know that you will develop a true wisdom-based mindset with the guidance of Rama. Remember that you do not have to find fault outside to protect yourself, OK? There is superpower in knowing *I am responsible* and living with that mindset."

With that, Mrs. Christine Yeo got in the car, smiled, waved, and was gone.

Responsibility—Learning Box

Wisdom	I am responsible for my life. If I want something in my life, it is up to me to make it happen.
	If I want to change things, I need to make a choice / decide what I want. Then I need to take actions that are in alignment with my goal.
	I am the creator of my own life.
	I participate in all of my life. I can either participate actively or I can participate passively.
Awareness	Your life is a continuous interaction between the outer world and your inner world.
	If life doesn't go your way, it is easy to find excuses and play the victim. This doesn't solve anything. In order to change things, you better ask yourself, what is *my* role?
	How can you *not* play the lead role in your life?
	Reacting in emotion does not result in the best outcomes for your life.
	Responding consciously to whatever life throws at you creates the best possible outcomes.
	Responsibility is a superpower. It is your ability to respond.
	Taking responsibility gives you power over your life. When you respond, you take control over the external stimulus. This way *you* lead your life, not the externals.
Story/Tool	The strangling fig.
	The outer world touches you with stimuli. Your power lies in your inner world. Think consciously before you touch back.

Practice	When assessing your life, ask yourself: where am *I* in the explanation?
	Use a yellow sticky to remind yourself "I am responsible"
	Become a *responder*.
	Get in touch again with your intuition.

4

Promise

Set Sail on Your Own Star

> There is no greater agony than bearing
> an untold story inside you.
> —Maya Angelou

> There is no greater gift than to honor your calling. It's why
> you were born. And how you become most truly alive.
> —Oprah Winfrey

I slept well. I had to be in the office early, so after a quick shower and breakfast, I gave Jane a kiss, and off I went. Traffic was still quiet. My mind was actively processing the events of the last few days. The short trip to Master Amir in New Delhi. The walk in the Singapore Botanic Gardens with Mrs. Christine Yeo. Inner power. Responsibility.

Too often, I realized, I had given away my power to external situations. I remembered the management meeting the week before where, in my view, some of my colleagues were not taking our lagging business performance seriously enough. I had made efforts to make the gaps visible, and I had challenged the team to find ways to step up. It had been like this for the past few months, and I did not see a lot of change. Last week, I had snapped. Out of sheer frustration, I had started shouting and blaming people. After my emotional breakdown, I had left the meeting, leaving my colleagues in bewilderment about my behavior and accusations. I was laughing now about it and thought, *So much for claiming your inner power, Dax. Nice example of being victim to external stimuli—not.* Things had to change. This was not the way. This had been very ineffective. The days before my trip to India had felt awkward in the office. People seemed to be watching me with confused looks on their faces. I had felt uneasy and small and had not made any efforts toward reconciliations with my team members. Now I knew better. I could immediately apply the lessons of Amir and Christine in my daily office life!

Many years earlier, I had heard an ancient Native American story. An old Indian chief is teaching his granddaughter about life. "Do you know you have two wolves inside of you?" the chief says to the little girl. "And do you know they are constantly fighting?" The young girl thinks about the questions and responds, "No, Grandpa. You are kidding me. There are no wolves inside me." The old man tells the child to close her eyes and find the wolves. After a minute, she opens her eyes and says triumphantly, "I found them!" Grandpa is pleased. "Now listen, darling," he says. "One wolf is the negative wolf. This wolf talks you down, it discourages you, it keeps you small. This wolf will always find excuses, is resentful and proud, and does not trust the world. The other wolf is the positive wolf. This wolf cheers for you, it tells you that you can do it, and it makes you grow. This wolf is hopeful, loving, and responsible and looks at the world with empathy and faith. You will understand why they are always fighting. Because they will never agree." The granddaughter thinks about it and then asks her grandpa, "Which wolf will win the fight?" The old chief smiles. "Great question, angel. The one that you feed the most will win."

We all have these two wolves inside. The wolves represent the positive and negative voices of the mind. The one you feed by giving focus and attention will get stronger and will win the fight. I reminded myself of the most important lesson from this beautiful story: *you choose which wolf you will feed.* I decided to consciously feed the positive wolf that day. *Putting my inner mind power into practice!* I thought. And I decided I wanted to be a deliberate responder in my discussions with the team. No more victim-type behavior.

The next few weeks were a joy. Focusing on the positive, focusing on what was good in my daily encounters, was paying off. It made me feel calmer, kinder, more deliberate, and also more decisive. Focusing my mind made me a more effective person in the office. Already on my first day back, I took the initiative to connect with my colleagues I had attacked the most. One on one, we sat down to discuss and harmonize our viewpoints and opinions. My more positive approach helped me to see more good things and opportunities. My colleagues became more receptive to my challenges due to my renewed focus. As it turned out, we were not thinking too differently about the performance of our business. Soon enough, we were aligned in a joint action plan to address the issues but also to work the opportunities. I made it a daily morning practice to remind myself to have a positive focus and take responsibility throughout the day. At evening time, I sat down for five minutes to reflect on my behaviors and actions. I noted that this daily routine helped me to grow my self-consciousness.

I was so busy practicing what I had learned and enjoying it that Rama's WhatsApp message on a Monday evening many months later felt a bit like a wake-up call.

> Hi, Dax.
> How are you?
> How is your mind? Are you responding to life?
> I would like to invite you for my Satsang this Thursday
> at 8:00 p.m.
> Hope to see you there.
> Sending you my love and hugs,
> Rama

I felt excited at once. "Rama!" I couldn't wait to share my amazing experiences with him. *Maybe he has a next instruction for me,* I thought.

On Thursday evening, I took a cab to Rama's training center. A large crowd had gathered by the time I arrived. Rama was nowhere to be seen, so I decided to just take a seat and await the start of the evening. I knew Satsang to be a Sanskrit word meaning "being in the company of truth." In practical terms, it is a gathering in the presence of a wise master. It was my first Satsang, and although I did not know exactly what to expect, I felt curious and enthusiastic, ready to be inspired. Rama appeared exactly on time, sat down on the ground, closed his eyes, and did not say a word. The atmosphere in the room changed from chatty and busy to serene and silent almost immediately. I also shut my eyes and enjoyed the peaceful and quiet mood.

Rama started talking in his calm and composed voice after a few minutes. There was a tranquil ambience in the room. People were listening intently. Some were taking notes. Others just sat to enjoy the experience. Rama talked about recent events in the world and how a wisdom mindset allows you to face challenges more easily and to enjoy life more. "You have all been given the greatest gift, the gift of life," Rama said. "Gifts are there to be celebrated, so the masters say, 'Celebrate life. Enjoy life.' That is what you are here for. You have also been given two superpowers." I was all ears when I heard him say this. Master Amir and Mrs. Christine had also been talking about superpowers. Rama continued, "Your first superpower is your innate ability to choose your thoughts, to choose your focus. Nobody will ever take this away from you. Your second superpower is your ability to take responsibility. Who wants to live like a victim? No one, right? Yet so many people live this way, finding excuses for what is not working in their lives. The master knows she has the ability to create her life. She also knows that this requires taking responsibility. The master deliberately responds to whatever life throws at her. She takes ownership. When you apply these two superpowers, you are set to live life to the max!"

It was a fantastically inspiring Satsang hour with Rama. I felt elated and energized. After the group session was over, Rama was engaging with the various people present. I stayed for a while, chatting and sharing experiences with other participants. When I was about to leave, Rama walked over to personally greet me and to ask how I had liked the Satsang. He could tell from my happy face, so without waiting for a response, he pulled out a little note and gave it to me. "Your next appointment, my friend." He smiled, as he almost always did. "The two superpowers are yours now to keep in mind and apply. It is time to learn about the mindset of the master. When you use your superpowers and follow the master's way of thinking, you will live your best life possible. When you meet my friend Olisa, she will introduce you into the next lesson. She is expecting you at the entrance of the Singapore Zoo next week, Tuesday morning at nine thirty. I hope this time works for you, Dax."

"It's a go, Rama. Thank you so much. Your friends' insights and guidance so far have been truly inspiring and valuable. I can't wait to meet Olisa and learn more!" We gave each other a hug, and I went outside to find a cab to go home.

At eight thirty on Tuesday morning, the taxi driver cruised through traffic, and I arrived well on time. Jane and I had been to the Singapore Zoo multiple times, but never did I feel the same eager anticipation running through my heart and stomach that I felt this time. I loved this learning journey, and I was convinced that my encounter with Olisa would be the next beneficial step. At exactly 9:30, a shining, vibrant young girl came walking in my direction. "Dax?" she asked.

"Why is it that everybody seems to know me these days?" I replied jokingly.

"Well, maybe it is because you look so enthusiastic and anxious to learn. I was observing you a little while just now, and you did not seem to be standing still for one second. Ready to explore, just like a kid. Hi. I am Olisa!"

We entered the zoo via the staff entrance. One thing was already clear about Olisa. She was a good observer. The way she had described me waiting for her arrival was spot-on. I was ready to delve into whatever it was she would be discussing with me. The excitement in my mind had transferred to my body, which was full of energy. "Where are you from, Olisa? I can see that you probably do not originate from Singapore," I said.

"Well noted, Dax," she said with a playful smile. "I am from Tanzania!" That made sense based on her appearance, and I was curious to learn how she had ended up in Asia. "You are not the only one who is surprised, Dax. What does a girl from Africa do here in Singapore? It is a question that many people ask. Happy to share my background.

"I was born and raised in a little village close to the border with Kenya and in the vicinity of Serengeti National Park. In Africa, you are surrounded by nature. I loved it. From a young age, you could find me exploring the outdoors. I would be wandering around, enjoying the beautiful flora and fauna. Many times, I made my trips with friends, sometimes on my own. We need nature, Dax. Nature is life. It provides us with oxygen, food, nutrients, medicines, raw materials, and minerals. What I also learned as a kid is that nature needs us. It is being exploited for short-term financial gains without consideration for the longer-term detrimental impact to all of us. Animals are being slaughtered for their skin and ivory tusks or as a hunting trophy. Forest is being reclaimed for wood production or to build new housing estates. The earth is becoming more and more polluted. And humankind is wondering why the amount of natural disasters is growing. Something has got to give, Dax. The universe will always strive for balance. The tsunamis, the forest fires, the viruses transmitted from animals to humans, they are all counterbalances to what humankind is doing to nature. Nature needs us, Dax.

"As I grew up, I desperately wanted to do my bit to protect and nurture our natural living environment. I was so glad when I reached the age of fourteen and I finally could become a nature reserve volunteer. That's what I did. My life has revolved around nature almost full-time ever since. I got a double master's degree in agriculture and veterinary sciences, but my real training I received from doing my work as a volunteer. My academic training, but especially this practical learning background, made me qualify for an international student's exchange program between my country and Singapore. So, to cut a long story short, for two years I have been doing my PhD at the Department of Biological Sciences here at the National University of Singapore. It is my aim to step up from making local contributions to the national reserve in Tanzania to making a global impact on the planet's well-being. This PhD and all the relationships that I am building will be of tremendous help in turning this objective into a reality."

I was impressed. A girl on a mission. Still I could not fully fathom what the Singapore Zoo had to do with all of Olisa's plans.

"Yes, the Singapore Zoo. Well, Dax, here is the thing: I love to be in nature, and I don't have too much time at the moment to be there. The zoo offers me an opportunity to connect with the world of fauna and some flora that I would otherwise miss deeply. So, like at home, I am doing volunteer work to contribute to the well-being of animals. I just *have* to be connected with nature, albeit in an artificial environment. But don't forget, Dax, animals are animals, wherever they are."

Our walk had brought us to the Wild Africa part of the zoo. I pointed at the signpost. "Yes, an African girl likes to reconnect with Africa," Olisa said. She beamed with pride. "All my time in nature has taught me so many lessons. One important one that we robots should all learn, I am about to share with you. Are you ready?"

I was laughing. "So you also know about the robot, Olisa?"

"Of course," she replied, smiling.

Wild Africa in the Singapore Zoo presents its visitors with animals like cheetahs, zebras, giraffes, lions, red river hogs, African painted dogs, leopards, and white rhinoceroses. Olisa was passionately talking about her encounters with many of these various animals back home in Tanzania, when she suddenly pointed me to a zebra. "You see that zebra, Dax? Why do you think she has such a big belly?"

I watched. "Is she maybe pregnant?"

Olisa confirmed. "I have a more important question for you. What do you think the little one is going to be once she is born?"

I looked at her with a *You're kidding me, right?* expression. "A zebra of course!"

"Very good, Dax. The little one is going to be a zebra. Now think about trees. My favorite tree in the Serengeti National Park is the iconic umbrella tree. This tree represents Africa. Its umbrella-type shape is visible throughout the flat landscape of the nature park. Giraffes and elephants love the seedlings of this tree. What do you think is going to grow out of the seeds that are not eaten by the animals?"

Again, I watched Olisa with a funny look. "An umbrella tree maybe?" I said humorously.

"Very good, Dax. Full marks. You are good at this. Of course, a little zebra is going to be a zebra. Naturally, the umbrella tree seed will turn into an umbrella tree. The same applies for all of nature on our beautiful planet, except for one species." That remark triggered me. I was curious now. "So I have one more quiz question for you. Which species is the exception?" Olisa knew she had asked me a funny, unfamiliar question and enjoyed the confused look on my face. "You thought this quiz was easy, Dax." She laughed. "Which species is it?"

"Humans?" I said with hesitation.

"Yes, Dax, you are right. Humans are the only species for whom it is not common to just become what they are destined to be!"

Olisa paused. She looked at me and then continued. "You were born one day. Suddenly, you were here. You were given the greatest gift: life! Your birthday is a great day, a glorious day. You come into this world crying, and everybody around you is laughing. The birth of a new baby is one of the big celebrations in life. The world rejoices. Rabindranath Tagore, the wise Indian poet, said, 'Every child that is born is proof that God has not given up on human beings.' When a child is born, we are all reminded of the beauty of life, the freshness of life, the potential of life. It feels as if we are reborn a bit ourselves. We feel excited, inspired, happy, full of joy.

"Then, the baby's life begins. But for what? Why are you here? Dax, what I would like to share with you today is that all of us are born with a magnificent promise. This promise is *who I can be is up to me.* The promise says that you can write your own life story. It says that your life is up to you! It says that you can decide and create the life that you want. You following?"

I most certainly was. I was intrigued and listening with great interest.

"Each baby arrives on the earthly plane with this beautiful, empowering promise. When you are small, though, you do not have the power yet to start living your promise. You don't have the conscious awareness or the physical ability to pursue your promise. The promise is there and will always be there, but it will take years for you to know it and to embark on your self-chosen quest.

"You probably wonder what happens in the meantime—what to be, what to do, when you are not aware of your promise. The world *fortunately* has a remedy. As a young child, you might not know your promise, but surely society knows what is right for you. The people around you have a clear view for your life. I trust you heard me being a bit sarcastic just now. Did you, Dax?"

Yes, I did. My mind was racing. If I had a promise, what was it? I doubted whether I was living it. It made sense that my life was up to me, but I could not forego the thought that my schooling and professional career choices had largely been inspired by what the world knew to be good for me. How would I know I was living my promise? Jane seemed to be more connected with her own choices. She was much clearer about her likes and dislikes in life. She had deliberately made choices in her life to leave places or relationships that did not feel good. Was this what living up to your promise was all about? I told Olisa that I was not sure that I was living my promise. I also shared with her my observation that indeed I knew of many people, me included, who had the habit of providing free advice to children and other adults regarding what they should do with their lives. Humans seemed more interested in directing the lives of others than in targeting their own lives.

"Good observations, Dax. Many people spend more time and effort in controlling the lives of others than in taking charge of their own lives. We think it is the right thing to freely share our thoughts and perspectives with others, whether the other is asking for it or not. We believe it is right to just always give our opinions and comments to others. Let me give a few examples of the kinds of things people think they know and frequently give to others:

"We are here to perform.
"We are here to get a *real* job like an engineer or accountant.
"We are here to fight and win.
"We are here to look beautiful.
"We are here to own and grasp and gather.
"We are here to please others.

"From a young age onward, you are told that you are here to get good grades at school, to excel at sports, to play an instrument, to graduate from a prestigious university, to pursue a successful professional career, to find a beautiful partner, to become a parent, to gather material wealth, to look gorgeous and young, to listen to other people because they know better."

"I recognize what you are saying, Olisa."

"I want to share with you an insightful little story about a recent event here in the zoo. I was walking around in Wild Africa, doing some chores, when I noted a nicely dressed young Singaporean lady walking behind a pram. I love babies, so I could not contain my curiosity. I walked over to her, and we started chatting. I welcomed her to the zoo and asked her whether she was enjoying her visit and whether she was just by herself. Of course, I looked in the baby stroller, and I saw two cute and cuddly babies, smiling and looking happily into the world. The topic of our casual conversation quickly changed to the little children. 'Wow, beautiful babies. Are they twins? Are they a girl and a boy? How old are they?' I threw many questions at the proud young mum, who kindly answered them. Then I asked her, 'And what are their names?' She looked at me a bit startled, and this is what she said, 'Well, we have not yet decided on the names, but this one'—pointing at the girl—'is going to be a doctor, and this one, the boy, is going to be a banker.'"

I had to laugh but also felt sorry. "Funny and sad," I responded.

"Yes it is, Dax. Other people know what is good for you. Or so they think. Without you asking, you will get the ideas of your parents, family members, teachers, coaches, friends, neighbors, preachers, professors, and colleagues. You are taught what life is all about and what it should mean for you. You get free advice on what to think, what to believe, what to be, what to do, what to aspire to. And you get all kinds of warnings and considerations about life that have a tendency to keep you small. For example, you need luck in life. Or life is not fair. Or it is better not to have big dreams because you can only get disappointed. Or you just need to adjust and align with others because otherwise you don't fit in.

"From the day you are born, you are being bombarded and indoctrinated with the mindset of the people around you. It comes with the right intent usually, but people do not realize that, by giving you their ideas about life, they are influencing you to live somebody else's life. They are not aware they are programming your mind into a robotic mind. You don't know all of this when you are a child. While you grow up, you don't know that the perspectives and plans for life that you are developing are not yours. You don't realize that other people are interfering with your promise for life."

I nodded. This all made very good sense. I had a serious expression on my face.

"Dax, have you ever noticed how sweet and vulnerable little children are? A little child is fully open, a big believer. Until the age of approximately eight, a child tends to accept and believe everything that is shared with him. The beautiful promise that it is your life, slowly but steadily, gets overshadowed by the ideas and expectations of other people. Let me visualize this for you. Imagine you are born with a blank sheet of paper, on which you can write and paint and decorate your own life story. By the time you realize that you are the artist, the sheet has been largely filled by others. Your sheet now represents what others think your life ought to be. It is not your work of art. It is not your story anymore."

"I know what you mean, Olisa. When I look at my life, I know that some of my choices and behaviors have not been truly mine. I have made choices based on the expectations from others in mind. I have acted to impress people, not because it was what I wanted to do but because I thought it was required. My parents left most decisions for my life to me, but I cannot say that my current life has been fully crafted by me. Jane knew at a young age that the guidance she was getting from her parents was wrong. As a teenager, she was already consciously making her own choices. Still, the imprint from her upbringing impacts her every day. She frequently doubts whether she is good enough because her parents never told her she was. She therefore does not always dare to make her own choices based on her heart's longing, and she is thus not writing her own story."

Olisa was listening.

"When I look around, Olisa, I indeed see the enormous impact from parents on their children. The father makes his child play tennis because it was once his own dream to become a great player. But the child might not like tennis. The mother believes that playing the piano or the violin is part of a proper upbringing because that is how she grew up. The child is forced to play an instrument, but it might not be what the child wants. The parents tell the child that she has to study hard in order to get a *real* job. She has to become a doctor or a lawyer or an accountant or an engineer or a banker. Parents write their children's stories without asking how the child wants to fill the blank sheet of paper."

"You are right, Dax. The consequence of all of this is that, slowly but steadily, your promise of *who I can be is up to me* fades away. It moves to the background. You start to forget it. Rather than living your own deliberately crafted life, you start to live the life that other people have designed for you. This is how humans are the only species who usually don't become who they are destined to be."

Olisa paused.

"That is a sad insight, Olisa, and it reminds me of the small novel *The Death of Ivan Ilych* by Leo Tolstoy. The main character is Ivan Ilych, who is reflecting on his life at his painful deathbed. He thinks about his childhood, his education, his professional career as a high-powered judge, his marriage, his children, and other relationships. He realizes that he enjoyed life much more in the early years of his life. Step by step, his joy had disappeared. *Maybe I did not live as I ought to have done*, is what Ivan Ilych ponders. He thinks about how he allowed others to make choices for his life—his father, his fellow students, his bosses, his wife. He thinks about the falsity of his life, the phoniness, the hypocrisy, the meaninglessness. He thinks about how much he has hated all of life's artificial decorum. He thinks about how deadly his official life has been. Tolstoy tells the reader that the mental suffering from these reflections is way more painful for Ivan than the agony from his physical disease. Then, in the final moments of his life, the following question appears in the mind of Ivan Ilych: *what if my whole life has been wrong?*"

"That is a very shocking question to come to when life is almost over, Dax. I don't know the book, but it seems that Tolstoy's main message is similar to what we are discussing here: we are here to live our *own* lives, to make our *own* choices, to write our *own* life stories, to live our promises. If you don't, you might come to the conclusion that your whole life has been wrong. Ouch." Olisa looked like she could feel Ivan's pain. Then she relaxed again and started looking hopeful. "But here is the good news, Dax. It is never too late. Once you realize your promise, you can start living it. Once you truly understand that it is *your* blank sheet of paper, you can become the artist who makes the painting of his own life."

"I love it, Olisa, but I am no longer a child, and only today I learned that I have this powerful promise. Can I please ask you two questions?

How do I know what my promise is? And how do I rewrite my story, given that it has partially already been written by others?"

"Let me ask you, Dax, do you think you are here in this life by mistake, or do you think you are here for a reason?"

I remained silent. Olisa continued. "We live in a perfect universe, Dax. Nothing in this universe happens as a random occurrence. The universe makes no mistakes. All is meant to be. You are here for a reason. The reason is life's purpose. It is wise to question your purpose. What are you here to do? If you want to live your promise, go within and ask yourself, who do I want to be in this life? What is my deepest, driving desire? What brings me love, completion, fulfilment? You are one of a kind. You are here to give your best self to this life. The universe thinks, *You are born an original. Do not die a copy!* But that is unfortunately what most people do with their lives. They become automated copycats. In the Bhagavad Gita, student Arjuna asks Master Krishna, 'What is the purpose of life?' Krishna answers, 'The purpose of life is for you to discover and follow your dharma.' Your dharma is your unique objective, your unique purpose for your life. Dax, if you want to find your life's promise, the question to answer is, who do you want to be? In Africa, we have a saying: do not set sail on someone else's star. Your answer to the question who you want to be is your guiding light for finding your own unique star."

"Thank you, Olisa. That is clear. I have never really thought about my life this way. I have never contemplated my life's purpose. I can see that different people have different purposes that are reflective of the unique individual they are. I have homework to do to get more clarity on the questions that you have framed."

"Nice, Dax. If you want to find your purpose in order to write your promise, take time for inner reflection. The clarity and the answers do not lie in the external world. They are available to you in your inner world. Be still and contemplate. That is the way to come to inner clarity."

I nodded.

"Your second question, Dax—how to rewrite your story since your life is already well under way? See it as a blessing that you are gaining this wisdom inspiration already now in your life. Some people never become aware of their promise. You still have plenty of time. When you do your homework and reflect on your life, you will find that there is no need to change everything. There is another African proverb: it is the one who lives in the house who knows where the roof leaks. It is your life; you know best what parts fit your promise well. And you know best what other parts you might want to change. The first five chapters of your story may have been written; it is your prerogative to become the deliberate author of chapters six and onward. Find your purpose, take up your pencil, and consciously write your purpose-based story. Leverage Rama's guidance, and I am sure it is going to be your best possible life story!"

I smiled. "You are an amazing girl, Olisa! Still so young and already so wise. I am going to write an amazing story of the next many chapters of my life. I will endeavor to find my purpose and to start living it. I will find out which ideas about life are truly mine and which adopted ones don't serve me. This is very exciting. I already know that this will result in some changes. If I am honest, that makes me feel a bit nervous, but I am sure Rama is indeed the right person to teach me how to feel the fear and make the change anyway!"

"Great, Dax, and thank you. Have you noticed, by the way, that while we were chatting, all the beautiful animals around us have spent their time just being themselves? That is also who you are meant to be. Buddha's last words before he died were *be a light unto yourself.* Everybody has a light within. Connect with that light, listen to that bright voice, and be who you want to be. If you follow others, if your aim is to be like somebody else, you will be nothing more than a half-baked copy. How can you be somebody else? It is valuable to learn from others, to be inspired by others, but only with the aim to grow and develop to be yourself. You cannot beat somebody else in being that person. But you will always be the best at being you. You are unique; there is nobody like you, ever. Nobody is a model for your life.

71

Nobody's life is a guide for your life. You know best what your best life is. Buddha says it is wise to live in your own light, to live your promise, to live life based on your own dreams and terms. It is foolish to follow others, to copy others, to imitate others, to want to be like others. It is your life, Dax, It is your choice how you want it to be!"

The energizing engagement with Olisa was coming to an end. Both of us had new appointments to attend. I felt inspired and motivated to start taking action on finding my purpose. I looked at the animals and noted their ability to just be. Olisa seemed to also have mastered this skill. She radiated self-assurance and confidence. She seemed clear of her purpose, certain to live her promise.

"Olisa, can I ask you a final question?" She confirmed calmly. "At what age and how did you become aware of life's promise?"

"I like that question, Dax, and it gives me the opportunity to tell you about my great-grandfather. He was already an old man when I was born. We had a special bond. He loved me dearly. When I was eight, his time had come to die. He was fragile, weak, and tired and spent his days in his bed. On a morning, he called for me. When I entered his little bedroom, he was as loving as always toward me. 'I dreamt last night, and I want to share my dream with you, dear Olisa.' I looked at him with my big brown eyes. 'In my dream, I was alone in my room. I had asked everybody to leave because I was tired and ready to die. I felt OK. I was enjoying the silence and solitude. Suddenly and slowly, the door of my room opened. This annoyed me because I had asked to not be disturbed. I snapped, "Who is there?" But there was no response. I watched the door as it continued to open. Somebody came in, and I immediately recognized the *person*. It was my life's promise! "No, not you!" I barked. "Not you! What do you want?" The promise spoke: "I have been with you your whole life. I have knocked on your door on various occasions. I have reminded you of my presence so many times. But every time, your response was to wait, to be patient. Every time I talked to you, there were other people and other ideas and other priorities to be addressed. Every time, you pushed me away." I knew my promise was right. I remembered the many times that my promise reminded me that it was supposed to be *my* life, that I was meant to be who *I* wanted to be. I remembered that I never paid any serious attention to my inner purpose. So I said, "You are right. I have abandoned you. I am sorry, but it is too late now. I am dying. Why have you come?" And my promise said, "I have come to die with you. I am joining you on your last trip of this life, and when you are born again, I will be there with you to remind you of your promise in your new life!"'

"My great-grandpa asked me whether I understood why he was sharing the story with me. 'Do you mean that you want me to live my promise, Bapu?' He laughed. 'Smart girl!' 'But how?' I asked. He told me in a child-friendly way to be who I want to be and how I could find my purpose. I listened and registered every word he spoke. Then he said, 'I know you will write your own life story, dear girl. Do you know why?' I shook my head, and he continued. 'I asked your parents to name you Olisa. Do you know what your name means?'; Again, I shook my head. 'Olisa means God's promise. I asked your parents to give you this beautiful name to ensure you never forget to live your God-given promise. I made that mistake, and that is why I had this dream. I don't want you to do the same! Will you promise me that you will choose your own life, dear Olisa?' I did."

I had tears in my eyes. Olisa noted. What an amazing story.

"I was very sad, Dax, when my bapu left the earthly plane that same day. Soon after, I resolved to live my life using his wise guidance and in the spirit of my name. I learned from nature, I learned from books, and I learned from coaches. I think I am on purpose, Dax. Since I was a young girl, my heart has been going out to the well-being of the environment. As humans, we have the most highly evolved consciousness of all species. It is my purpose and obligation to deliberately use my awareness to preserve the health and beauty of the planet. That is the story I am writing for my life, every day."

"This has been a magical morning, Olisa. Thank you. It feels like I owe it to you to start living my promise, but I know I owe it to myself. I will always remember your name as an inspiration to do so."

I gave her a big hug. While I felt the power of our wonderful embrace, Olisa said, "Thank you, Dax. It has been my pleasure. Don't be a preprogrammed robot living somebody else's life. Write your own life story. Be who you want to be. *That* is your promise and purpose for life!"

Promise—Learning Box

Wisdom	My promise for life: who I can be is up to me. I am here to live *my* life, to make *my* choices, to write *my* life story, to live *my* promise. I am here for a reason, and the reason is my life's purpose. I live in my own light. I live my promise. I live life based on my own dreams.
Awareness	Life is the greatest gift, and gifts are to be celebrated. Celebrate life. All of nature is on purpose except for one species: humans. Your promise gets overshadowed by the ideas and expectations of other people. *You* know best what is right for you, not the world. The purpose of life is for you to discover and follow your dharma. Don't be a preprogrammed robot. Write your own life story! You cannot beat somebody else in being that person. But you will always be the best at being you.
Story/Tool	The two wolves. Bapu's dream.
Practice	Be still and contemplate the question: who do I want to be? Remind yourself in the morning who you want to be and reflect on who you have been during the day in the evening. This exercise helps to grow awareness and to drive behavioral change.

5

Passion

Follow Your Heart

Let the beauty of what you love be what you do.
—Rumi

Passion is your power.
—Dr. Wayne Dyer

I went home after my inspiring encounter with Olisa and attended my afternoon meetings virtually. The last hour of my working day I used to go through my email inbox. Many years before, on my first working day, I had received valuable advice from my first line manager, Frank. When I walked into his office, he was looking at his monitor. He turned toward me, greeted and welcomed me, pointed at his screen, and said, "Dax, a first piece of advice: make sure you never become the slave of your email inbox!" This was the time before social media was keeping people hooked to their screens the whole day, so a very timely and visionary piece of advice. I often reminded myself of Frank's wise council when I was busy with too many emails and I started feeling uneasy and pressured. Receiving advice is nice; knowing how to implement it in your life is the important thing. My inbox had never gotten full control over me, but I also had not managed to be in control of the constant flurry of emails. I looked at my open items and noted a personal message from my boss in London. When I opened it, I read the following message.

> Hi, Dax.
> What about a next job in the Americas?
> There is a great opportunity based out of Houston, covering our business in North and South America.
> Let's discuss.
> Best regards,
> John

Living and working in the United States of America was one of my childhood dreams. I had always been attracted to America, land of the free, land of unlimited opportunity and hopes and dreams, land of beautiful nature and where people were crazy about sports. America had a great appeal, but my mind also conjured an immediate doubt: what would this mean for my learning with Rama? Jane grinned at my thought. "You know you can connect with each other without being in the same room these days. Remember, Dax?" Yes I did. "Great opportunity. Just ask Rama how to keep in touch." My sweet Jane, ever practical, ever supportive.

Rama was as pragmatic as Jane. "Your choice, Dax. You and I keeping in contact should not be a factor in your decision-making. Where there is a will, there's a way!"

Two days later, I talked to John. He explained about the business, the strategy, the objectives, the challenges, and the team. The possibility sounded even better than I had imagined. If I wanted to, I could visit a few of the countries in the region to find out on the ground. That was how I got to send Rama a WhatsApp message to inform him that I would be making a trip to the United States and Argentina a few weeks later. He was quick to respond: "Let's meet up for coffee this weekend!"

Rama and I met on a Saturday morning. "Life and its opportunities," was the first thing Rama said. "All your thoughts, including your dreams, allow you to spot the opportunity that life has on offer. Actions you took in the past, for example your choice of employer and you telling others about your aspiration to be in America, have resulted in this opportunity coming your way. Life is not a random roller coaster, Dax. You have the power to create, and this is nice evidence of it."

Correct, I thought. *Clarity of direction and a conscious mind can truly help to achieve your goals in life!* We ordered our coffees. I chose the usual cappuccino. Rama selected the coconut milk white mocha macchiato, the latest addition to the impressive beverage menu of the place.

"Did you have that drink before?" I asked him.

"No, I did not. First time," was his response. "To stay fresh and young in life, you've got to do new things, Dax. I have made it a habit to try new things out. Great way to explore life. Sticking to old habits can become a bit boring and keeps you away from new experiences," he said with a laugh.

"You got a point there, Rama. Still, I choose to enjoy my regular cappuccino now. Next time, I will open up my mind to the rest of the menu and make a different pick."

"Nice, Dax. I can see that you are making active use of your power to choose! From Asia to the Americas, from the East to the West! Your employer is providing you with wonderful opportunities. Do you realize how blessed you are?"

I had never really looked at my jobs that way. I had certainly enjoyed the various professional roles I had. They had provided me with fantastic challenges and personal development. They had brought me in touch with so many amazing colleagues. They had allowed me to make contributions to the growth and development of nations around the world. And of course they had provided Jane and me with a comfortable lifestyle. Still, in my mind, they were just jobs. But Rama was right. I was indeed very blessed with the company I worked for. The possibility to travel the world and explore different cultures and meet people from so many different backgrounds was an invaluable experience. My stay in the East had been such a learning experience for both Jane and me. Now we had the opportunity to also explore the West. The thought and feeling of gratitude was even more delicious than my cappuccino.

"There are great lessons to learn in both the West and the East, Dax. Over time, the West has been praised for its success in creating external material wealth. The East, on the other hand, has contributed significantly to the generation of internal spiritual riches throughout the ages. The objective of every human being is to find the source of peace and happiness in life. Human needs are physical as well as mental and spiritual. All these need to be met in order to experience calm and contentment. People around the world have been searching for everlasting happiness, but so far they have not achieved it. In the West, people try to find happiness through material possessions, and they suffer from anxiety and stress. In the East, people aim to find happiness through the spiritual path, and they suffer from the lack of worldly comforts. It does not matter where people are. Everybody needs both the lessons from the East on the inner world as well as the lessons from the West on the outer world. Your experience and learning in the East are now going to be complemented with the opportunity to live and grow in the West. This is great, Dax. Your company is helping you to establish the East-West bridge. This can be of immense benefit for you. I am sure it will help you to accelerate your personal growth. You will become a more balanced and understanding person."

"Your perspective makes the opportunity in the Americas even more exciting to me, Rama. I will make personal growth from the East-West combination one of my new objectives!"

"Sounds good, Dax," Rama responded. "You mentioned you will be visiting Argentina, right? When exactly will this be?" I shared my travel details. Rama looked pleased.

"Rama?" I said.

"Yes, Dax?"

"Can I ask you a personal question?"

"Of course. What is it?"

"You are such an inspiration. I see the immensely positive impact you have on the lives of so many people. How did you become like this? When was the moment you realized that it is your life's purpose to bring light to the world?"

Rama smiled. "Nice question, Dax. I don't usually talk too much about my life. I rather endeavor to inspire others by *living* my life in line with my teachings. But I am happy to share some of my background. I grew up in New Delhi in India in a well-to-do family. My father successfully built the family business from scratch. His childhood had been one of immense poverty, and at a young age, he had resolved to become a successful entrepreneur. Through a lot of hard work and tenacious perseverance, he achieved. By the time he was a father himself, he had made a small fortune. As a kid, I lacked nothing. I went to the best private schools, wore expensive clothes, and could participate in any hobby I wanted. I played a lot of cricket, for example. When I was a teen, my dad told me that I would have to take over the family business. From that moment on, my education became focused and directed toward this objective. It was also around that time that I had my first acquaintance with wisdom. My mum was a regular visitor of meetings with masters, and I accompanied her for one of these evening events. The words about freedom and happiness in life this gentleman spoke that evening touched me. They were like a spark that ignited my thirst for wisdom. From that moment on, I joined my mum every time she went out to be inspired. At a later age, I started my own search for life teachers I could learn from. I was taking two paths of training in my life: one for success in the external world and one for understanding my inner world. After I finished my master's in business administration, I joined my dad's company. I learned about all business aspects through doing jobs in all the various departments. Slowly but steadily, I mastered the business, and my father gave me more and more responsibility. When I was twenty-eight, he asked me to succeed him as the CEO of the company. I felt like I was on top of the external world. I had it all: career success, my own big mansion, many cars, servants, a gorgeous wife, and respect from society. My inner search under the guidance of various gurus has also continued. Master Amir, whom you met, has been my most important teacher. While I had all the outer success, I came to see there is more to life than material riches. At the age of thirty-three, enlightenment came over me. Everything became clear. I *saw* my promise. I could see that my life's purpose is to guide other people toward happiness and success in their lives. It didn't take me long to quit my role as CEO, and ever since, I have been teaching and coaching people how to live their best lives. How to be on purpose, how to enjoy life to the max."

Rama stopped talking. He looked at me with a truly happy face. "That, Dax, is the summary of how I came to be a life guide for other people. I have loved every day of my life since."

"Thank you for sharing, Rama. I love your story. What did your dad say when you told him you would be quitting the CEO role?"

"Hahaha," was Rama's response. "Yes, my dad. He was very disappointed and angry with me initially. He tried to convince me to change my decision. But I was not to relent. Once you find your life's purpose, there is nobody and nothing that can stop you from living it. For my dad and me, it meant that our relationship worsened, and for many years, my father did not want to talk to me. Only after some eight years, when he saw my happiness and joy, my positive impact on other people, and also my material success, he came around. Our bond has never been stronger since. I love him. He has been a most important teacher in the early days of my life."

Time was up. We both had to move on to other appointments. As I gave Rama a big hug, I said to him, "Thank you, Rama. Thank you for sharing your story."

A few weeks later, I flew to Buenos Aires via Amsterdam. My familiarization trip first brought me to Argentina for various introductory and get-to-know-you meetings. After three days, I then planned to travel to Houston, Texas, for another three orientation days. The normal schedule for these types of trips is: airport, hotel, office, restaurant, hotel, office, restaurant, hotel, office, airport. This gives plenty of time to meet people but no time to experience the surroundings. Whenever I traveled, I therefore used to ensure that I had at least half a day of free time to casually explore the new environment. Unfortunately, I had not found the time to do some preplanning ahead of my first trip to Buenos Aires. When I arrived at the airport, all I knew was the name of my hotel and the address of the office where I would have to be the next morning at nine o'clock. I had no clear plans for some exploration. The taxi brought me to my hotel. I was tired and not taking in much of the scenery. When we arrived in the city center, all I noticed was that the area where I was staying reminded me of Paris, one of my favorite cities in Europe.

I checked into my hotel, ate a nice pasta, and went to bed early, as the journey had been long and tiring. Despite the gigantic jet lag, I slept well. My phone alarm woke me up, and after a refreshing shower, I walked into the breakfast room at 7:20. To be on time for an appointment was the example my parents had always given me, so it had become a habit of mine. New office, new colleagues. I left the hotel early and arrived well on time at the company's security desk. I got my temporary visitor's pass and was allowed to go to the office floor and wait there for Andres, the local business manager. When I entered the floor, I noticed only one other person there at the early hour. When the gentleman saw me, he walked over and welcomed me enthusiastically. After he pointed me to a desk that I could use that day, he walked back to his own place. I sat down and observed the office environment. It was clear that our company's global real estate targets were also applicable here. Just watching the desk setup and layout, I could be in any office of our company around the globe.

As I was settling in, a second Argentinean colleague entered the floor. The lady walked over to the other colleague. She greeted him with a big hug and two kisses and went on to her desk. Then the third colleague arrived. He walked over to both colleagues present and wished them a good morning in the same, very personal way. Then he spotted me and walked over to give me a warm hug and welcome.

The lady, who came in second, now also noted me. She got up from her desk, stepped toward me, and gave me a personal embrace as if we were good old friends. The same ritual happened that morning in the Buenos Aires office every time a new colleague appeared. The new person walked to every other colleague and greeted each one in a very friendly, caring way. I was not left out. In a matter of thirty minutes, I received more hugs than I had received in the Singapore office in the five years I had been there.

Andres was one of the last people to arrive. After his good morning tour through the office, he came to me. He welcomed me in what I now knew was the standard Argentinean way. I got a big embrace and a most friendly verbal greeting. "Hi, Dax! Great to have you here. I hope you had a good night of sleep!"

"Thank you, Andres. Very nice to meet you too. Yes, I got a good rest, and I got a huge amount of fantastic hugs this morning!"

He laughed. "Yes, that is how we greet each other here in Argentina, Dax. Sounds like you have already gotten into one of our national habits. Clearly, you were open to experiencing it. Sometimes visitors are not ready for our personal way of greeting, and then we just shake hands. It is all good. Please come over to my office, and let's have a chat."

We drank a cup of coffee, and Andres took me through the introductory program that he had kindly put together with his team. There were business introductions, engagements with various teams, and many one-on-one meetings to get to know people. "Two more things, Dax," Andres added. "On your last day here, you are invited to join our management team meeting in the afternoon. It will probably help you to get a feel for what is currently on our business agenda, including our opportunities and challenges. It will also give you a firsthand encounter with team dynamics Argentina style. You are up for a treat!" He smiled.

"You mean a meeting full of hugs and kisses?" I responded.

"Something like that. You will see." Andres was a cool guy— charming, funny, organized, clear, and exceptionally well dressed. I had spent thirty minutes with him, and I liked him already.

"Was there another thing, Andres? You said *two more things*," I said.

"Yes, Dax. This one is very extraordinary. End of last week, we received this envelope." He reached into one of the drawers of his desk and pulled out a shining, dark red paper bag. "We had no idea what this was. Usually we do not receive such ardent envelopes. When we opened it, we found a brief letter addressed to me. The letter said that you, Dax, would be visiting us this week and that we were invited to join the dinner tango show in one of the most prominent places in Buenos Aires. There was one proviso: we had to bring you. In the package, we found ten tickets for the show of tonight. Of course, this was a wonderful surprise. But the much bigger shock is that Sofia Perez will perform. She is the best tango dancer ever, and it is sheer impossible to get tickets for her shows. We were astonished, Dax. This invite blew our minds. Most of us have never had the opportunity to see Sofia dance, and now we can. Don't know how this happened, but we are ready, and you should certainly join us. This will be magic!" Andres was obviously overwhelmed.

"Sounds fantastic, Andres. I am ready to join."

I returned to my hotel after an effective day with the Argentina team. I took time to relax and reenergize, and I dressed up for the big evening. Andres picked me up at 7:30 p.m., and together we drove to the theatre. He seemed even more excited than I was, probably because he knew what to expect. Dinner started at 8:30 p.m. This was a big event. The room was fully sold out. All visitors were beautifully dressed, especially the ladies. They were wearing the most impressive gowns, supplemented with gorgeous earrings and necklaces. Most men were wearing expensive-looking tuxedos. I felt somewhat underdressed, but Andres assured me that Argentineans were totally cool with that. There was excited conversation in the room. I could sense that people were enjoying the delicious dinner courses but were all eagerly waiting for the true main course of the evening: Sofia Perez's dance performance.

Fabian, one of Andres's management team members, shared a brief history on the tango with me. "Tango originated in the 1880s in

85

Argentina, Dax. We love this dance. We see it as a national heritage. Around 1900, it started spreading internationally. Tango is highly sensual. You will see that for yourself tonight. Because of this, initially tango brought a culture shock in the generally conservative cultures around the world. By 1915, tango had become accepted and very popular in fashionable European circles. The early tangos were spirited and lively. By 1920, the music became melancholic. Over time and impacted by many different cultural elements, many different styles of music and dance have developed. We Argentineans consider Argentine tango as the mother of all the tango. We are very proud of it." I could feel the love for the dance from Fabian's captivating story.

Suddenly, the lights were dimmed in the room, and a strange-sounding instrument started playing. Everybody became silent. Fabian quickly whispered to me, "The typical sound you hear comes from the bandoneon, a tango accordion. That is the tango's musical companion. The show is starting, Dax. Put all your senses to work and enjoy!"

I was in awe and in a trance for an hour and a half. The show was absolutely incredible and captivating from start to finish, touching my eyes, my ears, and my body. The music, the different rhythms, six musicians and two vocalists, the emotion, the temptation. The dancers, darkly handsome men, slim, stunning women, the couples becoming one. The dances, the energy, the power, the kicks, the spirals, hip-to-hip movements, the soul. The exercise, balance, skill, strength, physicality, precision, concentration, focus. The clothing, elegant suits, shining black shoes, amazing dresses, colorful, high designer heels. Sofia, the absolute star of the show, dazzling, leading, enjoying, on purpose. Ninety minutes of pure passion!

Sofia and her crew received a standing ovation of almost eight minutes from an ecstatic crowd. They smiled humbly as if to say, "Don't exaggerate, guys! This is what we love and do!" The honor and celebration bestowed upon them was more than deserved. What a show! I had never seen anything like this in my entire life. Very slowly, the room came to its senses after the dancers left the stage. You could still feel the excitement and admiration flowing through the room. The amazing performance seemed to be the topic of discussion at every table in the theatre. It certainly was in our group.

Some of my Argentinean colleagues had tears in their eyes. They were sharing their feelings and emotions openly and with broad hand gestures. I was silent and just taking in the experience. My inner reflections were disturbed by a sudden enthusiastic rumble on the other end of the room. I turned around and saw that Sofia Perez had reappeared to connect with the crowd. She halted at a few tables and was chatting with her fans. People's reactions were cheerful and euphoric, especially a young lady who was seated two tables away from ours. Sofia Perez and the lady were having an intense conversation that brought the young girl to tears. I could see Sofia reassuring her as she got back to her senses after a few minutes. Sofia gave her a big hug. The woman was shining again. She seemed deeply grateful.

"What was that all about?" I asked Fabian because I had not understood a word of the conversation in Spanish. Fabian explained that the young lady had become so emotional because Sofia was her idol. Her example in life. And she was so exhilarated to finally attend one of her shows and even to talk to her. Then she had burst into tears, saying, "I want to be like you, Sofia. How can I be like you?" Sofia had responded in a calming way, "Dear girl, do not want to be me. Want to be your best self. That is why you are here. Let me give you the secret how to be the best you: follow your heart and do what you love to do!"

Wise counsel, I thought, but before I could think further, Sofia had walked over to our table. She looked at me and asked kindly, "How did you like the show, Dax?" I was too flabbergasted to give an immediate answer, so she added, "You mind if I join you guys?" And before we truly realized what was happening, we were accompanied by Sofia Perez, the biggest tango star in the history of Argentina.

"How do you know my name, Sofia?" were my first words to the big star.

"Rama," she said with a smile. "He told me you would be in Buenos Aires and that you had never seen a tango show."

"Did *you* send the invite to my colleague Andres?"

"Well, I asked my personal assistant to do so, but yeah, in a way I did. And now that we meet, are you interested to hear my key life lesson?"

"I would love to, Sofia. Thank you so much." She smiled. My colleagues were also listening intently and in silent admiration.

"Do you have kids, Dax?"

I shook my head. "Not yet. It is one of my biggest dreams to be a dad!"

"Parenthood is the best, Dax. I can tell you that. My husband and I have a beautiful daughter. Her name is Eliana. She goes to primary school and frequently brings home a load of homework. After her cup of tea, she sits down, and she does her homework. Reluctantly. Exercises are OK for her. But learning for tests is a whole different thing. Eliana prefers dancing, playing with our dog, engaging with her friends, being outside in nature, creating beautiful pieces of artwork. Last week at dinnertime, I asked her about her nature and technology test the next day. Her response was. 'Yeah, I will look at it tonight.' After dinner, I observed her doing what she likes. When I reminded her, she said with a stern face, 'But what is the purpose of me learning this? I will have forgotten about it the day after!'"

I had to laugh. "Kind of makes sense, Sofia. Eliana must be a smart kid."

"She sure is! When you look at a child, Dax, you get valuable insight into how to live. A child will show you that we all prefer to do what we like to do. Naturally, we would choose to do what we love to do. Children live like this, if parents allow them. Many adults though, unfortunately, have long forgotten to choose based on what they like. They choose based on their conditioning. Let me share a story with you that Rama told me in one of our discussions. I love stories. They help to teach important lessons in a fun way. Ready?"

Yes, I was.

"Recently, more and more people are asking the wise, elderly master, 'How can I live more joyfully?' One evening, she comes home late and notices that she has lost the key to her house, so she can't get in. In front of the house, there is a lamppost. She walks over, sits down on her hands and knees, and starts looking for her key. People walking by notice, and after a while, one of them asks what she is doing. The master explains that she is looking for the key to her house. When the bystanders hear this, they immediately join the master in her search for the key. Soon enough, more than twenty-five people are crawling around underneath the lamppost lights. Nobody finds anything. After some time, a lady stands up, walks over to the master, and asks her, 'Where actually did you lose your key?' The master responds to say that she lost her key inside her house. 'Huh ... but why then are we looking here, outside of your home?' The master gets up and explains, 'Well, you have been asking me how you can live more joyfully, right? You have not been very receptive to the guidance I have been giving you to base your life on what you like. Joy is to be found in your life. Every day, you have the opportunity to find it. Ask yourself, are you looking for it in the right place?'"

My colleagues and I had to laugh. "That is a funny story indeed, with a powerful message!" I said.

"Think about it, mi amigos. You go to school. You study. You work. You fall in love. You marry. You grow a family. You interact. You find friends. You socialize. You have interests. You choose hobbies. You exercise. You live. You spend your time. But do you enjoy? Studies show that love for the subject is still an important reason for students to choose their course subjects. Other studies show though that a large part of the working population, up to 85 percent, are not happy in their work. The significance of joy appears to decline when we get older. Still, we all want happiness and enjoyment in our lives. You agree?"

Everybody at our table nodded frantically.

"If you want joy, you better search for it in the right place. If you want joy, you better spend your precious time on things that you like. You better spend your days on things that you love, things that give you energy, things that make you smile. Don't look for the keys to joy in places where you know in your heart you will not find it. Our robotic mindset does not help us in finding joy. When you were a child, joy was your nature. Children truly enjoy their days. Then you grow up, and somehow, some day, you lose this great skill of enjoying life. You get serious, you get focused on obligations, you start to regret the past and worry about the future. Do you remember when this happened? Do you remember when you moved from living joyfully to living without passion? Do you remember when basically you stopped living?"

We looked at one another around the table. I certainly recognized what Sofia was talking about. My life was joyful but not in comparison to the joy I had felt when I was a child. Every day was an adventure. Every day was playful and fun. I sensed my colleagues felt the same. "It makes sense what you are sharing with us, Sofia, but I have no idea when this change happened."

"There is no fixed date for the change, guys. The change happens step by step, and you accept it just like the frog in boiling water. Do you know this experiment? A frog is put in a pan with cold water. The water then is gradually being heated. The poor animal stays in the pan, adjusting to the increasingly warmer water until it dies because of overheating. You do the same. You adapt to circumstances that are not of your choosing. You adapt to the terms that society prescribes for you. As a child, you know you are here to enjoy, you are here to have fun. But society teaches you that life is about performing and accumulating. Society tells you to take life seriously. Slowly but steadily, you start to forget your innate knowing. Your focus shifts from having joy to doing things for the sake of achieving. You lose your playfulness, you become somber, and you become humorless."

The mood at the table had shifted from exhilaration after the tango excitement to silent contemplation. Sofia noted it. She stood up, circled her arms into the air cheerfully, and said with a beaming voice, "It is time to set things right and bring passion and joy back!"

"That sounds good, Sofia. Passion is advertised by almost every wisdom teacher as the basis for a happy and successful life. But it seems hard to find. Could you please explain how I can find my passion?" I asked.

"Good question, Dax. I am getting to it. The question that everybody should answer is: what do I *love* to do? Most people have no clue when you ask them. They have long forgotten. But your answer is there. It is hidden inside of you. When you want to find your answer, I have to warn you about your cunning mind. The mind can be the most powerful tool you have. It can also be an instrument that keeps you away from finding your passion though. You know why? Because of the robotic nature of your mind. Your preprogrammed mind carries many conditioned ideas about life that keep you away from your passion. The automatic mind has a tendency to reason. Finding what you love to do is not a rational thing. It is a matter of feeling and emotion. When you want to find the answer, it is wise to listen to your heart. Put your rational mind aside and feel the answers in your heart. Your mind can *fool* you, but your heart cannot. Your heart can *feel* you. Answers coming from your heart will make you smile. They will make you feel good, give you energy, and make you feel tempted to move into action. When you find your passion, Dax, nothing can stop you from pursuing it."

We were all hooked to Sofia's story.

"I know you have met Olisa. Wonderful, wise girl. She has shared with you that it is your promise and purpose for life to be who you want to be. Rama first sent you to her for a reason. Your best life starts with being. You are here to *be* the best you can be. That is step one. Step two is about doing. Loving what you do results from being what you want to be. When you do your life's purpose, Dax, there will be passion. Guaranteed. If you are who you are meant to be and do what you are supposed to do, you *are* on purpose, and you *do* with passion. When you live like this, life will reward you in the best way possible.

"My passion is tango," Sofia continued.

"I noticed," I said, and everybody had to laugh. "That was rather obvious, Sofia. You dancing is passion in action!"

"That is true, Dax. Very true. All my life, there was only one thing I wanted to be: a tango dancer. It is my passion to be out there on the dance floor and perform. It is great that people love it, but the most important thing is that *I* love it. When you love what you do, you will be your best self. When you love what you do, you will shine, and you will have unlimited energy. When you love what you do, you will not feel like you are working, and you will find joy naturally. When you love what you do, you will be successful. Jesus said, 'Where your heart is, there your treasure will be.' By *treasure*, he means the joy and results for your life. So here is the master's formula for life in the right order, Dax: be who you want to be, do what you love to do, and have what you want to have. It is exactly as I have experienced it."

For the second time that evening, we were in awe. The powerful insights Sofia was sharing made us silent and upbeat. Here was a lady at the top of the tango game. Her life was proof of everything she was telling us.

"If it is so simple in a way, Sofia, what goes wrong for so many people?" Andres asked. "Sorry, I forgot to introduce myself. My name is Andres. It is an honor to meet you. *Muchas gracias* for your time and inspiration!"

"Thank you, Andres. Nice to meet you too. Great you guys could make it tonight! The answer to your question is a sad answer in a way. Constant conditioning has created the idea in many people that they are not good enough. We have never been really accepted by our parents, our teachers, our friends, our coaches, our neighbors, society. All these people have been trying to improve us, to make us better, to turn us into somebody we are not. Much of the focus in growing up goes to our mistakes, goes to our weaknesses, goes to what we are not doing well. How many people emphasize how great we are, how beautiful we are, how totally unique and special we are? There are severe consequences from all the pointing out what is not good about us. It makes us believe that there is something else we should be, there are other things we should become, and there are other ideals to follow. We start to believe that praise will come later because apparently just being is not enough. We start to believe that we are only good when all these omitted things have been repaired."

All of us sighed because of Sofia's reflections. We recognized what she was saying.

"In the whole universe, human beings are the only species who cannot just simply enjoy being alive. Think about it. The rose is perfectly happy. The dog is perfectly happy. The mountain is perfectly happy. The clouds are perfectly happy. All of nature just thrives in being. Never does the rose question whether maybe it needs to be a lotus flower. Never does it get jealous of the beautiful sunflower because of its glorious height, its special orange color, and its unique characteristic to follow the sun during the day as the earth turns around the sun. The rose just is. How can it be something other than a rose? The rose only has one purpose and passion in life, and that is to be the most beautiful rose there is. But not humans. We are coached, from our childhood on, that we have flaws and that we need to change in order to be complete, in order to be fulfilled. We are taught how we should be. This does not work. Just like the rose who simply enjoys being a rose, we are meant to be just ourselves. Find what you love to do, just do it, and your life will be one of fulfilment and happiness. Follow your heart. Be yourself. That is the greatest achievement.

"Do you want to know what I tell my darling Eliana every day of her life? I tell her that she is perfect the way she is. I tell her to be who she wants to be. I tell her to do what she loves to do. I tell her to follow her passion and enjoy life. It is my intent to fill her mind with ideas and beliefs that will help her to live her best life, to live her life on her own terms."

I could see that all of us were making mental notes of the wise counsel Sofia was giving us. A few of my colleagues even took a pen to write down the powerful messages she was sharing with her darling daughter every day. *If only every child grew up with a mindset like that,* I thought. *It would make the world a better place!*

"Dear friends," Sofia continued, "you want to find your passion?" We were all desperately nodding.

"Find your answers to the following six questions:

"What do you really enjoy doing?

"What gives you lots of energy when engaged in it?

"When do you have the best time of your life?

"What do you and others think you are really good at?

"What can you keep on doing without getting tired?

"What, if all basic needs are fulfilled, would you want to do?

"You want to answer these questions intuitively. This is how you can best do this. Rama always says, 'To hear your inner voice, you have to silence the outer noise!' So find a quiet spot, sit down, and calm yourself. Here is a simple exercise to do that: close your eyes and focus on your natural breathing for a few minutes. It will calm your mind and connect you with your inner being. Now you take your pen and write down whatever you feel are your answers."

"Sofia, can you please repeat the questions once more so that we can all write them down?" I asked her. We all made detailed notes of her instruction on finding our passion.

It was past midnight. Sofia was still full of passion and energy. Passion gives energy—so much was very clear. And passion is contagious. Despite my severe jet lag, I did not feel tired at all. The whole team seemed very alive. But it was time to wrap up. Sofia's manager walked over and indicated to her that it was time to go home.

"Follow your passion, dear friends. Do not let society come in between. Become aware of your societal conditioning and dig deep inside yourself to find what you love to do. You can always change. Age is not an excuse for living without passion. You are here to do what you love. That is what I wish for you, Dax, and all of you. Now it is time for me to go home. I need to be fresh tomorrow morning to fill Eliana's mind with the right ideas about life, and I do not want to miss that. Enjoy Argentina, Dax, and find your passion!"

She left but not before she had given me a big, passionate hug. I thanked her and thought, *Rama truly has the most amazing friends all over the world.*

Back in the hotel, I sent Rama a one-word WhatsApp message: "*Sofia!*"

When I woke up, he had already responded.

> Dear Dax,
> I hope you liked Sofia's tango show, full of passion!
> And I hope you like the next step in your master mindset training.
> Enjoy Argentina,
> Rama

"Where does Rama not have any friends?" I asked myself. I remembered what he had once said: "Dax, the world is a small place once you understand the oneness in all. You can build lasting friendships everywhere." That certainly proved true for my wise teacher Rama.

The day in the office started with a full round of welcome hugs and kisses. Now that I knew about this intimate Argentinean morning tradition, I was an active participant and enjoyed it. The second day was productive. I got a good feel for our business in the country, and I met many people. Andres and Fabian took me out for dinner at a local steakhouse. The morning of my third day was as beneficial, and then it was time for me to join the management team meeting in the afternoon. Andres had asked me to just observe and share some feedback afterward. And of course I could contribute if I wanted. The team conducted the meeting in English so that I could understand. After some casual updates, the meeting went into business performance, risks and opportunities, and a number of investment proposals. These were the usual topics I was accustomed to. But the way the meeting was conducted was a whole new experience for me. In short, the participants spoke their minds in complete honesty and full of emotion. At times, it felt as if I had entered a war zone—one without deadly bullets but full of verbal firepower. People shared their thoughts and perspectives with a drive and intensity I had never seen before. When colleagues agreed, they cheered and applauded. When others had different ideas or opposing views, they brought their opinions forward as if their lives depended on it. I was spectator to a fierce spoken fight where every pro and con was heavily contested and debated. Andres did his best to manage the discussions toward conclusions but was involved himself in the intense sentiments and heated conversations at the same time. It was three hours full of fury and emotional energy. No time to breathe. A raging storm.

At 4:00 p.m., Andres called the meeting to an end. Most topics had been resolved. I had not spoken a word, but I felt adrenaline rushing through my body. It was time for drinks in another room of the office building. I was still speechless when I ordered my alcohol-free beer. The management team members were already there with drinks in their hands and were casually chatting, making jokes, and laughing heartily. The emotive fighting spirit had been replaced by a relaxed, friendly atmosphere. Andres came to stand next to me and asked, "Dax, any feedback?" He smiled.

I looked at him, probably still a bit shaken, and responded, "Andres, my friend, one word!" His eyes sparked, and exactly at the same time we both shouted, "Passion!" We burst out laughing.

"Yes, Dax, this is how we conduct our meetings. Full of passion, full of energy. It brings out the best of all of us, and it results in the best possible outcomes for our business. Immediately after the meeting, the intensity and disagreements are forgotten, and we are back to being very good friends again. Our joint love and respect is so big that we don't want anything other than the truth from everybody. This results in heated debates full of emotion, but all of that is forgotten when we have a drink afterward. In a way, we are just a bunch of little kids: open and honest, present in the moment, and not holding on to any grudges!"

We had some more drinks, and then it was time for me to say farewell. My flight to Houston was leaving that evening. Before I left, it was *gran abrazo* time. I hugged everybody present. As I left, I knew that Argentina, land of passion, would forever be in my heart.

Passion—Learning Box

Wisdom	I want to be my best self. I don't want to be somebody else. To find my passion, I listen to my heart. My (robot) mind can fool me; my heart can feel me. I am who I want to be, and I do what I love to do. When I love what I do, I will be my best self.
Awareness	Life is not a random roller coaster. You have the power to create. The objective of every human is to find the source of peace and happiness in life. Once you find your life's purpose, there is nobody and nothing that can stop you from living it. Passion is the basis for a happy and successful life. Just like the rose is here to be the most beautiful rose, you are here to be your best you. Your greatest achievement is to follow your heart and to be yourself.
Story/ Tool	The master and her missing key.
Practice	Go see a tango show! Sit down, calm yourself, and contemplate the passion-finder questions. Write down whatever comes up. Tell your child (and yourself): you are perfect the way you are, be who you want to be, do what you love to do, follow your passion, and enjoy life!

6

Priority

The Most Important Person

You can search throughout the entire universe for someone
who is more deserving of your love and affection than
you are yourself, and that person is not to be found
anywhere. You yourself, as much as anybody in the
entire universe, deserve your love and affection.
—Buddha

To forget yourself is the only sin. To
remember yourself is the only virtue.
—Osho

I also enjoyed my time in Houston. On my way back to Singapore, I reflected on the familiarization visit. Before I fell asleep in the comfortable airplane chair, I concluded that the Americas job opportunity was a fantastic one. Provided Jane would be supportive, I resolved to inform John immediately upon my return.

The plane landed in Singapore on a Saturday morning. Jane was there to pick me up. I shared my positive experiences with her in the car, and together we decided we would be making the jump from East to West. The only email I sent that weekend was my message to John to confirm my serious interest in the job. I used the remainder of the weekend to reconnect with Jane and get a proper rest.

It took a week for John to give me a call. He explained that he had been busy sorting out all kinds of approvals in the wider organization. It had all worked out fine. At the end of our chat, he said, "Dax, congratulations! You got yourself a new job. The Americas are waiting for you." I felt eager and enthusiastic. I thanked John for his support and asked him about approximate timing. "You will have to start early next year, Dax. That gives me the necessary time to find your successor in the East. You have a few months to wrap things up and plan some farewells." I told John we had a deal. As we ended our call, my mind started thinking about the many people in Asia who had touched and inspired my life.

It is funny, I thought. I had attended many farewell events for people moving on to new endeavors—from drinks with large groups of people, to events packed with activities like carting and hiking, to intimate dinners. Whenever the person saying goodbye took the microphone to say a few words, it was almost always about people. Yes, sometimes a bit about challenges and achievements was mentioned. But the majority of the address was usually about the bonds, the camaraderie, the teamwork with others, and the lessons, the guidance, and the inspiration received from them. Farewell events usually turned into very personal and touching happenings for that reason. *It is funny because people are so different. Still, what really matters for all of us are the relationships we have with others.* I was thinking about the many friends and colleagues who had been instrumental in making Jane's and my time in Asia so great.

It is said that moving places is among the most stressful events in one's lifetime. Other life situations that have a big emotional impact include death of a loved one, divorce or separation, marriage, starting a new job, financial problems, and illness. Jane and I decided to meditate daily in order to strengthen our inside. Choosing your mind's focus helps to sustain a stable inner foundation to be able to deal better with external changes. Counting our blessings was a prominent part of our practice. Consciously connecting with your mind and heart with everything good in your life is a simple yet powerful technique to stay calm in the storm. It gave us much inner strength, but still we both felt melancholic about our upcoming departure from Singapore. Saying farewell to places and people you have come to love wholeheartedly can be a difficult thing. As a remedy, we started our research on Houston and the Americas with a focus on all the things we knew we would fall in love with in our new environment. We also reminded ourselves of one of the wisdom lessons we had learned and knew to be so true: sometimes you need to close a door in life to be able to open a new one. Change gives opportunity.

Within a few weeks, we had made a comprehensive plan for our move from the East to the West. It was then a matter of working it step by step. One of my priorities for the remaining months in Asia was to visit colleagues in a number of the countries I had collaborated with intensively. These countries included the Philippines. One of Jane's and my joint priorities was to maximize our face-to-face connection with Rama. We knew we would keep in touch with him to continue our learning and growth. We also knew that opportunities to meet him in person would diminish. On one of those sessions with Rama, he asked me how the preparations were going. I told him about various elements of our plan in action, and I shared how we were leveraging meditation and wisdom to stay stable and focused.

"Sounds good, Dax. Change can challenge you. Therefore, it is even more important to manage your inner system deliberately. This helps to manage yourself, and it makes the transition easier. You mentioned you were going to visit the Philippines?" Rama had shown me on various occasions what a good listener he was. I was not surprised he had also picked up the details of my farewell travel plan.

"That's correct, Rama. It will be my last business trip in the region, the week before Christmas. For my friends in the Philippines, Christmas is the most important event of the year. They invited me to join some of their celebrations in previous years, but I had not been available then. I have been deliberate to plan this trip last so that I can join them this year!"

Rama smiled. "Good, responsible planning, Dax. What parties will you participate in?"

I shared the details of my program with Rama, including the charity event where I would be joining my colleagues to give out food and presents to the underprivileged.

"I like it," Rama said in his always positive voice. "Enjoy!"

So it was that I got on the plane to Manila with a packed schedule. As the plane was at cruising altitude, my mind went over the events of the previous months. It had been hectic. Jane and I had been working actively to settle our time in Singapore and to prepare for our move to Houston. Leaving Singapore meant cancelling the many commitments we had made, like our house lease, memberships at various social and sports clubs, and our mobile phone contracts. It also meant making decisions on our house inventory: what to ship to the East and what to leave behind in Singapore. Moving homes can be troublesome. It can also be a great help in sorting your material possessions before they grow over your head. We took the opportunity to give away a lot of our furniture to charity. Unburdening our life from stuff felt liberating. The biggest challenge had come from selling our car in the Singapore market, where car owners prefer to buy brand-new. But after we had started talking about the car for sale, we soon found an expatriate couple new to the country who opted for the economy car purchase. In between all the moving actions, I had made several farewell business trips to Malaysia, India, China, New Zealand, and Australia.

Now I was on my way to the Philippines. During my visits to the country's capital, Manila, I had come to admire and love its people. Poverty is visible everywhere, and the country is frequently ravaged by heavy weather conditions. Still, the Filipino people shine and laugh and enjoy. They seem to have a built-in resilience based on a positive outlook on life. I had observed this in the fancy business district, Makati. I had observed this in the poor living areas with hand-built houses from all kinds of waste materials and children walking barefoot. A smile on the face of a Filipino was never hard to find. I felt excited and sad at the same time—excited to meet my happy colleagues once more; sad because I knew it would be my last visit to this wonderful country with its beautiful people for a long time to come.

The days in Manila were filled with business meetings, one-on-one catch-up and coaching conversations, and social events. Life and business just continue when you are gone. As I discussed current and future business affairs with my committed colleagues, I was aware of this. I would soon be out, and I knew that nothing would really change. The awareness reminded me of a lesson that Rama had once shared: do not take life or yourself too seriously. You are just one little radar in an infinite universe. Life goes on whether you are there or not. Life goes on whether you achieve or not. "When you do not take yourself too seriously, anger will disappear," Rama had said. "When anger disappears, your joyfulness will grow, and you will be more compassionate and loving."

During the social events, we talked about beautiful memories of our years together. We thought of the significant business success we had achieved and the two global awards for our team's performance we had been rewarded. We laughed about the karaoke event where I had found that each Filipino has a talent for singing! We reviewed my appetite for all the typical Filipino food I had tasted, including the country's favorite delicacy: balut! Balut is a fertilized chicken egg incubated for a period of two to three weeks and then steamed. My initial response when I had been offered a balut egg had been "Not for me." Then I reminded myself of the important life lesson—to live with an open mind and to try new things. I ate my balut, which earned me an enormous amount of goodwill among my Filipino colleagues. We talked about how impressed I was with the selfless care that I had consistently observed in the team. Argentineans are passionate. Filipinos are caring. Help and support from others had always been available whenever a team member was struggling. Care seemed to be second nature for the local people, not only in the office. In Singapore, Jane and I had been blessed with the help of Rufina, our Filipino amah. Once I had asked my dear colleague Nancie for help to host Rufina when she had to be in Manila. Without even thinking, Nancie said, "Yes, of course! She can stay with us." I thanked her but also asked, "Why? Do you not need to meet Rufina first?" I will always remember her answer: "Because we care, Dax. In Philippines, we help other people!" All the memories made the social events that week magical and unforgettable.

The days passed quickly, and the last day arrived in a flash. It was time to join the company's Christmas charity event at noon. At 11:00 a.m., the team gathered to leave for the event. When we arrived at the location, it was full of people and joyous with Christmas decorations. The climate in the Philippines makes a white Christmas impossible. But decorated artificial pine trees, Santa puppets, green and red garlands, a sizeable nativity scene, cotton wool snow, and even three fluffy reindeer all contributed to an impressive Christmas experience. Volunteers were wearing seasonal sweaters and hats, a real Santa was engaging with children, presents were piled up on long tables, and Christmas carols blasted out of an impressive sound machine. It wasn't difficult to catch the joyful, festive spirit. My colleagues and I put on bright red Santa hats and joined the happy volunteering crew.

The event had been organized next to one of Manila's slum areas. These are densely populated settlements, crowded and with compact housing units. With an average daily income of two to four dollars, the slum citizens benefit from charity by companies and individuals. In the Philippines, support and help to the poor is a widespread phenomenon. There I was, participating in a Christmas benefaction event, giving out packages with basic necessities to underprivileged adults and some simple toys for the children. The company had also provided for a sumptuous yet healthy Christmas lunch for everybody. The atmosphere was not one of separation between the rich and the poor. It was an ambience of connectedness and care, with people mingling, chatting, and relating with one another as equals. Nobody seemed to feel superior. Nobody seemed to feel inferior. There was laughter and enjoyment. The volunteers were enjoying the Christmas celebration at least as much as the recipients of the gifts.

As I was participating in a most memorable Christmas event, I noticed one particular volunteer. She was a young local lady who had been working tenaciously and happily the whole time. She seemed to have an almost natural attraction to children, who were continuously gathering around her. She was kind and playful and made the kids laugh. One little boy especially had been staying close to her. Suddenly a woman who probably was his mother appeared on the scene and started shouting at him in Tagalog. The boy changed from a shining, cheerful little child to a sad and anxious kid. The volunteering lady noticed. She stepped forward and started a conversation with the mother. "Is there a problem, ma'am?" she asked.

And the woman explained in English so that I could follow: "I had told Diego how to behave at this celebration. He was not to spoil his best set of clothes. He was not to eat with his hands. He was not to shout and run. He was not to disturb the volunteers. He has done everything that I told him not to do." She gave little Diego an angry look, which made the poor boy cringe.

I was curious what the young lady's response would be. She looked kindly at the mother and said, "Your little Diego has been enjoying himself tremendously. He has helped me with various tasks. He has befriended many other children. He has been laughing, and he has positively touched others with his joyful and playful character. Allow me to give you a piece of advice: stop belittling your son with telling him what not to do. Start lifting him up by praising all that is unique and special about him. It will be of tremendous support in the rest of his life."

The mother looked at the lady for a moment with a who-do-you-think-you-are expression, but soon enough, a smile came on her face. "Thank you. That is one of the best pieces of advice I have ever gotten. I will remember. Merry Christmas!" With that, she picked up Diego and gave him a big kiss. The young lady waved at Diego and went back to work.

After a few festive hours in which thousands of packages were handed out, people started leaving to take care of other matters. Hugs and gestures of gratitude were exchanged, and soon enough, only the large group of volunteers was left. The young lady who had helped Diego suddenly approached me and asked, "Are you Dax?"

"Uh yes, and you are?" I said.

"I am Raquel Rivera. How did you like your first Christmas event in Manila?"

"I loved it, but I still do not really know who you are. Do I know you?"

"Not yet. But our joint friend Rama told me to see you here and tell you my story. Are you interested?"

I had to laugh. *Rama! This man is truly inimitable.* Then I said, "Very nice to meet you, Raquel. I would love to learn from your story."

She smiled graciously. "Good to hear, Dax. Let's help clean up, and then we will go for a walk, a drink, and an inspiring chat!" Raquel could notice that I was ready to meet my next teacher.

We did the chores, and I took my time to say a last farewell to all my dear friends from the office. I was flying back to Singapore early the next morning, so this was the last time we were all together. Parting with a grateful heart is difficult and wonderful at the same time. Difficult because you experience a sense of loss. Wonderful because you have had the opportunity to engage and connect with people you have come to love and because the beautiful memories will last forever. I felt both emotions running through my veins.

Raquel was waiting patiently. When we finally left for our get-together, she kindly said to me, "I can see that you and your colleagues not only had a business relationship but also a true friendship bond. That is wonderful, Dax. The most effective professional teams are built on a foundation of trust, respect, and care for each other. I am sure you guys made an amazing team together."

"We did, Raquel. The team will always have a place in my heart," I responded. "Thank you so much for spending time with me this afternoon. Can we first get ourselves a nice beverage though? I was so engrossed in the Christmas activities that I forgot to drink sufficiently. Not a smart thing in this climate," I said jokingly.

After we purchased sufficient liquids to survive the afternoon, I asked Raquel about her purpose and passion in life and where she had met Rama. "Nice questions, Dax. I am happy to share my story. I was born and raised in the southern part of the country, on the island of Mindanao. My family was poor, and my father did not have a permanent job. He was always out to find a day job to earn a few dollars to feed our family. But he was never able to sustain us on a continuous basis. When I was five, it was necessary for my mum to become an amah. That is a foreign helper in a family of a relatively rich family abroad. She has mainly worked in Hong Kong and Singapore for a period of more than thirty years. She was never around, but I loved her because I knew it was her intent to take good care of us. My five siblings and I were pretty much raised by our grandparents. My grandmother had also been an amah, and so had my great-grandmother been one. It kind of runs in the family. For many Filipino girls from poor backgrounds, it is like a programmed destiny. You may have dreams for your own life, but gradually they disappear, and you start to believe that being an amah is the only possibility to provide for your family. You have heard about the robotic mind, right? Well, here you have a good example how such a mind turns into a self-fulfilling prophecy."

I confirmed my awareness of the robotic mind, and I shared with Raquel that Jane and I had had the pleasure of a Filipino helper, our dear Rufina, during our time in Singapore.

"I hope you have been taking good care of her, Dax! Every Filipino amah deserves proper treatment, as they are away from their loved ones and taking care of you. As a girl, I was pretty obstinate and independent. I was clear that I wanted to make my own choices for my life, but as I grew up, my resolve to do so became weaker. I did not observe much change in my environment. For most people, life seemed to be predestined. I started to think that maybe I would never be able to realize my dreams. Would I have to accept a future in the footsteps of the women in my family and just become an amah? Nobody in my direct family made an effort to change my fatalistic thinking. To the contrary, people were telling me that this was my fate as a girl from a lineage of amahs.

"Then one day a man came to our school. I must have been fourteen. His name was Jay. I still remember. He told us he had been fortunate enough to grow up in a rich Filipino family. After university, he had started working as an investment banker at an international bank in Manila. After a few years, he had been offered a job in Singapore, which he had gladly accepted. Then the story he was telling us changed. He was not there to talk about his career in banking. He was there to talk about life lessons he had learned from a wise master called Rama while in Singapore and how it had changed his life. He talked about the power of the mind and how the right mindset can be the most powerful tool in our lives. He told us of our promise in life, the fact that we all can be who we want to be. He explained that we all have a purpose for being here and that finding your purpose is the objective of life. He said that knowing your passion will help unearth your purpose. He inspired us to find passion and purpose in our lives. And I still remember the last words of his talk. Words I will never forget. Jay said to all of us, 'Never forget: it is *your* life. You owe it to yourself to make it the best life possible!'"

"That sounds like a student of Rama," I said. "And it shows the consistency in Rama's teachings, as this is exactly what he wants me to learn." I grinned.

Raquel continued. "The lessons from Rama had inspired Jay to make significant changes in his life. When he left Singapore, he quit the bank. He went back to the Philippines to inspire children to live their best lives. To live the life of their dreams and passions. And to teach them how to do this. He said to all of us at my school, 'Children are our future. You are the future of the Philippines. The better your lives are, the better will be the future of our country. It is my purpose in life to teach children to be who they are destined to be!' When Jay was done talking, all my schoolmates and I burst out in cheering and applauding him. He had opened our eyes, and he had given us a vision for our best lives. I felt so happy, exhilarated, and grateful. That was the day that I decided again to live my life on my own terms."

I was listening to Raquel. Again I had met one of Rama's students and friends who was on a mission to take life in her own hands and inspire the world with her fantastic example. While telling, she was shining and full of energy. Her words were flowing as if inspired by the universe itself. "I am getting goose bumps from your story, Raquel. Please continue. I would love to hear how, after listening to Jay, your life evolved. But maybe you can first quickly tell me how you and Rama became such good friends."

"I certainly can, Dax, thank you. After his empowering talk, Jay stayed at the school for a few hours to meet individual students. I was determined to talk to him, so I lined up and had the opportunity to meet him. We had an immediate connection when I opened our conversation by saying, 'Thank you so much, Mr. Jay. You have changed my life already. Now I want to learn how I can create the life that I want!' Upon hearing this, Jay looked at me with the most loving and empathetic expression I had ever seen, and he replied, 'Raquel, I love your determination and clarity. The masters say that clarity precedes achievement. You are on your way! I would love to teach you how you can live the life of your own choosing.' That is how Jay became my teacher, my coach, and my friend. One day Jay invited me to join him for a trip to Singapore, where he would be participating in an inspirational training from Rama. I gladly accepted, as I was very curious to meet the man that Jay had talked so lovingly about all these years. I met Rama when I was nineteen years old, and ever since, he has been my wise mentor and guide in life, as well as a cherished friend."

"Nice story, Raquel. Great you have different people in your life who inspire and guide you. Now tell me about your best life."

"I will, Dax. When you grow up in the Philippines, you are surrounded by people in need. When I met Jay, I knew in my heart that I wanted to spend my life caring for other people here in the country that I love. I did not want to become an amah taking care of foreigners abroad because I saw so much opportunity close to home. I became a nurse out of passion. Every day, I give my love and care to hospital patients. In my free time, I do voluntary work like today's Christmas event. I love to bring a smile to the faces of children and adults by doing good. When I was twenty-one, I started a shelter for homeless people in Manila. This organization has grown to become the biggest contributor to the people in need here in Manila. We feed and care for thousands of underprivileged human beings every day."

I was impressed. Raquel was approximately thirty-five years old, and she clearly was on a mission to follow her passion. She radiated an energy that you don't see in many people. "It sounds like you are the Mother Teresa of Manila," I said.

"Actually, Dax, that is the name that people have given me. I don't like to mention it. I am Raquel. I am very happy my life has turned out exactly as I dreamed it to be. I am enjoying every day of my life to the maximum. You can't imagine how much satisfaction it gives to be a force for good in the lives of adults and children." She beamed with joy as she was speaking. I could feel her passion.

"So, in short, Raquel, your life revolves around taking care of other people," I said.

"Yes and no," she responded. "This is a good bridge to what Rama would like me to share with you! Have you ever heard of Professor Abraham Maslow, Dax?"

"Do you mean Maslow who is famous for his five-tier model of human needs?"

"Yes I do, Dax. Maslow's theory states that humans are motivated to fulfil their needs in a hierarchical order, starting with physiological needs at level one and ending with self-actualization needs at level five. This is a frequent learning topic in marketing classes all over the world."

"Yes it is, Raquel. It certainly was part of my training!" I said.

"It is a nice insight, but Maslow shared many more valuable lessons with his students. There is one message in particular that I believe is way more important than his human needs model. It is my favorite teaching, and I really think that everybody should be made aware of it!"

Raquel was being earnest. I was more and more fascinated, so I asked her to continue.

"Ever since I started learning from Jay, it has been my objective to master myself. It is my goal in life to be the master of my own destiny, and it all starts with mastering myself. Professor Maslow defined self-mastery in a very intriguing way. Simple yet complex to reach, clear yet challenging to achieve. You want to know, Dax?"

I nodded.

"Maslow states that self-mastery is to become independent of the good opinion of other people."

"Becoming independent of the good opinion of other people?" I repeated. "That can't be too hard, Raquel, can it?"

Raquel laughed. "You think you are free from what other people think of you, Dax?" she asked teasingly. "Think about it. Do you always speak your mind honestly? Or do you hold back because you are afraid of other people's reactions? Do you always make your own choices? Or do you take into account the expectations other people might have in making up your mind? Are you always unshaken when people critique or challenge you? Or do you sometimes feel insecure or emotional when people don't agree with you?"

I was reflecting, and I had to admit that I was not master of myself in the way Maslow had described it. "I guess you are right, Raquel. Living up to this definition is a serious challenge indeed. Why is that, because it sounds so simple? And why does becoming independent of the good opinion of other people result in mastery? Can you please explain more?"

"I have asked myself these questions, Dax, and I spend a lot of time studying myself and others to come to an understanding and also a resolve. Believe it or not, your mindset again is the big player in all of this."

"The robot mind, I presume, Raquel."

"Yes, Dax. The robot mind! I want to make you aware how a most detrimental belief develops in the minds of many people. I have to start at the time a human is born. Babies are so cute, so adorable. Everything the little one does is considered fantastic and is cheered upon. Pulling up the little baby legs. Discovering the baby's own hands. Burping. Making pretty noises. Even a full diaper is seen as a major achievement. A baby is allowed to be. She will not tell you, but she enjoys is. It allows her to develop naturally. But little ones grow older. At toddler stage, the little boy or girl will start to experience opposition for the first time. You know why? Because the little kid starts to develop willpower and learns to say no. It drives many adults mad. Why is this kid not doing what I want? What happens is that adults start telling the child what to do and what not to do. This is how the brainwashing of the kid on what is right and what is wrong begins.

"I want to tell you a story, Dax. Listen. I regularly visit schools to talk to children. I want to inspire them just like Jay did with me. One day, I was at a preschool in a class full of youngsters. I introduced myself, and then, as always, I asked the kids to tell me their names. It is all part of making the children comfortable but also to challenge them to speak. They started giving me their names. Some spoke with a soft voice. Some shouted their name. Some spoke clearly. Some mumbled their name. And then it was time for a little boy with beautiful brown eyes and dark hair to say his name. He said, 'My name is Luis Don't.' I was surprised, so I asked the little boy to repeat what he had said. Once more he said, 'My name is Luis Don't.' I had heard the name for the second time then, and I asked little Luis: 'Is that really your name?' He looked at me with innocent eyes and said, 'Yes it is, Miss Raquel. My mum calls me 'Luis Don't' the whole day!' I grinned, but I felt sorry for the little boy.

"This is what little children often hear, Dax. Don't shout, don't run, don't eat with your hands, don't speak with only one word, don't enter the table with unwashed hands—don't, don't, don't. What do you think little Luis takes from this? He learns that he cannot decide for himself. He learns that there are rules about what he can and cannot do. He learns that he is not a good boy when he is behaving in a way that is not allowed. The consequence is that Luis starts to believe that his choices and ways do not matter. That others apparently decide." Raquel spoke the last sentence in a cynical tone.

I recalled her brief conversation with Diego's mum. "This is why you advised Diego's mum to refrain from telling him what not to do, right?"

"Correct, Dax. The *coaching* doesn't stop at kindergarten age. When the child is at primary school, he starts to bring home test results. The standard way these are received is that when the grade is great, the child receives compliments, recognition. But when the grade is disappointing, there is none of that. The child receives disapproval, criticism. Children take messages literally. They don't argue. For them, the disapproval is true. The result is that children develop a belief that they are not good enough. They start to think that their value is dependent on how they perform because that decides the opinion of other people.

"The kid grows older. Other people are then getting focused on their results. At school. At sports. In friendships. Results count to get approval from others. Peer pressure to be, to do, to look like the norm increases. Adolescents feel the need to belong. Their behaviors and appearances are led by their friends because that is the way to be accepted. The approval from others has become the primary objective in the lives of high school and university students.

"It never stops. The graduate makes his self-worth dependent on the success of his career. The wife makes her life experience dependent on the feedback from her partner. The businessman goes on accumulating material things to attract admiration from other people. Life has become a race for the approval of others. We have become prisoners of the idea that the most important thing in life is what other people think of us. In the words of Maslow, we have become totally *dependent* on the good opinion of other people.

"So here is what we do. We don't speak our mind honestly because we are afraid of other people's reactions. We make our choices and actions dependent on what other people expect from us. We feel bad and uncertain when other people disagree with us or criticize us. *What will they think?* has become a leading thought in all that we are and all that we do. And we are not aware of it."

Raquel paused for a while. I was silently contemplating the insights she was sharing. They were so true. The priority in the lives of many seems to be to ensure others like them. People are more concerned with the happiness of others than their own. They are afraid to upset others and are focused on pleasing them.

"I recognize what you are sharing, Raquel. Society indeed teaches you that it is very important what other people think. More important than what you think yourself."

"Yes, Dax, that is correct. And this is not helpful at all. When you think, *I am good if others think I am good*, you have basically given your control over how you feel away. You have put your view of yourself in the hands of others. Whatever they think, you accept it. I am so glad Jay helped me to understand this at a young age. It is not how I have chosen to live my life!"

"Can you please tell me more, Raquel?" I responded.

"Yeah, but first I have another question for you, Dax: who is the most important person in your life?"

I hesitated, and without waiting for my answer, Raquel continued. "Most people will respond with somebody else based on the conditioning of their mind. They will say, 'My mum, my dad. My sibling. My partner. My child. My boss. My coach.' When I ask this question and I get these kinds of answers, I always immediately follow up with the question, 'Are you not forgetting someone?'"

"You mean me—right, Raquel?"

"Yes, I absolutely mean you!" she said cheerfully.

"This is what I would like the whole world to know: you yourself are the priority in your life! Everybody should have a mindset that says, *I am priority. I am the most important person in my own life!* It is your life—right, Dax. Do you agree?"

"I guess I do, Raquel. Yes I do!"

"Just think about it. You know your dreams and aspirations for life much better than anybody else. You know who you would like to be and what you love to do. Other people don't. You know how you feel and how you experience your life. Nobody else does. You deal and communicate with yourself the whole day. Much more than other people talk and listen to you. Better to listen to yourself, I would say. What do you think, Dax?"

I was thinking and I couldn't agree more with her.

"How can you *not* be the most important person in your life? I want everybody to realize this. *You* are the priority in your life! It is good to have your own views. It is good to make your own choices. It is good to support yourself. It is good to have positive self-talk. Your life starts with you. *You* have to make it your best life; nobody else will."

"It is true, Raquel. I totally agree. But I do see a problem. Many times when people prioritize themselves, they are blamed for being egoistic. What is your view on that?"

"Unfortunately, you are right in that observation, Dax. Here is the thing though. The person who calls you egoistic suffers from the same robotic mindset that most people have. It is the mindset that says that other people are more important. Whenever this person sees you behaving in a way that is independent of the good opinion of other people, he simply does not understand. His mind cannot fathom. In his life, he always puts others first. When he sees that you put yourself first, he calls you egoistic. Deep down, that is exactly what he would like to do himself, but he has not yet connected with me to become aware that *he* is priority!" Raquel laughed.

"Dax, you asked me whether my life revolves around taking care of others. And my answer was yes and no. Yes, I am a nurse in the hospital. And yes, I take care of others as a frequent volunteer and through my charity organization. But also no. Because, first and foremost, I take care of myself! I want to tell you a story. I am sure you will love it.

"A long time ago, in ancient India, there was a wise guru. He spent his days walking from one village to another to share his light with many people. One day he is walking through the desert when he suddenly sees a tree in the middle of nowhere. *This is a good place to rest,* the master thinks. *Here I will sleep for a while in the shade of the tree.* The saint has a good, reenergizing nap. When he wakes up, he feels eternally grateful to the tree. So he hugs and thanks the tree with his whole heart. The tree says to the guru that it is all good. 'This is my purpose in life.' And the master asks the tree, 'How? What do you mean?' The tree explains that it is there in the desert for people like the guru. 'I provide shelter and shade for travelers. It is my endeavor to be as big and wide as I can.' The wise saint listens and says, 'I understand, but are you happy? Happiness is the key purpose of life after all!' The tree responds, 'Of course. This is what my life is about, so I am happy.' And the guru says, 'If that is your purpose, then take away your focus from your branches and your leaves that provide shelter to others. Focus on your roots instead. Shift your priority from giving through your branches to nourishing your roots! First take care of yourself. Then you will be able to give even better care to others!'"

"I love the story, Raquel. The message is very clear. Life starts at your roots. In other words, life starts with myself. And we all want to give. But to be able to give the best to others, I must first give to myself. Nice way to illustrate that I should give priority to myself!"

"You got it, Dax. And do you know what your roots are? Your roots are your thoughts. It is your mindset. That is why I want to imprint the mindset *I am priority* with everybody I meet. Putting yourself first is not egoistic at all. It actually helps you to do more for others!"

"That is a great insight, Raquel. Fantastic!"

"There is more, Dax, that you need to understand so that it becomes easy to accept the *I am priority* mindset. One day I was approached by a beggar while walking on the streets of Manila. I could see he was thirsty and hungry. He asked me for some money. Almost immediately, I told him that I would give him some, and I reached to get my purse from my handbag. No purse! I had left my wallet at home that morning. There I was—I wanted to give the poor man some cash, but I could not do it. I am telling you this, as it demonstrates a very important life lesson: you can only give what you've got yourself. I wanted to give some cash, but I could not give it because I did not have it. This applies to everything in life. If you want to give out maximum empathy and care to others, you better make sure you first have it inside. When you give priority to yourself, you fill your own purse. Then you will be able to give to whomever you want. That is the optimal order for life. It does not work the other way round."

"Raquel, so what you are saying is that when I give to myself first, I create the ability to give that which I give myself also to others. That is another very good way to explain why prioritizing myself is not egoistic at all. Rather, it is the opposite. Everybody else will actually benefit from it."

"That's it, Dax. And I have one more nugget for you in case you are still not fully convinced that it is good to give priority to yourself. There is nothing wrong with your wish to feel appreciated by others. Positive attention and feedback can be nourishing for you. It can help you to thrive and grow. But you will only accept compliments and admiration from others if you first appreciate yourself. If you do not think positively about yourself, you will not believe the praise and approval that other people are giving to you. If you don't think you are good enough, no feedback from others will be sufficient to convince you otherwise. So if you want to get maximum value from other people's positive opinions on you, you better first work on yourself. When you train your mind, you can build an inner foundation of self-love, self-worth, and self-esteem. This opens the door to experience the ultimate benefit from other people's reactions."

"Wow, Raquel, you are making it so clear why life should truly start with putting yourself first. It allows you to give more to others. It enables you to give what it is you would like to give to others. It helps to gain and blossom more from positive input from others. And I guess it protects you from criticism and negative views that others express to you."

"Correct on all accounts." Raquel smiled. "You got it. So who is the most important person in your life? Who should get priority?"

"Me!" I shouted. "It should be me!"

"Here is my lesson to you, my friend: *I am priority!* Change your mind's software from *others first* to *me first*. It is the greatest gift you can give yourself and others! So next time when you are doing volunteering work and you are thirsty, make sure you gift yourself a drink first. Then you are ready to help others even better!" she said with a big grin.

"Hahaha, you remembered me being thirsty," I responded.

"Yes, I did, Dax. When you said that at the beginning of our chat, I already knew I would mention it at the end of our afternoon together."

"Sharp mind, Raquel."

"Yes, Dax, a trained and focused mind. I am gifting myself my meditation every day. That is part of me giving priority to myself. You now understand why!

"Maslow was so right, Dax. When you become independent of the good opinion of other people, you make your own choices for life. You write your own story, not the story that someone else has made up for you. When you allow yourself to be guided by your inner voice, you will live on your own terms and conditions. When you give priority to yourself, you will first take good care of yourself, and then you can take care of everybody else. When you develop the mindset *I am priority*, you are in position to maximize your life. Then you can truly enjoy the ride, Dax. That is what life is for!"

I looked at Raquel Rivera. So young, so wise. Shining and so full of energy. On purpose, following her passion. An inspirational teacher. "Thank you so much for your heartfelt care for me, Raquel. I have loved every minute of our get-together. Your life is testimony to the value of your advice and guidance. I will make your lessons part of my mindset and my life. And I am sure it will be of massive benefit for me. Salamat, Raquel. I wanted to say take good care of yourself, but I guess that is unnecessary in your case!"

"Thank you, Dax. I still appreciate your well wishes, although indeed I do not think I will ever get rid of my *I am priority* belief." She looked at me confidently, and we both started laughing.

Priority—Learning Box

Wisdom	It is *my* life. I owe it to myself to make it the best life possible. I am the most important person in my life. *I am priority!* My roots are my thoughts. I take good care of my roots. As I give to myself, I create the ability to give more to others. As I give to myself, I can enjoy positive feedback so much more (because I will believe it).
Awareness	Change gives opportunity. Sometimes in life you need to close a door to be able to open a new one. Clarity precedes achievement. Know what you want. Don't be a prisoner to the idea that the most important thing in life is what other people think of you. Self-mastery is to become independent of the good opinion of other people. You can only give what you've got. As you develop the mindset *I am priority*, you are in position to maximize your life.
Story/ Tool	(Little) Luis Don't (is that really your name?). The master and the desert tree.
Practice	Count your blessings. Develop the *I am priority* mindset.

7

Self-Belief
The Secret Ingredient

The only thing that matters in life is your
own opinion about yourself.
—Osho

Self-belief is the catalyst for spectacular achievement.
—Robin Sharma

You are what you believe yourself to be.
—Paulo Coelho

My visit to Manila had been a rewarding last trip in Asia, the part of
the world that I had come to love so much. Great people, great nature,
great work ethic, great hope for improvement, great chaos sometimes,
great resilience, great growth, great care, and of course great food.
Jane and I would miss our beloved Asia. But we had learned how to
handle such loss. From Rama, we had learned about the power of our
minds. There had been a time in Singapore when I had quoted the
phrase "the mind is a powerful tool" several times every day—until
Jane made me aware of my new habit and told me kindly that she had

gotten the message. I stopped spreading the message. But I kept the wisdom.

The power of the mind can be summarized by one word: focus! My power is in choosing my focus deliberately. Master Amir had made this key lesson for life very clear. When you choose your thoughts with focus, you can influence how you feel. When you use your mind with awareness, you can be the conscious creator of your life. The mind is a powerful tool indeed. Jane and I had learned how to use this tool. We would not be focusing on missing Asia or regretting we had left. No, we would deliberately think of all our experiences and people in Asia that we felt so grateful for. That way, we would not be feeling sad. We would focus our minds on all the good that Asia had given us. We would be filling our hearts with beautiful and positive memories to keep amazing Asia always alive for us.

The weekend I came home from my trip to the Philippines was our last weekend in Singapore. Thanks to Jane, we had completed all the moving preparations. When I was in Manila, the container with all our stuff had been filled and taken to the harbor for shipping to the USA. We had left our rental home. All our subscription ties with Singapore had been cancelled. We were free agents. We had five more nights in one of the beautiful Singapore hotels before we would be boarding the plane. We would take it easy, relax, and get ready for our move to the West. There was only one appointment left—one that we were looking forward to very much. Rama had invited us for a celebration dinner on Sunday evening.

The easy weekend went by slowly. If you don't allow yourself to be rushed by the external world, time appears to be moving more leisurely. Time is on your side to enjoy and relax if you choose to do so. Unfortunately, it also works the other way. When you allow yourself to be pressured by the world around you, and you feel the stress, time seems to be moving faster. It adds to your anxiety. We enjoyed the weekend. We took a dip in the hotel pool and had a nice nap on Saturday afternoon. On Sunday, we slept in, had a casual breakfast, had coffee in the city, enjoyed lunch at our favorite hawker center, and dozed off on a lounger next to the swimming pool. After a refreshing swim, we went to our room to get dressed for dinner. I knew Rama would not mind our attire. He had once told us an intriguing riddle.

A master is invited to a party. The women in the room wear beautiful evening gowns. The men stylish tuxedos. The master shows up in T-shirt and shorts. The question is: what does he do?

We had started speculating about the possible answer, applying the wisdom lessons we had learned. "The master knows that the inside is more important than the outside. He just sits down and stays calm. The master does not react. He does not feel insecure. He *responds* by walking over to the hotel concierge and asking for a loan tuxedo. The master knows about the power of focus. He deliberately chooses to focus on all the positive things in the room. This way, he manages how he feels."

Rama had listened patiently. He seemed pleased but not satisfied. When our ideas had stopped flowing, Rama said, "Great answers. I can hear how much you have learned. I applaud the development of your wisdom minds! Still, none of your answers represents the master's mind. The answer to the question is *the master does not even notice!*"

We had been stunned. Then Rama continued mysteriously: "Analyze the question with your robot mind, and you will never come to understand the answer. Silence your mechanical mind through meditation. And use your wisdom mind to reflect on this riddle. One day, you will comprehend the deep yet simple answer."

This is why I knew he did not mind the attire in which we would show up. As Jane and I were choosing our clothing, I reminded Jane of the riddle. She remembered. Then she said with a big smile, "I do care though, Dax! So you better put on something nice."

A taxi took us to a charming, little Italian restaurant. Rama had shared the restaurant's name and address via WhatsApp. We had never been there. There were only some fifteen tables. Grapevines were hanging on the ceiling, and there were lush plants scattered around. The smell of the woodfired pizza oven and typical Italian kitchen herbs like basil delighted our noses. Dimmed lights gave the place a romantic atmosphere. A waiter appeared, and when we mentioned Rama's name, he beamed. "Ah, friends of Maestro Rama! Come, I have reserved the best table for you." He guided us toward a table near the window, surrounded by impressive potted plants. "A table in nature, as Master Rama calls it, and with the best view of the house!" The waiter pointed outside, and there we saw a large, well-maintained pond filled with lotus flowers and what appeared to be Japanese koi carp. We sat down to wait for Rama.

Rama arrived perfectly on time. He was wearing casual Western-style jeans with an Indian kurta, a loose, collarless shirt. Jane and I noticed simultaneously and started laughing. "What is the laughter about, my friends?" Rama asked. We recounted his riddle. He smiled and said, "Masters might not notice, but that does not mean they can't have style!" He sat down and admired the lush plants around the table and the lively pond outside. "We got the best table. I love it!" Then he turned to us and asked kindly, "How are you, Jane and Dax? Are you ready to trade the East for the West?"

Yes, we were ready. We shared our updates with Rama, including my recent trip to Manila and my unexpected but very inspiring engagement with Raquel. "Great you met her, Dax," Rama said with a playful look on his face. "She is an impressive young lady indeed. I am glad you now know your priority in life!"

The Singapore and Asia chapter of our lives had been fantastic. We felt that we were ready to turn the page and start writing a whole new chapter in the Americas. "Sounds good, my friends," Rama said. "You have maximized your time in Asia. And you are ready for new adventures. Now, let's first order some of the delicious food." Rama smiled like a happy child in a candy shop when he looked at the menu. "The food here is so good. Choose what you like. Anything will impress your tastebuds!"

As we were studying the menu, the chef of the restaurant appeared. "Maestro Rama, so good to see you again!"

Rama stood up and said, "Luigi, my friend!" and gave the chef a big hug.

"What can I delight you with tonight?" Luigi asked, and we placed our orders. "Excellent choice, *scelta eccellente!*" Everything we said was welcomed by the chef's infectious enthusiasm. "*Grazie amici*, I will do my best." And with that, Luigi rushed back to his kitchen. Shortly after, the most delicious dishes started filling our table. Now and then, Luigi personally came to check in to see whether we were enjoying ourselves. We definitely were. It was clear that Luigi wanted to make sure we had the perfect evening in his amazing restaurant.

"Italian hospitality and Italian delight in Singapore. You probably understand why I love this place so much," Rama said to us. "Simply fantastic!

"I am grateful we met, Jane and Dax. You are a blessing to me. You have been wonderful students. Enthusiastic. Open-minded. Curious. Courageous. Responsible. You have grown your mind awareness and your wisdom mindset. You have grown your life, and I don't mean in material terms. I know you have been successful in the external world, and I even know you have grown your wealth during your time here. That is great, but it is not the ultimate goal of life. You are not here to gather and accumulate. You are here to be happy. To experience joy. We all want happiness and joy, and everything we do eventually is driven by this desire. The primal root for life is happiness. Most people apply the so-called more, more, more strategy to become happy. They think that when they acquire more, they will be happy. They live in a beautiful house, but they have spotted an even more beautiful home. Their minds tell them that if they own the other house, then they will be happy. So they work and work to earn and earn. And finally the day has come to purchase the place. They feel exhilarated. They are so happy when they move homes. Until they find the next property they desire. Their happiness is gone, and life has again become a pursuit for more. This does not only apply to homes. It applies to cars, to jobs, to jewelry, to clothes. It applies to relationships, to spouses and friends. Your desirous mind will always want more. The more, more, more strategy gives you temporary happiness at best. It will never satisfy your inner longing for structural happiness and joy."

We were listening.

"Happiness, my friends, is not something external. It is an inside job. When you train your mind to focus on things that make you happy, you choose happiness. You will be happy, irrespective. But when you allow your mind to focus on things that make you unhappy, you unconsciously choose unhappiness. You will be unhappy. Do you spot the difference between happiness and unhappiness? It is just the *verb*! You can either take active charge of your mind and create happiness, or you can passively allow your automatic mind to create unhappiness. The untrained mind unfortunately is more attracted to lack and negativity than to blessings and positivity. When you don't take control over your focus, your mind usually attracts negativity. Your untrained mind gets distracted by the world around you, where there is much that makes you unhappy. A master's mind can ignore and focus, Jane and Dax. With such a mind, you can choose your thoughts, and you will be the master of your own happiness."

It was a wonderful evening. Our stomachs were loving the amazing Italian food. Our souls were being nourished by the wisdom that Rama was sharing. Wisdom always made us feel good. It inspires and empowers. Wisdom had helped us to grow our lives in many aspects. Happiness and joy. Our relationship and other relationships. Peace and calm. Focus and decisiveness. Health and energy. And also success and results. Wisdom truly was, as Rama had once remarked, the optimizer of life. Wisdom never bored. You always wanted more. Probably the only worthwhile more, more, more strategy in life is the pursuit for more wisdom. "Thank you, Rama. That is such a powerful reminder," Jane said. "We will miss your company tremendously." She sighed.

"My dear Jane, inspiration does not require face-to-face connect. You can always remain in touch with wisdom and guidance, no matter where you are. You carry your mind with you wherever you go. Keep the beneficial and valuable thoughts and perspectives in your mind. You don't need my physical presence or that of any other teacher.

Become the master of your mind and fuel your mind with wisdom. That, my dear Jane, is the greatest gift you can give yourself."

Rama's words, spoken so selflessly and lovingly, brought tears to our eyes. "Still, we will miss you," I uttered.

Rama smiled and said, "But of course we can always *choose* to keep in touch, albeit at a distance! How is the food anyway?" It was easy to understand why this was one of Rama's favorite restaurants in Singapore. The food and the ambience were truly amazing and magical. "Good," said Rama. "Glad you are enjoying your last supper!

"Did you notice the pond outside?" Rama suddenly changed topic. We nodded. "I also chose this place because there are two more valuable lessons I would like to give you. You see the lustrous lotus flowers and the colorful koi fish? They have great life lessons for all of us. These I want to give to you as a kind of farewell gift."

"We are all ears," Jane said happily. We were both ready to be inspired.

"Koi are carp fish that originate from East Asia. The name *koi* is a Japanese word that means affection or love. Koi are considered symbols of luck, prosperity, good fortune, and also perseverance in the face of adversity. There is an old Asian myth about koi. It is told that koi fish who live in a small pond and among small other fish will not grow big. They will keep small and will not become bigger than the fish surrounding them. Koi, on the other hand, who live in a large pond and are accompanied by large fish will grow big. They will reach their true potential. Although the premise of the legend is not proven scientifically, the story has big meaning. Your circumstances, including the people you surround yourself with, have a massive impact on your life. You will never be bigger than your environment. So the lesson is: choose your surroundings and the people you associate with wisely. They can block but also unleash your growth."

"Great lesson to remember and apply, Rama," I said. "What about the lotus flower?"

"The lotus, my favorite flower!" Rama was beaming. "In the East, the lotus symbolizes divine birth and purity. It lives in shallow water with its roots in the mud. Its stem rises above the water so that everybody can enjoy the blooming of its gorgeous flower. The lotus teaches us how to live: be in the world but remain above it. You live in the world, my friends. We all do. The mud in which the lotus flower roots represents the world we live in. It can be a muddy place. It can be a bewildering place. It can be a place that pulls you down. But the lotus flower stays above it. It stays true to itself. It shines and blooms above the water. This fascinating flower will not be pulled down by the mud. It will rise above it. The lovely lotus shows its best self to the world. The flower lives up to its promise: to be the dazzling flower it is supposed to be. We can all learn from this powerful lesson. Yes, live in the world, but make sure the world does not own you. Live your promise. Live your purpose. Be who you are destined to be and show it to the world!"

Jane and I were staring at the pond outside, admiring the various lotus flowers, contemplating. "Be in the world and be myself," I said.

Jane said, "Thank you, Rama. You have an amazing ability to inspire. We have learned so much from you. Your lessons have elevated our lives. I love you. I thank you from the bottom of my heart."

I felt the same gratefulness for this kind, loving, wise man who had given us so much. "Thank you, Rama," I said. "Thank you so much."

"Thank you, my friends. Remember: you are here to *live*. Everyone is existing, but not everyone is living. A mind fueled with wisdom will help you to live. To be happy, to enjoy, to thrive, to shine and bloom, no matter the mud around you. Be like the lotus. Live! And continue your growth so that you will enjoy life to the max!" We were silent. Rama continued, "Oh yes, Dax, before I forget. Here, a note with the name and contact details of my friend Ace in Houston. Contact him when you are settled. He has a fascinating story to share. Your next lesson for your how-to-live-life-to-the-max mind!" Rama handed me a little note with scribbles. "No surprises this time." He smiled.

The magical evening came to an end. Luigi checked once more to see whether we were all completely satisfied. We were. Our stomachs and souls were in bliss. "*Grazie*, Chef Luigi. It has been *magnifica*, as always!" Rama said. We ended the evening with big hugs. Luigi joined in. He told us to come back whenever we were in Singapore. We did not think about the next delicious Italian dinner though. We thought about Rama and how much we would miss him. We thought about all the wisdom gifts we had received from him. The best gifts. Gifts that had become part of our being and life. Gifts that nobody could ever take away from us.

And so our memorable and cherished time in Singapore came to an end. We spent some time in Europe before we flew to our new destination: Houston, Texas! It was a smooth transition. After a month in a temporary accommodation, we found a nice place to live in the green Memorial area. A new home with an impressive swimming pool, a useful comfort in a climate with eight steaming-hot months per year. Soon enough, we had found our ways. So two months after we arrived, I took Rama's now crumpled paper from my purse. I picked up the phone and dialed the number. Two ringtones later, I heard a strong, deep voice: "Ace speaking!" Ace and I agreed to meet at Rice University campus on Tuesday afternoon, two weeks later.

I drove my car to downtown Houston. After a short drive, I reached the impressive campus of Rice University. I parked my car. Ace had said that I could find him on the indoor basketball court. I had always imagined American university campuses to be the best in the world. Now I was visiting one for the first time in my life. Our appointment was at 4:00 p.m. I still had plenty of time to explore the Rice campus. It impressed me, as I had expected. Efficient residential lots, beautiful college buildings, top-notch sports facilities, spacious walkways, towering trees, and neatly moved lawns. The atmosphere was serene yet buzzing. People everywhere—engaging, playing, studying, discussing, preparing, relaxing. An inspiring setting for sure. A place for students to grow, develop, and thrive. I thought, *It would have been really nice if I had had the opportunity to study in an environment like this.* I felt happy for all the American and international students who had this kind of life-enriching opportunity. At 3:45

p.m., I started making my way toward the basketball courts. With guidance from a group of students, I found the Tudor Fieldhouse.

I entered the indoor basketball arena expecting loud activity, but there was none of that. I saw basketball players and a whole team of what I assumed to be coaches and support staff. Everybody was sitting cross-legged on the ground, with eyes closed and in complete silence. My footsteps were the only noise I registered. I sat down and waited. Exactly at 4:00 p.m., one of the members of the support team blew a whistle loudly. Everyone opened their eyes and stood, still not making a sound. On the hand signal of another staff, all of them shouted, "Yes I can! Yes we can!"

A tall, bold man concluded the training by saying, "Good practice, gentlemen. Y'all can be proud of yourselves. Always remember: it is belief that will make us perform at our best. We need our bodily physique, yes! We need our skill, yes! And we need ..."

He stopped abruptly, but then the whole group yelled together, "Our mind, yes!" High fives were exchanged, and the arena was now filled with enthusiastic chatter, laughter, clapping, and screaming.

The big, bold man came walking my way and said, when he was close, "You must be Dax!"

I nodded and said, "You must be Ace."

He walked me outside, in basketball attire and with a towel around his neck to catch his sweat. "Pleased to meet you, Dax. Always good to meet friends of Rama! It has been a while since I met my most inspiring coach. Hope he is well."

"He certainly is, Ace. Happy, stable, calm, and wise as always. Enjoying life every day. And ever passionate about inspiring others to live their best lives. Thank you for having me. I love sports. I love this university campus. And I loved the unusual end of the team's training session. Is that something you learned from Rama?"

Ace laughed. "Oh yes, Dax. I have incorporated many of Rama's lessons in my life and in my role as a coach. Not sure Rama told you, but coaching is my big passion. I was a reasonable basketball player myself but always uncertain. I never made it to the absolute top. I choked at the deciding moments of the game—frustrating, but something good has come out of it. In my search to address this issue, I found Rama. He has helped me to overcome my inner anxieties and fears. It was at the end of my career as a player, so I did not really experience the benefits on court. But I resolved to share the treasure I received from him to inspire other players. And so I became a coach. I love to win games as a coach. But deep down in my heart, I love it even more to give these young kids an inner foundation so that they can win in life, on *and* off the court. *That* is my biggest passion. To inspire others to live happy and successful lives."

It was a beautiful day. We had gotten ourselves a nice, refreshing drink. We were sitting outside on a wooden bench. Some mighty trees provided a cool cover against the powerful sun. Coach Ace clearly was a well-liked man, as students were greeting him continuously. Some of the kids asked for a selfie with the coach, and he calmly and kindly obliged. "You are on popular demand, Coach Ace," I observed.

"You see, Dax, after almost twenty-five years of coaching in the NBA, I have now been the coach of the Rice Owls for the past ten years. I have been around, which helps in becoming known a bit. It is my objective to give my positive best to others every day. When you give your best, you usually receive the best."

I liked Ace's humble and calm demeanor. This was one of the most successful coaches in the history of basketball. But he didn't show it. Ace exuded a patience and kindness that indicated a strong inner balance and contentment. "I agree with you there, Ace. I am curious and excited to learn about your coaching secret."

"Happy to share, Dax. But I always have one condition. That is probably my American nature. We just love to make deals." He laughed. "The condition is that anybody with whom I share the secret ingredient for success must also share it with at least ten other people. I want to spread the word, you see. And I can use any help I can get. Do we have a deal, Dax?"

I smiled. "A man on a mission," I responded. And then I said, "You bet!"

"I want to tell you a story first, Dax. Interested?"

"Definitely! I love stories. Effective way to get lessons across."

"An old man in China knows that he is about to die. A happy and contented man. He has grown from a poor farmer to be a rich man, based on discipline, hard work, and service to his community. He has called for his two sons to settle his legacy. His oldest son is lazy and only after pleasures in life. His younger son is like him, hardworking and kind. Ancient Chinese custom prescribes that the oldest son inherits everything. Although in his heart he feels it is not right, the old man has decided to follow this practice.

"He informs his sons. The oldest son will inherit all the property and belongings, with one small exception. The younger son gets a small piece of land, including a little hut. And he receives a small gift, wrapped in paper. The old man once received that gift from his father, who called it the secret ingredient. 'Put it on the wall in your bedroom, dear son, and use it every day!' the father says. The younger son takes the gift but hardly hears the suggestion. He is disappointed and quickly bids farewell.

"The old man passes away. Normal life kicks in. The older boy enjoys life while underpaid laborers are working his lands. He is spending money, throwing parties for so-called friends. The younger son has quickly given up on his anger and thinks lovingly about his deceased father. He lives in the little hut and works his small piece of land tenaciously. Soon, he is earning some money from selling the crop he does not need for his own consumption.

"Time passes. It comes to the situation that the older son finds himself short of cash, and he decides to sell a piece of his land. *Who cares? I will just pay my laborers less money,* he thinks. His workers suffer. The younger son buys the land with his hard-earned savings. This happens a few times. The land owned by the older son shrinks. The unhappiness of his laborers is growing. The land owned by the younger son increases. His ever-growing workforce is well treated and increasingly happy. The older son notices. He remembers the secret ingredient. *Could it be magic? I have to turn things around. I better find out.* He goes to the hut of his younger brother and finds a simple, poor place. One table, two chairs, a bed, a small cupboard, and a tiny mirror on the wall. 'Nothing here,' he concludes, and he leaves.

"A few years later, misfortune strikes—dry season and a spreading infectious disease. The older brother's land has no produce. His laborers, with no loyalty, decide to flee. The younger brother, together with his motivated workforce, manage to deliver some production, sufficient for survival and some income. Pondering how unlucky he has been, the older brother gets outraged. 'Why me? Why not my younger brother? Is it this special ingredient?' Once more, he rushes toward his brother's little hut. He bursts out, 'Why are you so lucky? What is the secret? Tell me or otherwise,' he threatens.

"The younger son remains calm and says, 'Come.'

"They walk toward the bed. The younger brother speaks. 'Every evening when I go to bed, I count my blessings. When I wake up, I look in the mirror and tell myself that I am going to have a great day! Then I enjoy my day and give it my best.'

"The older son is astonished. 'That is it? That is what you do? What about the special ingredient? What is it?'

"And the younger son says, 'The secret ingredient? It is the mirror I got from Father. It is where I see the secret every day.'

"The older boy is confused. 'But what then is the special ingredient?'

"The younger brother looks at his brother confidently and answers, 'Me!'"

Ace became silent. I looked at him. "I love the story, Ace!"

"Yes, Dax, the secret ingredient for success in life is belief in yourself! It helps to overcome fears. It gives you the courage to make your own choices and to take action. It gives inner strength, inner stability, inner fearlessness, inner persistence. Self-belief allows you to pursue your dreams and to deal with the challenges you face. Here is the thing, Dax: we don't learn it. I did not learn it. I wish I would have had the inner foundation of self-belief at the time of the one NBA final I played. I missed the deciding shot in the dying seconds of game seven. Because I got nervous. Because I lost focus. Because I did not believe ..." Ace stopped talking and remained silent for a while before he cheerfully continued. "Never mind. Something great came out of it. I already told you that my insecurity brought me to Rama, where I found the greatest treasure of all!

"Children are born with an intuition that they are good exactly the way they are. We knew it all, but we forgot. You know why? Because the people around the child give the impression that the child is not good enough. Think about schools, Dax. Intuition gets replaced with intellect. Children are made to believe that when they score well on tests, they are smart. If not, they are stupid. What do you think happens with your self-belief when you frequently hear that message? We don't learn how to develop self-belief at schools. But that is not even the worst thing. The worst thing is that the school system can destroy the intrinsic self-belief each child has."

"Wow, Ace. I never thought about the impact of education that way. But it seems true. Schooling gives many kids the idea that they are not good enough. That is certainly not a helpful idea to have in your mind."

"Correct, Dax. Self-belief has a major impact on your life. Let me give you an example. As a coach, I have to evaluate my players regularly. Feedback can help the player. It can also be detrimental. The difference though does not result from the feedback. The difference comes from the way the player handles the feedback. And that depends to a large extent on the person's self-belief.

"Last year, I had to tell two of my talented players, Chris and Scottie, that they were not going to be part of the Owls team that season. These conversations are not easy. The kids feel disappointed for obvious reasons. But you better be honest with them. When I give feedback, I also give encouragement and advice—how the player can improve and what is required. Chris and Scottie pretty much got the same message from me. This is what happened.

"Chris took our conversation negatively. Already during out chat, I observed his low self-belief mindset. He told me that he had expected this. That he never deemed himself good enough anyway. He had been surprised to be selected for the tryouts. He had always had the impression that the rest of the team did not understand why he was there. Then he told me that he expected this to be the end of his basketball dream. That he felt he was a disappointment. He would never be good enough. Since that day, things have gotten worse. The guy has so much talent, but he does not believe it. He has talked himself down to such an extent that his game has deteriorated. I did not select him for the preseason tryouts this year. He has such a great talent. I still think he can make the NBA but only if he believes it himself."

"Wow," was all that I could utter. "Too bad for Chris. What about Scottie?"

"Scottie got the same feedback. But his mindset is different. He took it positively. Yes, he was very disappointed. Yes, he needed time to handle the message. Still, his almost immediate response was one of self-reflection. He acknowledged most of the feedback. But he felt he had grown his skill in almost all areas of the game. He saw opportunity for further improvement. He asked my advice and guidance how he could continue to grow and get better. Already in the meeting, he showed a resolve to train and practice harder to be prepared for the next opportunity. He was determined to make the team this season. And guess what, Dax? He did. I expect him to be one of my star players. He has improved so much. Scottie has turned the adversity of last year into his advantage this year. His positive self-belief has truly helped him to step up."

"Two talented boys, same feedback, very different outcome," I reflected.

"Yes, Dax. Both have the potential to be great players. But they do not have the same mind. The different experience for Chris and Scottie results from their different internal beliefs systems. It is not the feedback that makes the difference. The difference is made by their internal processing system. Chris saw evidence for his already lacking self-belief and made it worse. Scottie took the disappointment as encouragement to work harder and improve himself. He could do that because he believes in himself."

"So what you are saying, Ace, is that self-belief is a kind of filter through which I process my life. If the filter is positive and healthy, it will help me to deal with whatever happens to me. But if the filter is negative and unhealthy, it can pull me down and discourage me when faced with adversity."

"Spot-on, Dax. Your self-belief can become a self-fulfilling prophecy. When you have low self-belief, you have low or negative expectations. A negative expectation will never make you perform at your best. It results in less effective behaviors and actions—or even no action. This leads to suboptimal results, which reinforce your low self-belief. When this happens frequently, your self-belief spirals further down, and the self-fulfilling prophecy is a fact of life. It also works the other way. A positive self-belief gives positive expectations. Positive expectations result in positive behavior and actions and thus a high likelihood of strong results. These positive results help to grow your belief in yourself. And the positive reinforcement continues from there."

I was all ears.

"Dax, what I want everybody to understand is that self-belief is at play in every situation we encounter in our lives. When we think negatively about ourselves, this can work against us. Positive self-belief, on the other hand, is a great help in life. It is one of the key qualities of highly successful people."

"I get it, Ace. This is really valuable insight. Thank you so much. Can I ask you a few questions please?"

"Go ahead," was Ace's gracious response.

"What exactly are beliefs? How do they develop? How do I know what my beliefs are? And how can I change them if they don't support me?"

"Those are all the right questions, Dax. Good thinking. I will go straight into each one of them. What is a belief? A belief is a thought that you keep thinking. Once your self-belief was just a thought. When you continue to give attention to the thought, it can develop into a belief. A belief is much stronger than a thought because of its repetitive nature. Rama would say that beliefs are the main building blocks of your robotic mind. Your beliefs are embedded in your subconscious mind. From there, they drive your mechanical behaviors. Without you knowing, your beliefs steer your life, because much of what you do, you do without awareness. You better make sure, therefore, that your subconscious software program is the right program!"

"I like that comparison, Ace!"

"So, how do you develop them? Pretty much unconsciously. Most people are not aware what self-belief they are growing. Your surroundings have a big impact on the development of your belief system. You don't know this, and you are not aware of how important positive self-belief is. If you knew, you would want to take the development very seriously. But we don't know. We think outer appearance is way more important. Look at the kids on this campus. They want to impress. They think that being cool depends on their outer appearance. Cool clothes. Swell shoes. Awesome accessories. Plastic surgery. Boasting language. Expensive cars. Of course it is nice to look good and receive admiration from others. But it does not set you up for life. Outer identity is nice, but what you need is a positive and stable inner identity. I always say *outer identity looks nice, but building inner identity is wise.* That is what will truly serve you in the storms of life. Pretty much all these kids are unaware of the importance of their beliefs for their lives. It is my mission to make them understand and to coach them to develop a conscious, winning belief system!"

"I like it, Coach. I am listening and learning," I said.

"How can you know what your beliefs are? That requires some serious self-reflection, Dax. You have to become more aware of your thoughts. Connecting with your thoughts is not so easy. But I have a helpful suggestion for you that you can use to get to know your beliefs. First a question: what do you get when you squeeze on orange?"

"What do you mean, Ace? You get orange juice, right? Or is this a trick question?" I responded.

"No, Dax. It is not. Indeed you get orange juice. But why?"

"Because that is what is inside, I would say."

"Absolutely, Dax. What comes out of the orange is what is inside."

"Yes?" I confirmed questioningly.

"The same applies to you, my friend. When you are squeezed, what comes out is what is inside you. What comes out is your robotic belief system. You will not see it in the good times. It is easy to contain yourself when everything is going smoothly. But when the going gets tough, that is when people will show you their real face. What they show is a good indicator for how they think, for their inner beliefs."

"That is a nice tool, Ace. It is very much in line with something I once read from a wise master. He said that you can make out the inside of a man by listening to the words he speaks and by observing the actions he takes. What comes out is what is inside. This is good. So if I become more aware of myself in times of challenge, I start to learn about my hidden, subconscious beliefs—right?"

"Absolutely, Dax. You will get to know yourself by observing who you are in times of adversity. It will take some time, but if you are honest in your self-reflection, you will gain great insight into your inner system. And you will start to see what parts of that system do not serve you or are not to your liking."

"This is great, Ace. I will use the orange idea to grow my self-understanding!"

"That brings us to your last question: how to build a healthy self-belief? Or how to change your self-limiting beliefs? Growth and change starts with awareness. That is always step one. Oftentimes, you need somebody else—for example, a coach—for this. It is my passion to make people aware of the power of self-belief, Dax. Once you are aware, you need clarity. Step two is to define what you want. What kind of self-beliefs do you want to develop? Which limiting beliefs do you want to change? A practical way to do this is to decide on at least three empowering *I am* thoughts about yourself. It is up to you. You choose your thoughts that feel good and are powerful for you. Let me give you a few examples, Dax: I am good, I am beautiful,

I am strong, I am calm, I am stable, I am free, I am powerful, I am unique, I am positive, I am blessed, I am abundant, I am persistent, I am courageous, I am amazing, I am able, I am me. I guess you get the gist. Such statements feel good, right?

"Now you move to step three. You want to program your mind with the *I am* statements. The steps so far are relatively easy. You become aware, and you create clarity. Now it is time for implementation. This is the time that your mind might start to trick you by telling you that change is not possible. Your mind will bring in doubt. It will tell you that you are who you are. That you cannot change. Like the Buddha said, your mind can be your best friend but also your worst enemy. Your doubting mind, your mind that stops you from believing what you want to believe, is a trait of your enemy mind. Don't be distracted by it. *You* have created your existing beliefs. Maybe unconsciously, but still you are the creator. This also means that *you* can change them. And it does not need to take long. Change starts with a new thought. You can change your thinking any moment, so you can initiate change now! Cool, right?"

"That is cool indeed, Ace. I can change now. Great insight. Wow."

"Step three is about reprogramming your robotic mind. This requires repetition. Remember, a belief is a thought that you keep thinking. Through repeated thinking, you can build the beliefs that you want. I have a change recipe for you. It consists of two daily actions. Are you ready?"

"I am, Coach," I said enthusiastically.

"Action one: repeat your three *I am* statements three times a day. Think, feel, and speak each statement a number of times in the morning, afternoon, and evening. The more intensely you can feel the statement, the more effective you are in developing your new self-beliefs. Don't think and speak like a robot, emotionless. Think and speak and truly feel it, even if you don't fully believe it in the beginning. Your mind is capable of holding any belief you want. The thoughts you have chosen might feel strange in the beginning, but in time *I am good* will feel as natural to you as riding your bicycle or drinking a glass of water. Are you with me so far, Dax?"

"I certainly am. I can do this!"

"Great. Action two: take three daily actions in alignment with each of your new beliefs. In total, this would thus be nine daily actions. Three times three. Practice discipline and persistence to take action over a period of time, and this will make the change real."

"Also can, as they say in Singapore. But just to make sure I understand specifically, Ace, can you give me an example of an aligned action if I want to create, for example, the *I am positive* belief?"

"Sure can. Being positive means that you are focused on what is good in your life. So here is what you can do daily to develop that belief: compliment yourself on something you did well today. It does not have to be big. Cooking a nice meal is worth a compliment. Taking care of yourself is worth a compliment. Taking an action from your action list is worth a compliment. Be positive toward yourself. You can also be positive toward your partner, your children, anybody. Taking the action to compliment yourself or somebody else is an action in line with your aspired belief to be positive. It will turn your aspired belief *I am positive* into reality."

"Thanks, Ace. That is very clear."

"Dax, there is an ancient wisdom definition of who you are. It says *you are what you think you are.* That in a nutshell is the secret of self-belief. We should all replace our subconscious, limiting, unhelpful beliefs with consciously chosen, empowering, uplifting beliefs. Don't be a full-grown elephant that is conditioned to believe it cannot break free from its chains installed by humans. The elephant could not when it was small and did not have the power. Now this mightily strong animal cannot because it *believes* it cannot. You don't want to be locked up by your beliefs. You don't want to be chained by limiting, detrimental, disempowering thoughts about yourself. Whatever you believe, you are right. Henry Ford once said it nicely: 'If you think you can or if you think you cannot, you are right.' You are what you think you are. This is a universal law. So you better choose and install your beliefs wisely."

"I am what I think I am," I repeated. "That is a powerful mantra."

Ace continued. "It is fantastic to see what my players are capable of when they grow the right belief system. You asked me about the end-of-practice exercise with the team. Dax, you don't win games on the basis of impressive physique and technical skills only. Competing to a large extent is a mental game. Winning or losing often depends on the team's performance in the dying seconds of the game. Do you have the inner calm and inner confidence to make the deciding shot? That is what differentiates the great players from the good. They have the inner belief system that supports them. You need to be prepared for it. You don't develop positive beliefs when the heat is on. You develop them in advance. That is why mind training has been part of my practice sessions ever since I learned about the power of self-belief. We use the last fifteen minutes of every practice game to prepare the players' minds to be ready for the winning shot. I want my players to believe in themselves. I want my players to have the inner knowing that they can. I coach my players toward an inner belief system that lifts them up in the challenging moments on court and in the rest of their lives. Remember this, my friend: you are what you think you are. With that knowledge, make sure that what you think of yourself is positive. Grow a supportive self-belief that allows you to live your best life possible. Develop a self-belief that sets you up to score in life whatever the circumstances. Make sure that when you look into your mirror, you look at yourself with gratitude and confidence. Just like the younger son in the story I told you. You can. We all can! Your belief system is the secret ingredient for your life!"

This man was amazing. Truly passionate about giving his players the self-belief to succeed in the game of basketball and in the game of life. And now he had shared his inspiration on the power of self-belief so graciously with me. "Fantastic afternoon, Ace. I love your energy and lessons. Thank you so much. I can see why the kids love you. Self-belief truly is the foundation for life. Do you have time for one more question?"

"Shoot," Ace responded as a true basketball coach.

"What if you have developed a healthy and supportive mind, but you still miss the last-minute shot?"

"Hahaha, good question, Dax. That can happen of course. Even Michael Jordan has missed last-second shots. But here is your answer. You might have missed that shot. But you have the inner belief system to deal with this in a positive way. You stay strong and resilient, and you remain confident on the inside. With that mindset, you will leverage the missed shot to grow so that when the next opportunity arises, you will win the game for the team!"

"I got it, Ace. Thank you! Your story is so inspiring. I will take your lessons and grow an empowering inner belief system, step by step. I already know the first three thoughts that I want to cement in my mind: *I am positive, I am able, and I am me!*"

"Sounds good, Dax. That is a great foundation. You are on your way, I know. I also have a last question for you. Do you still remember my condition for my sharing?"

I smiled. "Yes I do, Coach Ace!"

"That is good, Dax. Please add one *I am* statement to the list then: *I am sharing the secret of self-belief with as many people as possible!*"

"I will, Coach! I might include it in a chapter of a book I intend to write."

Ace smiled, and soon enough, we were both laughing.

Self-Belief—Learning Box

Wisdom	My mind is my most powerful tool. I carry my mind wherever I go. I am like the lotus; I live in the world, but I remain above it. I choose my surroundings and the people I associate with consciously, as I realize that they can block but also unleash my growth. I not only want to exist; I want to *live*! I process my life through the filter of my self-belief. Self-belief is at play in every situation of my life. I am what I think I am.
Awareness	You are here (in this life) to be happy. To experience joy. The primal root for life is happiness. The difference between happiness and unhappiness is just a verb! You can *choose* happiness or *allow* unhappiness. Wisdom is the optimizer of life. Mastering your mind and fueling your mind with wisdom is the greatest gift you can give yourself. Once you fill your mind with wisdom, the gift of wisdom is always yours. When you give your best, you will receive the best. Outer identity looks nice; building inner identity is wise. Your belief system is the secret ingredient for your life. You can change your beliefs. It takes focused mind training and persistent action in alignment with your aspired beliefs.

Story/Tool	The myth of the koi carp.
	The lessons of the lotus.
	The young son and the mirror.
Practice	The orange (observe yourself in times of adversity to get to know yourself).
	Three times three (repeat your three *I am* statements three times per day and take three aligned actions for each statement every day).

8

Perspective

Trip to the Moon

You don't see the world as it is but as you are.
—Talmud

If you change the way you look at things,
the things you look at change.
—Dr. Wayne Dyer

Coach Ace and I had parted with a big hug and with Ace inviting me to some of the Owls' seasonal games. As I was driving home after another inspiriting encounter with one of Rama's friends, Rama's wise words on the myth of the koi carp resonated in my ears: "You will never be bigger than your environment." Ace had taught me another important, related life lesson: you will never be bigger than you think you can be. *Man,* I thought, *our mind, this great tool, can be our most powerful tool. But if we are not careful, it can also be our biggest limiting factor in life. It all depends on how we use it.* The more I learned, the more determined I became to use my mind consciously. To choose its focus deliberately. Mindset and thinking truly were the basis for your life. I resolved to use the next three months to get more insight into my robotic belief system. I wanted to understand my supporting beliefs and also my beliefs that were holding me back. And I was going to train my mind in the empowering belief system of three that I chose—*I am positive, I am able, I am me*—using Ace's advice.

Back home, Jane enjoyed my sharing of the coach's lessons. "Even more important for me, Dax. You are pretty positive about yourself already. I have quite a way to go." I agreed with my darling. Despite the fact that she was a wise, smart, kind, caring, beautiful girl, she had never really believed in herself. Jane had not grown up in a supportive and encouraging environment. To the contrary, her family members had been more busy with their own struggles than in guiding a little girl to become a self-confident woman. At the age of eighteen, Jane had left her parental home and started taking her life in her own hands. And she had done well. She had been a passionate, successful student. She had built up a successful professional career. She had grown a number of fantastic friendships. But still, she held herself back because of limiting beliefs. She never thought herself good enough, and she was always doubting her intuition and contributions. I had told her so many times what a wonderful person she was, but my message never really landed. *Self-belief is what you think about yourself*, as Coach Ace had so clearly explained. Not what others might think. Positive feedback and compliments can help, but they will never be stronger than your own ideas about yourself. "Let's jointly work our belief system, Dax," she said to me. "I am going to start by defining the three *I am* statements that I want to live by."

Dinner plan that evening was steak at the Taste of Texas, presumably one of the best steakhouses in town. We had received an invite from some of our new American friends. The restaurant is located next to the I-10, the most southern cross-country highway in the American interstate highway system. It runs from Santa Monica, California, to Jacksonville, Florida, and stretches almost four thousand kilometers. More than a third of its entire length runs through Texas, including through Houston. I was a frequent visitor of the I-10, and I had spotted the Taste of Texas. Until our friends' invitation, I had never considered going there. *A restaurant next to a sixteen-lane highway can't be good,* had been my closed-mind thinking. When we visited the place that evening, I was impressed from the first moment we entered—well-organized entry; friendly, welcoming staff; spacious surroundings; impressively high ceilings; positively buzzing ambience; fantastic food. The best steak I have ever eaten in my life. We were treated with on-loan cowboy hats and stylish neck bandanas to make the experience even better. It was a wonderful evening. We were certain we would be back.

In bed that evening, I reflected, *Never visit restaurants next to highways? This is how a judgmental mind can keep you away from great new experiences!* Without our friends' invite, we might have missed the opportunity. I gave myself some advice: "It is good to make up your own mind. But it is also good to keep an open mind and listen to others. It can enrich your life significantly."

In the months that followed, I practiced the lessons from Ace. I wanted to become more conscious of other limiting beliefs I was holding. At the end of every day, I sat down to reflect on my experiences and emotions that day. My prime attention went to the challenging moments, the moments in which I was the squeezed orange. As Ace had said, these are the moments the real you comes out. Through my practice, I definitely got to know myself better.

I became very aware of the effect criticism and opposition had on me. When these happened, I felt shaken and insecure. My robotic reaction was to pull back, to avoid confrontation. I started noticing the pattern. I found that I had a way to go to live up to Raquel's lesson: mastery is to become independent of the good opinion of other people. I was not independent. I was carrying the belief that I had to win arguments. It impacted my professionalism and personal effectiveness. Whenever challenged, I lost sight of the broader agenda and purpose at play. I became tense and stopped listening well to other people. My robotic mind and behavior took over. It was not me consciously leading myself when disagreement and pushback happened. I made a first note of my self-reflection. I intended to seek Rama's guidance.

My second note came from my self-observations after the company announced the next reorganization. I felt disappointed and frustrated. This was organizational change number ten in the twenty years I had been working for the company. I felt I rejected yet another change. And I noted that my mind started worrying about job loss this time. It made me anxious and uncertain. I inquired with myself. *Why? Why did I feel squeezed? Why did this announcement take me off balance?* I experienced that when you go inside, you can unravel your thinking patterns. I found that I was worried about money. In case of redundancy, would I be able to sustain our life financially? I also found that part of my self-image was built on what I do and what I have. My confidence was partially built upon my corporate job and the material wealth it provided. "Unhelpful beliefs," I said to myself. "You are not free!" My second point for discussion with Rama.

The uncertainty also triggered something else: a step up in my inner search for my purpose and passion. I questioned whether my job, in which I was spending a large part of my life, fulfilled my deepest driving desires. More and more, I felt that I was not in the right place. Olisa and Sofia had inspired me into inner contemplation, to be in search of my purpose and passion. My heart was telling me that I loved to inspire and empower people. Yes, I was listening to my heart, but I noticed that my mind was interfering. My heart was longing to share my learnings and wisdom with others. My mind was objecting and introducing all kinds of reasons why this was not a good idea. I added a third note to my Rama consultation list.

Life in Houston in the meantime was good. Jane and I had found our ways. We loved our swimming pool. We had met a number of friends and were regularly engaged in discussions on America's heritage, freedom spirit, developments, and customs. We had made a number of city trips and visited natural parks to explore the vast, beautiful country. And we had experienced a number of professional sports games, where we had witnessed America's love for sports. Life certainly was good.

Approximately half a year after our inspiring encounter, Coach Ace sent me a message.

> Dear Dax,
> I hope you are enjoying your time in our country.
> And I hope you are working your inner belief system :)
> Time to visit the Owls!
> I have reserved tickets for you and Jane for this week's Thursday game.
> Will I see you there?
> Ace

After checking with Jane, I confirmed our presence to Ace. We were excited. Ahead of the game, I checked the Owls' season performance online. It appeared they were doing well and could still make March Madness, the NCAA playoffs tournament. I noticed one predominant element in the team's press coverage: its strong end-of-game performance. Statistically, the Owls were the best close-game finishers. *Ace's beliefs coaching is working. Yes we can!* I thought.

We arrived on time to purchase Owls caps and shawls that turned us into real fans. The stadium was on fire when we entered. The crowd was ready for the next Owls home game. We purchased large sodas and a huge bag of popcorn, just like everybody else, it seemed. Then it was time for the speaker to announce tonight's teams. Every Owls player was welcomed by deafening cheers from the crowd. Scottie was in the starting lineup. The game was an easy one, and Scottie was excellent. The fans loved him, as they were continuously chanting his name. He led the team to a convincing lead after two quarters—a lead the team sustained in the third, and by the start of the fourth and last quarter, the Owls were ahead by twenty-six points. Coach Ace was calmly active on the sideline, giving instructions to his team in the field and talking to his bench players.

As the speaker was announcing a number of substitutions, suddenly his voice rose: "Ladies and gentlemen, I am proud to present the debut of Chris Turner! He has come from far, but this man can be the next NBA sensation. Tonight, for the first time, he will show y'all what he's got. Give it up for Chris from Galveston, Texas!" The crowd was cheering. An impressive-looking athlete entered the field. He exuded a remarkable confidence and certainty for a debut appearance. When he scored his first three-point shot, he ran to Ace and gave him a big hug. The coach was beaming with pride and joy. The Owls won with a comfortable nineteen points, and Scottie was voted man of the match.

After the game was over, the team gathered around Coach Ace. We couldn't hear his speech, but when he was done, the whole team started dancing while yelling, "Yes we can. Yes we can!" Soon enough, the whole stadium was shouting, "Yes we can! Yes we can!"

We met Coach Ace after the game, and I congratulated him on the victory. "Great game, Coach. And I liked the end-of-the-game practice," I said with a smile.

"Glad you could make it, Jane and Dax. Glad you liked the game. I like your fan outfit!"

We started chatting, and then I remembered the debut guy Chris Turner. "Was this *the* Chris?" I asked.

"Yeah, that is him, Dax. I am so happy for Chris that he has got his act together again, after his mental downturn. Remember he didn't make the preseason tryouts? A few months thereafter, I started seeing the light in his eyes. His inner talk had changed. His basketball talent was still there, and the two were coming together. When one of my players got injured, I brought Chris into the team some eight weeks ago. Tonight was his first game. I am so proud of him. He is ready to compete at the highest levels now, I am sure. Emotional moment tonight, especially when he came running my way after his first points for the team." I saw happy tears appearing in the coach's eyes.

Ace continued, "I never gave up on Chris. We continued our conversations, and he continued a bit of basketball practice. He found his power. We all can change our mindset, Dax. *We are born with a mind, not with a mindset.* Sometimes it takes a coach to get you into a healthy state of mind. Chris practiced my guidance to develop a supportive inner belief system. His mind has changed to the positive, and he is now turning his amazing talent into performance. The guy is ready to shine. I am sure he is going to win us games this season. And I am so glad for him. Mark my words, Dax: this man is going to be the next big NBA star. I just love it when my coaching helps to improve the lives of my players!" Ace was full of energy, even after the game.

The power of passion. Passion gives positive energy! I thought. Then I said, "Great job, Coach! The right beliefs *do* drive results!"

I was keen to further strengthen my own belief system, so a few weeks later, I contacted Rama. I had plenty to seek his guidance on. We met virtually for the first time a week later. "Lots going on with you, Dax," Rama said after I had shared my life's updates. "Sounds like you are having a good time. And you are definitely learning about yourself. I like your three coaching points. Good self-reflections. Growth always starts with self-awareness, Dax. So you are doing yourself a big favor by analyzing your feelings and associated thoughts. When you get to know your robot mind, you are on your way to change its programming in case you don't like it."

I just loved the ever-positive perspective of Rama. He would never tell you that you were doing badly. He would never point out your failures. He always saw life as a big, exciting learning journey where there are always opportunities to grow and develop. A truly empowering coach! Rama asked, "Ready to start, my friend?"

I nodded.

"You've got some fundamental life questions, Dax," Rama started. "About relationships and people interaction. About change, uncertainty, and inner stability. And about finding purpose and passion. I can wholeheartedly say, solve these three, and you have mastered life." Rama was laughing. He was always able to keep serious topics lighthearted and fun to create a relaxed and inspiring learning environment. "Since we only have forty-five minutes for this call, I would like to suggest we leave the purpose and passion question for the next time. Also because I feel you have not yet deepened your inner search. Get clear, Dax. Seek inside your heart and find your purpose. Don't let your rational mind interfere. It is *your* clarity. Nobody else's. Take a pen and write down your inner calling in a mission statement. Who are you here to be? What are you here to do?" I listened. "Are you OK to work this one a bit more?"

Yes, I was. Rama was right. I needed more time to conclude my inner search for clarity.

"All right then, let's start with change, uncertainty, and inner stability. Listen, Dax, life *is* uncertain, unpredictable. Life *will* always change. Understand this. Did you ever wake up and know what the day would give? No, right? When the day starts, you never know what it will bring. This is a good thing. How fun and exciting would life be if we knew exactly what would happen every day? The uncertainty keeps life exhilarating, inspiring, and, yes, also challenging sometimes. It is wise to have a mindset that accepts this fact of life. When confronted with change like a reorganization, your acceptance gets tested. *You* get tested. Do you have the confidence and trust to know that things will work out fine for you? Are you stable enough to remain positive and focused on the opportunities? The reorganization trigger has given you some useful insight into your mechanical thinking patterns. Deep down inside, you think shortage. You are concerned with money. And you found that your self-image is dependent on what you do and what you have. Right, Dax?"

I nodded. "Yes, Rama. Correct. I know these are unwise beliefs, and I would like to change them. How can I do that?"

"No need to be harsh with yourself, Dax. As I said, change starts with awareness. Becoming more aware of your robot mind is a great thing. It is the start you need. Without such awareness, you will forever suffer from these self-limiting beliefs. So, actually, you are doing great!"

"Thank you, Rama. You are too kind. I just love your ever-existing positive focus!"

"*Practice makes positive*, Dax. We can all develop such a mind. Let's talk money first. For many, money is both the source for temporary happiness but also a source of structural concern. People tend to continuously worry about it. Do I have enough money? Will I have sufficient money in the future? The reorganization has revealed this hidden concern of your mind, Dax. The best way to address the worry is to consciously fill your mind with good-feeling thoughts about the subject. I will ask you a few questions. You will give me your answers. All right?"

"All right."

"First question: when in your life did you ever experience a lack of money?"

"Uh, never, Rama."

"You can take some assurance from this. You agree?"

"Yes, I can."

"Second question: assume you will be made redundant as a result of the reorganization. Will you still have your talents, your skills, your experience, and your mind to work with?"

"Obviously yes, Rama."

"Excellent. So you may have lost your current job, but you still possess everything that made you successful in life. Not a bad thing to remind yourself of, if you ask me!"

"True," I said.

"Question number three: what mindset do you think will be most beneficial for you in times of change? A mindset of concern, worry, anxiety? Or a mindset of hope, opportunity, positivity?"

"Also an easy question, Rama. Clearly the latter. As I think, so I shall be, right? A positive mindset will create a positive life. I like the way you are shifting my mind."

"Right answer again, Dax. The people who create opportunity from change are the people with an opportunity mindset. The people who turn change into positive outcomes are the people with a positive mindset. They are guaranteed to make the most effective decisions and then take action accordingly to create the best possible outcomes.

Do you think they allow their minds to be stuck in the swamp of anxiety? No, they don't. They use their minds to create the next chapter of their lives deliberately. From such creation, money will flow naturally. When you focus your mind on a lack of money, in a way that is what you are creating. When you focus your mind on who you are, who you want to be, and on taking the best possible actions, you will create what it is you want. This includes money, but more importantly, it includes joy, excitement, opportunity, happiness."

"That sounds very good, Rama. Does this translate into a master's formula for handling change?"

"It does, Dax. You want to know?"

"Yes, please."

"The master's formula is: *manage yourself*! Do not try to manage the inevitable change. Manage yourself!"

"That's it?"

"That's it!"

"No reference to money?"

"No reference to money! Money is just an outcome, Dax. An external result. The ancient masters say, 'As within, so without.' They mean to say that life starts with you. So when you create a mindset of opportunity, positivity, and abundance on the inside, that will be your external reality also!"

"I love it, Rama. Your wisdom basically always brings the matter at hand back to me. Me first, and the rest will follow. Is this also the case for me handling criticism and opposition?"

"It sure is, Dax. Ace has been so clear to you: you are what you think you are. If you make your self-image dependent on what you do or what you have, you run a big risk. It implies that if you don't have a high-profile corporate job or if you don't own a fancy sports car or whatever, you will think you are nothing. A nobody. Is that what you want? Your train of thought is common though. Our egos get trained to think that who we are is what we do and what we have. But the master says that who you are is what you think you are. Managing your ideas about yourself is the fastest road to improving your self-image,

Dax. Develop a positive set of thoughts about yourself, no matter what. Apply Ace's guidance, and I guarantee you your self-image and self-confidence will become stable as a rock!"

"Thank you for the reminder, Rama. I will certainly do this. Just watched the clock though. Time flies when you are being inspired. We only have five more minutes."

"That is all right, Dax. I do have some more time available. Let me share a few words on your other note: handling criticism and opposition. We are all familiar with this challenge. We all meet other people who have different views and opinions. Objection, disagreement, and conflict are unavoidable in life, just like change. People have different perspectives. That is a fact of life, and it is fine. Diversity of thought in general helps to deliver better results. Just think of the power of teams. Together, teams can achieve more, when the diverse power of its team members is truly unleashed. But controversy and discord can be painful if you make the pushback personal. Negative feedback can hurt if you carry a deep-rooted belief that you are not good enough. Because it triggers that self-reducing belief. Dispute can make you feel bad if you have an established belief that life is all about winning. Because it can give a sense of losing. So, just like with change and uncertainty, criticism and opposition can awake detrimental beliefs that you might be carrying. That simply hurts. When you don't want to be shaken by the feedback from others, there is only one remedy, Dax: work your inner foundation!"

"It is always the same answer, Rama!" I had to laugh.

Rama was smiling. "Yes, it is, Dax. You know how to do this. Get to know your limiting robotic thoughts. See how they don't support you to remain calm and stable. And see what thoughts you would like to replace them with. We all have the ability to develop an inner foundation that makes us unshakeable, whatever other people say or do."

"Rama?"

"Yes, Dax?"

"Can I ask you a personal question?"

"Yes, Dax."

"Have *you* always had an unshakeable inside?"

"No, Dax. I have not. Just like you, I became aware of unhelpful thinking patterns after I started my inner search. Master Amir was the one who guided me toward self-understanding and growth. I also had many robotic traits that did not serve me in my life. Let me give you two examples. In my early twenties, I was quickly irritated with other people. They could annoy me tremendously if things did not go my way. Amir said to me, 'Rama, you can try to carpet the whole world to walk softly or you can put on the right shoes!' He helped me to find the right shoes, or, in other words, he taught me how to manage myself irrespective of the behavior of others. Another lesson related to my liking of material possessions, especially watches. I thought I needed them to feel good, and I had become attached to Rolex watches. Attachment is the root cause for all suffering in life, but I did not know that at the time. One day, when I was wearing my newest Rolex watch and I was visibly proud of it, I visited Amir, and he noted it. He must have thought it was time for me to learn about the negative consequences of attachment. After we had talked, he said to me out of nowhere, 'Nice watch, Rama. Can I have it please?' My attachment mind immediately started objecting, but intuitively, I knew that Amir was right and that he was teaching me an important lesson for life. I gave Amir the watch. He smiled and said, 'You think you can still be happy and contented, my friend?'"

"Wow."

"Wow indeed, Dax. The *way of wisdom*! Masters sometimes have unexpected ways to teach their lessons. I am so glad I started walking the path of self-realization. Just like everybody else, I had to learn a lot, and I am still learning because life is never stagnant. I have grown my unshakeable inside over time and under the guidance of the right teachers. Step by step, I became aware of my inner power and how to exercise it for the benefit of my life."

"Thank you, Rama."

"You are welcome."

Time was up. *Some more homework to do,* I thought. But I did not mind. This was the type of homework I loved. I was more and more convinced it was the best investment for my life.

"Any plans for the next couple of weeks?" Rama asked. I told him about my planned visit to NASA Space Center. "Interesting. When do you plan to be there?" I shared the details. "Nice, Dax. Good choice. A visit to NASA can give you a whole new perspective on life. Explore and enjoy!"

So it was that I was driving the I-45 South toward the Space Center on a Saturday morning a few weeks later. I-45, I-10, the 610, I-69, the 290, the 35. The myriad of highways surrounding Houston initially had confused me a lot. But once I got to know the numbers and the respective directions of Houston's road infrastructure, I managed to find my way around efficiently and effectively. The I-45 South was a new road for me, but I had found it easily. Traffic was quiet, and I was one of the first visitors to arrive.

At reception, I bought a ticket and was advised that a group tour would start in fifteen minutes. I figured I could learn more efficiently by listening to a seasoned tour guide, so I waited. More people were arriving, and within ten minutes, a good crowd had gathered. A few minutes later, a relatively small man in a NASA uniform arrived. He immediately introduced himself. "Hi, y'all. I am Wayne, your tour guide for this morning. Hope you are ready to explore and learn!" The guy spoke with a beautiful southern accent. Various "good morning" and "pleasure to meet you" well-wishes were exchanged, and soon thereafter, Wayne got us going.

"Good morning again, ladies and gentlemen. My name is Wayne, your tour guide this morning. I am the man with the best job in the whole wide world!" I was looking at Wayne, and I was listening. I believed what he was saying. The passion and enthusiasm he was exuding were contagious. We were blessed with a tour guide on purpose.

"It is my pleasure to be introducing y'all into the wonders of space and science and technology. I have been intrigued by the solar system ever since I was a kid. I started reading about it when I was nine years old. I was in awe of the massive size of the system, its orchestrated structure, and its unimaginably long history. The solar system was formed 4.6 billion years ago. Can you fathom, guys? And can you imagine that mankind only started understanding its structure a few *hundred* years ago? The Polish astronomer Copernicus was one of the first to propose a mathematical predictive model, with the sun as the center of the solar system and the planets circling the sun. This was some five hundred years ago. Since then, step by step, scientists from all over the world have deciphered the solar system. My physics teacher accelerated my interest in space. I was hooked, and I chose to study aerospace engineering. My passion must have been convincing and infectious because I was admitted to six well-known universities here in the US. I spent my college years at Stanford in an attempt to contribute to the exploration of space myself." The tour guide beamed.

"I am still more than passionate about exploring the unexplored. It not only has been the recipe for mankind to learn about our universe and past. It also is the way to grow and develop yourself. If there is one valuable thing that I have acquired from my space investigations, it would be to always have an open mind, because there is always more to explore and learn. NASA has been a great lifelong employer for me in this respect."

Wayne was a fantastic tour guide, mixing personal stories with explanations of the various elements of the monumental Space Center. The group was all ears. It is impossible to lose attention when you are being guided by such an inspiring person. Wayne introduced us to the many secrets of space and space travel like an enthusiastic kid. We saw the world's only space shuttle replica as well as various other spacecrafts and modules. We touched the Lunar touchstone, one of only eight moonstones in the world that can be felt. We walked through Rocket Park with a display of a variety of space-launch vehicles. We listened to John F. Kennedy's speech at Rice University in 1962 where he spoke the historical words, "We choose to go to the moon." We explored the Mission Mars exhibit where NASA reveals its plans for future travel to Mars.

Wayne lent his expert voice to every part of the impressive science museum. Two hours passed in a heartbeat, and it was time for Wayne to wrap up. "Ladies and gentlemen, I hope you have enjoyed the tour, and I hope your minds have leaped a bit. Never think you know it all and never underestimate the human potential. These are two lessons that NASA is proving to be true every day. Are there any questions?"

As people started raising their hands, Wayne added, "I have a rule when it comes to asking questions. I like to make things personal, you know. So if you want to ask a question, please first introduce yourself with your name and then ask me anything you like." Many people shared their name, and many questions were asked.

I also had questions. I raised my hand when the questions and answers were almost coming to a close. Wayne nodded in my direction. "Thank you so much, Wayne, for the tour. Your passion is contagious. I feel like joining NASA now. Oh sorry—my name is Dax."

"Hi, Dax. Nice to meet you. How can I be of help?"

I asked, "Have you really worked as a tour guide here at the Space Center your whole life?"

"Well, Dax, I have been a NASA employee ever since my graduation. But I only became a guide after a few different jobs. I have walked on the moon."

Many people in the crowd could not contain their admiration. "You've been on the moon!"

"Yes, I have, ladies and gentlemen. Defining moment in my life. That though is a whole different story for which I don't have time now. Hahaha!" With that, Wayne thanked the group for their active and interested participation, and people started leaving.

I was hesitating, overthinking Wayne's unexpected answer. *The man had been on the moon.* Lost in thought, I did not notice that Wayne was walking toward me. Suddenly he was standing in front of me and said, "Dax, interested to hear about my trip to the moon and what I learned?"

"Huh?" was the only response I could bring out.

"If you have time, my friend, I am happy to share. But first let us get a nice cup of coffee at the Grounds Control Coffee Bar. You ready?"

"Yes please, Wayne. But why the honor?"

"Don't worry about it, Dax. You seem like a guy who is interested in adventure stories and their life lessons. And I do have a few hours in my schedule available."

I was too much in shock of this sudden opportunity that I did not ask any more questions. "I would love a nice cappuccino!"

We walked over to the coffee bar, and after we sat down, Wayne looked up at the sky. He sighed. "My trip to the moon and back. I was one of the crew of the *Apollo 15* mission in 1971. Trip of a lifetime." Wayne shared about his training as an astronaut, the preparation for the mission, and the mission itself. "The moon visit changed my life, Dax."

"How, Wayne? How did it change your life?"

"It changed my perspective, Dax. It opened my eyes. When I stepped on the immaculate bone-white surface of the moon, I watched space and realized that everything is in good order. The vast universe is not a random collection of objects but rather a perfectly orchestrated system. A system with a place and purpose for all. A system in which everything is connected. Ever heard of the word *epiphany*, Dax? An epiphany is an instant awakening, an instant seeing or understanding. My visit to the moon was an epiphany for me."

Wayne paused for a few seconds and then continued. "As I walked around on the moon and observed, my mind opened up. I realized that we are all connected. We are all one. We come from the same Source. I realized that when you are in conflict with someone, you are basically fighting with yourself.

"I saw planet Earth in a very different light. I looked at the earth and thought, *Funny that people think that earth is the center of the universe. It is nothing more than a tiny spec in the whole. A drop in the ocean. Funny that people believe they are the center of the universe.*

That life revolves around them. That the purpose of life therefore is to compete and fight and win.

"I saw the magnitude of the universe, and I realized there is so much we don't understand. Mankind thinks we know and lives with a closed mind. Believing that he is right. Not open for new lessons and experiences. Man keeps himself small. It is futile, Dax. There is so much to be learned and explored. We are here to remain curious and to grow through life.

"Man thinks that life is about conquering and proving yourself right. This is all based on our limited perspective. If we would understand our perfect place in the vast universe, we would know that all is well. We would know that we are here to live in harmony with all. To collaborate and support each other. We are here to enjoy. Our conditioned minds limit our experiences of life. We are here to juice out life. To be the best we can be.

"Standing on the moon, my mind got stretched. I returned from the journey a changed man. I saw the world and its people in a whole new perspective."

I was listening in awe. Some of the things Wayne was sharing reminded me of meditation experiences Jane had shared with me. "Sometimes when Jane meditates and silences her mind, she arrives at a knowing and feeling place that all is one, that all is good exactly the way it is, that nothing needs to be changed. It sounds similar to your epiphany, Wayne."

"It does, Dax. And it *is* similar. I have learned and experienced since that when you go beyond your thoughts in meditation, you will have the same beautiful experience that I had on the moon. You don't need to travel in a rocket to feel calm and peaceful and bliss."

"I have also seen glimpses of it in my meditation practice, Wayne. I am continuing with my practice in order to experience more silence and joy. This is a good reminder! But please tell me, what happened next?"

"When your mind gets stretched, Dax, it will never regain its original dimensions. Oliver Wendell Holmes once said this so eloquently. It is very true. My mind never returned to mediocrity and misunderstanding. Still, I got confused. Because my old mind started questioning my new vision. Never underestimate this robot mind of yours."

"Wait, what? Did you say *robot mind*?"

"I did, Dax. You familiar with the robot mind? Then you probably know that it can create confusion like no one else can. I started doubting my experience. Had it been a dream? I was in need of guidance from someone with an even higher perspective. That is how I found Rama."

"Sorry, who? Rama?"

Wayne smiled. "Yes, Dax. Rama."

"You mean wisdom coach Rama who nowadays inspires the world, based out of Singapore?"

"That's the one!" Wayne responded.

"Does Rama have anything to do with our get-together here and now, Wayne?" I asked with a smile.

"Well, I guess," Wayne responded. "Recently he told me that I would be meeting a guy called Dax. And he asked me to talk with him about the topic of perspective. Do you also know Rama?"

I started laughing. "This man! Always good for a pleasant surprise."

Wayne said, "Yep, must be the same guy. You want to hear more?"

Yes, I definitely wanted to hear more.

"Rama appeared in my life, Dax. What a blessing. He has helped me to understand my epiphany in easy and practical ways. He has helped me to turn my perspective-changing journey into a much improved life."

"How, Wayne? What did Rama teach you?"

"He taught me that *my perspective decides my reality*!"

"Come again?"

"My perspective decides my reality. That is your key lesson for today! Let me illustrate. I recently visited my son and his family. My son told me they had Wi-Fi connection problems and he had to urgently call the help desk. So he did. He ended up in the usual waiting line. It annoyed him. He put the phone on his desk with the speaker on. We all heard music playing, intended to ease the wait. Still, my son's agitation grew. He started grumbling and complaining about the lack of speed, the service, the wasting of his time. He got really frustrated. My granddaughter of five also heard the music. She did not mind her dad's desperation. She liked the music. She started dancing. She was totally engrossed in the music and her dance. Enjoying herself.

"Perspective decides reality, Dax! My son's frustration perspective created a negative and angry reality for him. My granddaughter's playful perspective resulted in dance and joy. Same situation, different perspective, different reality."

"That is a nice story, Wayne. I appreciate it. Tell me more."

"Rama introduced me to the power of my mind. He taught me that I have the power to choose the focus of my thoughts. To choose my perspective. Thus, I have the ability to create my own reality. We live in a dual world, Dax. Every person, every circumstance, every event, every location, everything has two sides. There is good in bad situations, and there is bad in good situations. We can all choose what we see. Think about the famous glass half-full or half-empty. Rama explained that my moon experience had given me a whole new perspective on life. Because I had seen the grandeur and the perfectness of the universe, I became aware of the irrelevance of much what we robots struggle with. You know the robotic mind, right?"

"I certainly do!" I smiled.

"Well, if perspective decides your reality, then the question is, what is your perspective? Most people believe that the world is as they see it. But different people see the world differently, so how can that be? The Talmud helps us to understand. It states, 'You don't see the world as it is but as you are.' In other words, Dax, your inside is the basis for your perspective. Your thoughts, beliefs, convictions, and ideas decide what you see. Our perspective thus reflects the program of our robotic mind. That program is mostly conditioned. Colored by our upbringing, our learning, our experiences. And then we think we are right. We don't accept other views. But we don't know that we see the world as we are, not as it is."

"I get it, Wayne. You are saying that I am looking at the world with my own perspective. I see the world in my own unique way. Right?"

"Yes, Dax, correct. It is as if all of us have a unique pair of glasses. And although we look at the same things, the reality we observe is different because of these glasses. People perceive different realities dependent on the coloring of their glasses. Now, if you don't like the realities of your life, you might want to change them. Trying to change the outside world will not get you there. You can only change yourself. When you change your inside, the realities of your life will change. Guaranteed."

"Rama told me the exact same thing. The solution is always on the inside, never on the outside. Now tell me: how did your epiphany change the reality of your life?"

"With Rama's help, I understood that my reality had changed because *I* had changed. My visit to the moon had instantaneously changed my inner program. It usually takes more time to reprogram yourself. But throughout time, there are many examples of people who changed in an instant. It happened to me. My inside changed, and my perspective and my reality changed. I will give you a few examples of how, Dax.

"I had been a fighter my whole life. I grew up believing that life is all about winning and competing. My dad had been a convincing example. When I saw the superb balance of the universe, I realized the futility of this belief. The need to be better than other people is stupid. You are here to learn and grow. To be better than you used to be. To express your best self. Besides, we need each other. To keep the balance. To join. To complement. To help. Life is not about kicking ass and beating others. Life is about togetherness, love, and support. My first mindset shift was from competition to collaboration.

"For most people, life is contending. Striving. Aiming. Struggling. Up on the moon, I noticed the perfection of everything. There is nothing to be improved. I wondered why on earth we have come to believe that achieving is the purpose of life. It is not. All our life, we are running. We are chasing. Hardly ever do we stop to see the perfect wonder that life actually is. We forget to enjoy the gift of life. I came home with a knowing that we are here to celebrate and to appreciate. My second mindset shift was from achievement to appreciation.

"As I was walking on the moon, it occurred to me that everything just is. All is as it is supposed to be. The universe is in perfect order. Humans seem to believe that we first have to proof ourselves before we are worthy. We need to show before we accept ourselves and before we are accepted by others. We cannot just *be*. We think we have to *do* first to earn our right to be. I realized that we are human *be*ings, not human *do*ings. We are here to *be* the person we would like to be. There is nothing we have to demonstrate first. We are, and that is perfectly fine. My third mindset shift was from doing to being.

"In space, the universe showed me its real face. No masks, no role-play, no appearance. The universe just authentically is. It became clear to me that pretending takes away from who we truly are. We are born unique individuals. But then we start to believe that we have to be like other people. We start to think that we are not good enough the way we are. We start to play roles; we act. Dax, the purpose of life is not to be like somebody else. Life is about becoming your best self. You are here to be your authentic self. My fourth mindset shift was from acting to authenticity.

"My mind swirled through space, Dax. It became filled with a whole new mindset of who we are and why we are here. What you see depends on the veil of your mind. That veil is your mindset. My mindset leaped. It changed in an instant. I have seen the world in a new light since then. I see the beauty, the order, the potentiality of each person, the connectedness. My new mindset has given me a joyful new perspective. It has elevated my life in all aspects. My life is full of love, purpose, happiness, positivity, freedom, truthfulness, and success. Life has become a celebration, exactly as it is supposed to be."

I was taking in all the lessons that Wayne was sharing, processing them and firing back questions. "Fascinating story, Wayne," I said to him when at 3:00 p.m. we finally sat down to have some lunch. "I loved the space education during the tour. And I love your lessons on the mind's perspective. Your epiphany has also been an awakening for me. I really appreciate it. Can I ask you a question about practical application in my life?"

"Of course, Dax. Fire!"

"I was talking to Rama about people interaction challenges the other day. It seems that you have found the key for effective relationships. Can you please share your insights with me?"

"That is an important question for life, Dax. Because life is all about relationships. They can be bountiful blessings but also big burdens. I sure can give you my SPACE perspective. It describes my key principles for effective human interaction. You want to hear?"

"Yes please!"

"SPACE! The S stands for *self*. You are here to be yourself. Don't wear a mask; be your unique self. That is the best you can give into a relationship. The P, as you can imagine, Dax, is all about *perspective*. Be aware that your perspective decides your reality. So choose your perspective wisely when you observe the people around you. Focus on what is good. What you like. What gives you energy and inspiration. It will elevate any relationship. The A is about *accepting* the fact that other people have their own perspectives and realities. Don't fight these. See how they complement your views and ideas. An accepting mind brings empathy. Empathy helps to bring out the best of people. The C represents *collaboration*. Together trumps tournament. Life is not a competition. Through collaboration, you will achieve more. See how you can help and lift each other in your personal relationships. Finally the E, which describes *enjoyment*. You are here to celebrate your life and to enjoy the presence of other people. We can all add so much to each other's lives. Put your focus on what you can contribute to others and enjoy. It will enrich your life."

"I like it, Wayne. Self. Perspective. Acceptance. Collaboration. Enjoyment. SPACE. That is a mindset that will help me in relationships but in other aspects of life too."

"It sure will, Dax. See the world as it is, not through your limited eyes but through your SPACE eyes."

"Your wonderful lesson on perspective says that my reality is all about me. I set my mind. My mindset directs my perspective. And my perspective decides my reality. Correct?"

"Correct, Dax. It all comes down to you, just like Rama always clarifies. All solutions can be found within. It has been a great couple of hours together. Let me leave you with a compelling story that will allow you to easily remember. Are you ready?"

Yes, I most certainly was.

"An alien had recently moved to a new planet to live. The alien was not happy at all, so he was grateful when a space master visited the planet. 'How can I help you?' the master asked when the alien came to seek counsel. 'I moved here only six months ago, but already I am very unhappy. The place is dull. There is no entertainment. The other aliens are not inspiring. The food is terrible. What should I do?' The master said, 'Do you have an idea?' Yes, the alien knew another planet that was just fantastic. He would be happy there. The master said, 'What stops you? Pack your stuff and go!' Half a year later, the space master visited that planet and met the alien. 'Nice to meet you again. You have moved! How are you?' he asked. The alien answered, 'That's why I came to you. At first, I was very happy here. But after two months, my experience changed. I started noticing many things I don't like. The architecture. The lack of ambition of the other aliens. The kinds of jobs. Basically, I feel as miserable as I did on my previous planet. What to do?' The master asked whether the alien had an idea. Yes, he had done extensive research this time and found the perfect planet. The alien was certain that that was the place to be. 'What stops you?' the master said. 'Go find your happiness there.' Six months later, the space master met the alien again on the new planet. 'Great to see you. Are things good now?' the master asked. And he received the same answer from the alien. The place had been good. But then the alien had found many things that were making him unhappy. 'What to do?' he asked the master. It was time for the real answer, so the master told the alien, 'You have to stop changing planets, my friend. You have to start changing yourself!'"

I repeated the master's advice: "Stop changing planets; start changing myself. This is all about perspective—right, Wayne?"

"Yes it is, Dax. You got it. Circumstances do not make you unhappy. Your perspective, your focus does. If you want to change your reality, you have to change your perspective. What the master tells the alien is, 'Put down your glasses with negative, what-is-wrong-here lenses and replace them with spectacles that help you take the positive, what-is-right-here perspective."

"I like that metaphor, Wayne. When you put on the right glasses, or in other words, when you change your perspective, your reality will change. What you see is what you are. I think I really got it."

"You do, Dax. Choosing the right perspective has another major advantage for your life. When you develop a mindset with a positive perspective, your reality will be positive wherever you are. Remember, wherever you go, there you are!"

"I love it, Wayne. Wherever I take my inner perspective, that will be the reality I will experience. It is not about the externals. My life experience depends on my internals. Perspective is everything."

"It is. My epiphany on the moon changed my perspective, and it has changed my life. I have loved every second of my life since I returned from the moon so much more. I have made choices based on my purpose and passion. That is why I never left NASA. After my astronaut career, I spent twenty years as lead of the space command center. Then, when it was time to retire, I asked to become a tour guide here at the Space Center. I love to talk about space, and I love the engagement with people. My life is great. I am enjoying every day. My perspective leaped. Here is my advice to you, Dax: choose your perspective wisely because *your life is your perspective becoming real.*"

Before I drove home on the I-45 North, I sent a message to Rama.

Dear Rama,
I feel like an astronaut today.
My perspective has leaped.
Thank you!
Dax

Perspective—Learning Box

Wisdom	I accept that life is uncertain. I accept that life will always change.
	I manage myself. I do not try to manage the inevitable change.
	I have to manage *me* first, and the rest will follow.
	I come from Source. I am connected with all. I am one with all.
	My perspective decides my reality.
	As I choose my perspective, I create my reality.
	I move from competition to collaboration. From achievement to appreciation. From doing to being. From acting to authenticity.
	My life is my perspective becoming real.
Awareness	Your mind can be your most powerful tool, but it can also be your biggest limiting factor in life.
	Sometimes you may need a coach to get to know your (robot) mindset.
	You can try to carpet the whole world to walk softly, or you can put on the right shoes. The master's formula for dealing with life: manage yourself!
	You have the ability to develop an inner foundation that makes you unshakeable.
	When your mind gets stretched, it will never regain its original dimension.
	Beware of your robot mind. It can create confusion like no one can.
	Circumstances do not make you unhappy. Your perspective does.

Story/Tool	SPACE (self, perspective, acceptance, collaboration, enjoyment). The alien changing planets.
Practice	The glasses—get to know the glasses with which you look at life by examining your experience of life. Apply a SPACE perspective in your relationships (and life in general).

9

Lifetime

Did You Have Fun?

If you miss the now, you miss life.
—Vikas Malkani

Happiness is a creation of your mind. Both memories
of the past and anxiety for the future rob your
happiness. Learn to live in the present.
—Swami Rama

Tomorrow does not exist. Life only happens now.
—Abraham-Hicks

NASA Space Center—done! What a blessed visit it had been, thanks
to Wayne. He had enriched my tour of the US space history with
his expert commentaries and explanations. And he had inspired
me with his important lessons on perspective. I was determined to
develop a SPACE mindset—a beneficial perspective to have not only
in relationships but in many aspects of life. In my morning mind-
training practice, I reminded myself of the elements of SPACE and
envisioned how I would apply them in my life.

Time passed. Life kept Jane and me busy. But we always managed to find time to sit down together and share what we were truly thinking. About anything. Each other. Our relatives and friends. Our home and garden. Travel plans. Shopping. Work. The news. Anything. It varied. Our self-reflections, personal well-being, and personal development, including our questions, were a fixed item on our agenda. In one of those conversations, Jane told me she had decided on the three empowering *I am* statements she wanted to have as her foundation: *I am beautiful, I am free, I am good just the way I am!* I gave her a big hug and a kiss, and I said, "You are, Jane. You definitely are. It is time you believe yourself!" We were on the same path. The path of self-understanding and personal development. We were growing together. And we simply loved it.

Sitting next to our garden pool on another such occasion, Jane asked me about the status of my learning experience under Rama's guidance. I had shared many details of the various encounters I had had with the amazing friends of Rama. That evening though, she asked me for a stock-take. How was the inspiration coming together? What was the impact on my life? Was I enjoying the experience? Great questions! My mind swirled back to the evening with Rama in Singapore.

Rama had opened my eyes. We are robots. I was a robot. A robot who was living his life based on the software I had gathered in my mind over time. Rama had basically been saying that my software might be out of date or might contain errors. Just like we do with computer software, it is wise to regularly check our inner programming for bugs and viruses. It had been a confronting wake-up call that evening in Singapore but also a valuable one. It had inspired me to go on my journey of self-reflection and self-realization under the loving and selfless guidance of Rama.

I had met Master Amir in India. Amir had introduced me to what I considered the most fundamental life lesson—namely, that my power is in my thinking. My power sits in my ability to take control over my mind. He had helped me to unravel the intriguing wisdom line "as you think, so your life shall be." I had left New Delhi promising myself to grow my mind awareness and to train my mind to become a deliberate thinker.

Mrs. Christine Yeo had given me the second key building block for life: responsibility. I still remembered the story of the strangling fig, her favorite tree in the Botanical Gardens. We can live life complaining, moaning, and finding excuses. It will not make our lives better. Or we can apply the question that Christine's PE teacher had asked her when she was only seventeen: where am *I* in the story of my life? Responsibility is a true superpower. Upon reflection, I had found myself applying victim behavior in certain situations to no avail. I had resolved to be more like the fig.

I said to Jane, "I see the two lessons that I have learned from Master Amir and Christine as the basic building blocks for life. Thinking is the basis. Taking responsibility is the requirement. Rama first wanted me to know these before he put me on my quest for clarity."

That is how I had gotten to meet Olisa in Singapore Zoo. A powerful girl on a mission. Very clear about her purpose in life. She had inspired me to find my dharma. To be who I am supposed to be. Not to spend my life like her dear bapu, whose sad end-of-life dream I remembered vividly. She had taught me to be true to my promise, irrespective of the ideas that others had implanted in my robotic mind. Based on her inspiration, I had intensified my search to find my life's purpose.

Next, Rama had made me find Sofia in Buenos Aires. Her tango show had been breathtaking and thrilling. Her passion for passion had been a lesson I would never forget. When you follow your passion, you will be the best you can be. Passion gives energy and inspiration. Passion drives performance. Passion makes you fearless, resilient, and persistent. I had experienced the effectiveness of passionate and intense team dynamics among my Argentinean colleagues. It had further cemented Sofia's lessons on the power of passion in my inner system.

"Jane, I believe Rama wanted me to meet Olisa and Sofia to get clear on the direction for my life. He once told me that you first need to know your destination before you can start taking effective action to get there. Direction comes from finding your purpose and passion. I am implementing the lessons I have learned. I am starting to understand my unique promise and purpose and to find my passion."

In the Philippines, I then met Raquel *I am priority* Rivera. I reminded myself of her key lesson every day. Whenever my robotic mind would challenge me being the priority in my life, I would consciously bring up the question "Who else?" This soothed my conditioned mind. I had become more and more convinced that giving priority to yourself is necessary to live your best life. And it is the only way to be able to give your very best to others. Just like caring Raquel had explained to me.

Coach Ace then enlightened me on the power of beliefs. Oh man, wrong beliefs can make your life hell. They can limit your life experience. But beliefs can be changed. As Ace had taught me, I am what I think I am. And I can choose what I think about myself. Coach Ace had given me a practical tool to become aware of my inner belief system. And he had taught me how I can build a healthy, empowering belief system. I was practicing his guidance every day. My self-image, self-confidence, and self-belief were growing steadily.

Astronaut-turned-tour guide Wayne had shared the amazing story of how his walk on the moon had changed his mind's perspective. Perspective decides your reality. Wayne's life had changed for the better in so many aspects after his epiphany. He had opened my eyes. If I want to make changes to the reality of my life, I have to start on the inside. I have to first change my mindset. All the lessons that Rama wanted me to learn were complementary and consistent. The more I learned, the more sense they made.

"It is an amazing journey with Rama as the invisible tour guide, Jane. He is making sure the lessons he wants me to learn are all coming together nicely. We need building blocks for our life. We need direction for our life. We need inner stability based on the right mindset for our life. Rama is making sure that I am getting all the ingredients for creating my best life. I am curious to learn what might be next!"

Jane had lovingly listened to my reflections. She was on her own journey to grow through life. At a young age, she had seen many examples in her direct family of how not to live. Jane had been a natural in her own change journey because she was very clear on what she wanted. Ever since we met, she had been articulate about her wishes for life and from me, her partner. Enjoyment, love and support, acceptance, care, and celebration. Her search for a better life had been the prime inspiration for me to start reading wisdom lessons from masters. Journeying together had made our experiences a lot more enjoyable and also a lot more effective. I was learning from Jane's experiences. Jane was benefiting from my adventures. She looked at me. "I love the way Rama is imparting his guidance into your life, Dax. It is fun. It is practical. And it is based on encounters with truly fascinating people. What might be next? Maybe how to apply all the lessons in your life?" I did not know, but I knew that Jane's gutfeel usually was very right.

A few days later, Rama sent me a WhatsApp message.

Dear Dax,
How is the reality of your life?
I was wondering whether you would be in Europe in the next few months?
I would love for you to meet my friend Ernst in Holland!
Sending you my love,
Rama

Holland was well-known to us, although we did not have any travel plans at the time of Rama's message. But this changed quickly. One of the benefits of working for a multinational company is the frequent opportunity for international travel. It allows you to see the world. Shortly after Rama's question, the business I worked for announced a global leadership meeting in Istanbul, Turkey. I was invited. For me to get there, I would fly via Schiphol, Amsterdam, and I would thus be in Holland. They say that there are no coincidences in life—only universally orchestrated, rightly timed events. That is how the invite felt to me. I sent Rama my update and travel plans. He organized my next visit to undoubtedly another one of his inspiring friends.

Weeks passed. Jane and I spent a few days in Dallas, where we visited the Sixth Floor Museum at Dealey Plaza, the place where JFK had been shot in November 1963. The Owls kept up their strong season performance and were heading toward the playoffs. Hurricane season brought some serious rain to Houston, flooding the streets like we had never seen before. We kept our perspective in check and connected regularly with our blessings. The day of my trip to Europe was quickly approaching. My visit to Ernst was planned the weekend after the Istanbul meeting, such that I would have time on my hands. Rama had given me address details in a little city in the western part of the Netherlands, north of the country's capital, Amsterdam.

The global leadership meeting reminded me of previous such meetings. Much time for human connection. Celebration of achievements. Inspiration from external speakers. Priorities and plan discussions. And change. Somehow we were always telling ourselves that things were never good enough. Change was always required. And the resolution always seemed to have to come from organizational and process change. I observed in myself that I had grown a bit tired of the ever-existing optimism about the impact from such peripheral adjustments. They never seemed to work. If you don't change the *mind* of the business, the outcomes will just stay the same. I had started seeing the wisdom that I was learning and incorporating into my life also at play in the corporate environment. Of course, the universal rules applied. *As I think, so I shall be* also works at the aggregated *as we think, so we shall be* level. The meeting was great because I had the chance to meet many old friends and colleagues, but it was uneventful and boring from a content perspective. As I boarded my plane to the Netherlands, I felt somewhat drained. To recharge myself, I closed my eyes and connected my mind to my purpose and passion that was becoming clearer and clearer. I envisioned myself on a stage and sharing wisdom to inspire a large audience. It worked. The thought of benefiting others brought a smile on my face. I started feeling better by taking conscious control over my thoughts. Upon arrival in Amsterdam, I was full of positive energy again. Although the meeting with Ernst was not until the next morning, I decided to take the evening easy. I had a light dinner at my hotel in Amsterdam and retreated to my room immediately thereafter. A good night of sleep was always welcome.

After breakfast the next morning, I took the train to the city of Alkmaar. From there, a bus delivered me at almost the doorstep of the address in the little village of Bergen that Rama had given me. Public transport in the Netherlands is well organized and efficient and allows you to visit pretty much the whole country. The last kilometer or so, I traveled by foot, and I arrived at my destination at coffee time. It was not a single home. Rather, I had reached a living community consisting of three ten-story residential towers, each painted in a unique color. The apartment with the number of the address from Rama was in the turquoise tower, so that was where I rang the entrance bell. As the door opened, I entered a general area, where I immediately saw the elevator that would bring residents to their homes. I also spotted two hallways, one of which was the connection to one of the other two towers. Cheerful music came from the other corridor. I decided to enter that corridor, and I arrived in a group area full of tables and chairs and filled with elderly people. The room was beautified with colorful garlands and other festive ornaments. As I entered, I noted a man facing the crowd and standing on a table. He was dancing happily to the song that the other people were singing. There was another table filled with various delicious-looking cakes. One of them was decorated with the number ninety-three. After a few songs, the people present cheered three times with their arms and hands high up in the air, and then the room became quiet. *This must be a Dutch birthday celebration,* I thought.

The dancing man had noted me and started waving his arms as if to invite me in his direction. I pointed my finger at myself to ask whether he meant me. The man nodded, and I started walking toward him. He came down from the table, and when I was near, he stepped forward and gave me a big hug. "Dax, you lucky man, you have arrived at exactly the right moment. Celebration time! It is my ninety-third birthday today, and you can choose your piece of cake now!" The man looked triumphant and walked me toward the table with the cakes.

"You must be Ernst?" I uttered.

"Yes. Sorry, my friend. I forgot to introduce myself. I am Ernst indeed!" And so our engagement started with eating a nice piece of Dutch apple pie, together with a large group of elderly people who had joined Ernst for his ninety-third birthday celebration.

The address Rama had sent me to turned out to be a private home for elderly people. It was beautifully situated in the picture-perfect village of Bergen and surrounded by forest, dunes, and the sea. "Nice place indeed, Dax," Ernst said when we sat down on the wooden bench in the park of the senior residence. "The environment you live in has an important bearing on your well-being. Through your mind's focus, you can turn any environment into a blessing, but nature all around certainly helps!" At that moment, Ernst's mobile phone beeped to indicate the arrival of a WhatsApp message. "Listen, Dax. You will like this one," he said after checking it.

> Dear Ernst,
> Congratulations on your ninety-third birthday!
> You long ago found the secret of perennial youth: young at mind, young at heart and body.
> Be young and keep celebrating life, my friend, every day.
> With love,
> Rama
> By the way, say hi to Dax, who must be with you now!

Ernst started laughing after reading Rama's message. "This man misses no opportunity to share his wisdom and love. He even remembered your visit to me today, Dax. Isn't it amazing? Thank you, Rama!" he said.

"He is amazing," was my response. "But so are you, Ernst. Ninety-three, dancing on the table? A lively birthday celebration with at least sixty other people? How do you do this?"

Ernst looked at me with a mischievous expression. "That, Dax, is exactly the topic that Rama asked me to talk about with you. How to live life!"

What a man, I thought. I said, "I would love to hear your story!"

"Let's go then, Dax!" Ernst said, full of energy. "And let me be honest with you: I have not always been celebrating life. I have learned to live through my experiences and with the help of other people. Like most people, I grew up with adopted ideas about what is important. I lived a pretty regular life. School, sports, studies, job, relationship, house, child. When I was thirty-four, I thought I had it all. Then our son Tom was born and I was certain: my life was complete. Are you a parent, Dax?"

I shook my head. "No, I am not, Ernst. But I am most definitely an aspiring parent! I love kids."

"Same here, Dax. Children are wonderful. And your own child is even more wondrous and magical. Being a parent has been the greatest privilege. Tom was the light of my life. Being privy to a growing-up child truly is one of the most fantastic gifts. Tom grew up, developed well, and turned into the young man he was supposed to be. I watched, I enjoyed, I loved every day with him. Then disaster struck. I still remember July 23, 1972, a hot summer day. I was fifty-three years old. Tom had just turned eighteen. He had been going to the beach with friends that day. When driving home on his bicycle in the evening, he was hit by a car. The driver was drunk. Too much beer at the beach. Tom died instantly, on the spot. At 22:14, police officers rang our doorbell and brought us the terrible news. The world sank under my feet. I was completely shattered."

Ernst became silent. "Wow, Ernst, I feel your hurt and pain. That is absolutely devastating. What happened next?"

"I fell in a dark hole. My whole life felt useless. Without purpose. Exactly as other people with similar experiences are telling. I got paralyzed. Not physically but mentally. My life came to a hold. There was no more joy. No more happiness. My wife, Eva, was coping a bit better. At least she kept her eyes open to the external world to find help. A man from India came to Amsterdam to inspire his audience with a talk named 'Heal Your Life.' It must have been some five years after Tom's passing. Eva wanted to go. Somehow she knew we needed the insights of this man. I did not want to go. Who could help me? Without Tom, my life was over. Eva basically dragged me there.

"It is where I met Rama for the first time, Dax. He must have been in his midthirties. I did not want to be in that hall. I did not want to listen. Still, when he appeared on stage, something happened in me. The calm and stability that Rama radiated got my attention. I still remember his first few sentences. 'Dear friends, life can present us with beauty but also with almost unbearable pain. Whatever the circumstance though, it is possible to be happy and peaceful. Masters throughout time have done us a huge favor by unraveling how. Who wants to learn?' Eva and I looked at each other. Tears in our eyes. Simultaneously, we raised our arms. My skepticism disappeared. Instantaneously, I was present. Would it be possible to live joyfully after what happened with Tom? I wanted to hear more from this mysterious man."

I was doing the math in my mind. If Ernst had met Rama in the midseventies, it meant that they had known each other for more than thirty years. It also meant that Rama was around sixty-five years old. Sixty-five years? The man looked at least twenty years younger! "Tell me more, Ernst," I said.

Ernst continued. "Ever heard of the word *synchronicity,* Dax?" He did not wait for my answer. "Synchronistic events are visually unrelated occurrences that appear significantly connected. These happen. Synchronicity happens. And not at random, Dax. This amazing, invisible universal order that brought Wayne his epiphany is at play at all times. We cannot always fathom why, but fact of the matter is that seemingly random events happen together for a reason. Synchronistic experiences leave us with a sense of curiosity. An intuitive knowing to pay attention. That is what happened with me and Eva that morning in Amsterdam. We knew we were in the right place to hear the inspiration we so desperately needed for our lives."

See, there are no coincidences, I contemplated, remembering my thought upon receiving the invite for the Istanbul meeting.

"Amazingly, Dax, one of the examples that Rama used was about parents losing a child. 'An unimaginable event that still can happen,' as he described it. If you allow it, the death of your child can destroy the rest of your life. That was pretty much my experience till that day. Then Rama said, 'We all want to live. We all want happiness and joy in our lives. Even in the face of such a dreadful event like the loss of your child, this innate longing remains. You might not be consciously aware of it, but it is there. Humans want to enjoy life. So after pain and drama, someday you will have to pick up your life again. It is up to you. You can. And you can decide your own timing. You can choose whether it is going to be sooner or later. My friends, if you are in a similar situation, you can ask yourself the following two questions: Do I want to live again? If your answer is yes, then ask yourself, When?' That is where he paused for a moment, Dax. It felt as if he was talking to Eva and me. And that is where my inner candle started burning again a little bit. I looked at Eva and said, 'Yes, I want to live with joy, and I want it to be sooner!' We were both crying."

I could not say a word. The emotion was running through my inner system. I looked at Ernst and was longing to hear more.

"That day, Dax, I learned a big lesson about death. As humans, we are all so afraid to die. Death is the biggest fear that people are carrying in their minds without openly talking about it. We forget that death is a normal part of life. Birth and death are part of the same circle of life. When there is birth, there will be death. It is inevitable. And it is all good. Rather than seeing death as your enemy, you can also see death as your friend. Death is in fact a very important teacher for all of us. Yes, we will all die one way. We can't change that. The lesson that death wants to teach us is to live *now*. Death is here to remind us to live today. To remind us to make sure we enjoy life now because one day we will be gone! Death is not here to scare us. Death is here to wake us up to make the most of life now. I have not felt afraid of dying ever since. No, I have made the lesson that death is teaching us the guiding principle for my life."

"I love it, Ernst. Choosing your perspective on death deliberately. Death as a teacher is an empowering thought!"

"Rama shared something else that morning in Amsterdam that I have never forgotten," Ernst went on. "The topic of his inspiration was 'Heal Your Life.' Rama said, 'All healing starts with a happy mind!' Many people are broken for different reasons. Health problems. Relationship problems. Self-esteem problems. Financial problems. Lack of meaning problems. We are looking for healing of many aspects of our lives. All healing starts with a happy mind, Dax. When you change your mind, you will change your life. When you claim your inner power and *choose* happiness, you will find that your external reality of life will completely change. I was in desperate need to heal from the immense pain that I was feeling ever since Tom had left this earthly plane. I basically had stopped living. I was immersing myself in the tragedy and my inner suffering. I was not connected with my power. I was blaming life for my misery. That day, I welcomed death as my friend and teacher, and I made a start to take responsibility for creating inner happiness."

"Looks like you have been very successful in your pursuit for life and happiness, Ernst. Look at you. Ninety-three, vibrant, shining, laughing, sharing, and enjoying. You are leading by example," I said in admiration. "It is clear that you have found the key to live! Please share more."

"My connection with Rama started that day. He still is my most important teacher in life. Sometimes, Dax, we need somebody who inspires us. Someone who helps us to challenge our conditioned ideas and gives us the wisdom perspective on life. In a way, the rebooting process of my life started with the 'Heal Your Life' inspiration. I have been keeping in touch with Rama to get regular upgrades and keep the inner software of my mind healthy and happy. You work for a large corporation, right?"

I nodded.

"In the corporate world, capital is key. Agree? A company needs capital to achieve its objectives. There are different types. Financial capital, of course. Human capital, absolutely pivotal. Intellectual property capital, for differentiation. Asset capital, for efficient production. Companies take their capital resources very seriously. Every capital decision is analyzed, weighed, considered, tested, and risk assessed. Every decision receives major scrutiny. Makes good sense because the various capital sources are the lifeblood of the company and are costly. Let's now look at humans, Dax. To run our lives, we also have various sources of capital to spend. The human sources of capital are time, energy, effort, and money. How serious are we in deciding how we spend our human capital? How much consideration do you give to how you spend your time, energy, effort, and money?"

"Uhm ... that is a good question, Ernst. I think I give quite a lot of consideration to how I spend my money. I take a lot less thinking time about how I invest my energy and effort. And to be honest, I hardly look at time as a scarce resource. I am not very conscious about how I am using my time."

"Dax, that pretty much sums up how most people spend their available resources. Pretty serious about money. Less attention for energy and effort. No focus on time. Why do you think time gets no attention?"

"Not sure, Ernst."

"It is because we all think we have plenty of time. We think time is an abundant resource. But it is not. I would like you to become aware of the fact that we are all on a countdown. After every day we have lived, we have one day less to live. Time is life capital. It is a scarce and uncertain resource. Scarce because our time is finite. We are eating up our available time every day. Uncertain because we do not know how long we will live. Tom did not know the morning of the day of his death it would be his last day. Nobody knows. It is wise to pay attention to your time and to spend it consciously. Don't take your time here on earth for granted."

This made a lot of sense. A simple lesson but not one that I had heard so explicitly before. Ernst was serious about time. So much was clear. "How to do this, Ernst? How can I spend my time in a better way?"

"I would like you to think about your life, Dax. Life is time, and time is life. Are you with me?"

I nodded.

"If you want to make the most of your time, it helps to have the right perspective. There are important things about time that I would like you to understand more consciously. If you do, you might want to spend your time more deliberately. That is certainly what I have been doing after my awakening about the preciousness of life and time by Rama. First thing to realize, Dax, is that your life only happens in the now. Think about a timeline that started the day you were born. You were born in the now at that time. From there, you have existed every moment. And every one of these moments was *now*. We are here now, in beautiful Bergen, sitting on this bench. From here, the now moments will continue. What is currently still the future one day will be your now. To say it briefly, your life is a continuous flow of now moments. Are you following, my friend?"

I was. I said to Ernst, "You mean to say that if I want to make the most of my life, I better make the most of my now moments, right?"

"Correct. I am coming to my formula for optimizing your time. But first, there are other things I would like to share with you. So your life is this continuous flow of now moments. Yet we do not spend much time in the now."

I was confused. "Come again, Ernst. How do I *not* spend my time in the now?"

"Let me ask you a question: where is your mind during the day?"

I was certain what Ernst was explaining was important. But it did not yet make a lot sense to me. "Uhm, Ernst. Not sure I am following you. My mind is just where it always is. It is not like my mind can go traveling!"

"That is a great way of indicating what your mind actually *is* doing all the time, Dax: traveling. It is moving from the past to the future and back to the past again. Your robotic mind spends most of its time in the past or in the future. It is hardly ever present in the now. Am I making sense to you?"

I was thinking hard about what Ernst was saying. "You are, Ernst. Now that I think about it, it is true indeed that my mind is frequently occupied with past events and future plans. What does that mean?"

"You heard what you said, Dax? *'Now* that I think about it.' Good use of the now." Ernst was laughing.

Ninety-three and still so sharp, I thought before he continued.

"Most of our precious mind space we spend on regretting the past or worrying about the future. You might have heard this before. Without awareness, we waste our mind power thinking about all the errors of the past or all the things that can go wrong in the future. How do you think this makes you feel? And how do you think this helps to maximize the use of your now time?"

I was starting to see where Ernst was going. "Makes me feel bad and angry or concerned and anxious. Certainly does not make me feel good and positive." Ernst nodded. "And if my mind is wandering in the past or future all the time, I cannot make the most of the now moment. My mind is busy with other things."

Ernst nodded again. "Yes, Dax, you are getting it. Here is a secret about the mind that I would like you to always remember. *Your mind can only be in one place at a time!*"

"My mind can only be in one place at a time?" I repeated.

"Yes, correct. Recall that I already said that life only happens in the now. So if your mind is in the past, your mind is not in the now. You are basically missing life. Same if your mind is in the future; it is not focused on the now, and life will pass you by. We cannot see life, Dax, if we allow our mind to roam in the past and the future all the time. Our untrained mind has the tendency to get stuck in the past and the future over and over again. Our robotic mind bores us with the same regrets and the same concerns all the time. It stops us from making the most of our now."

"So I better learn to live in the now, right?"

Ernst confirmed.

"But what then about the past and the future? They are still part of my life."

"Oh yes, both are part of life, and they both have a specific, important purpose. Let me explain how you can leverage your past and future to optimize your use of the now. Got a question for you, Dax. Where would the past be if you didn't think about it?"

Ernst was looking at me, waiting for an answer. "It would not exist?" I responded hesitatingly.

"Correct, Dax. If you don't think about your past, it is as if your past does not exist. If you suffered from sudden amnesia, the past would not be there anymore. Rama has a nice phrase to make this clear. He says, 'The past is dead, except in your head.'"

"I like it, Ernst."

"We keep the past alive in our minds. Our untrained, automatic mind tends to remember all the negatives. An illness of twelve years ago. A broken relationship of seven years ago. A failure of twenty years ago. We carry the burdens from the past with us on our journey of life. This is not an effective use of our mind. The *only* purpose of the past is to learn from it and to use its lessons *now* to make your life better. This way, the past has great value for you."

Nice perspective, I thought. *Wayne would be pleased.*

Ernst went on. "Also thinking about the future can be beneficial. But do not waste your time and mind worrying about it. Rather, use the now to set your goals. To decide your objectives. To get clear on what it is you want. To imagine the future you want to create. That is it, Dax. Clarity is the future's only purpose."

I gave Ernst a thumbs-up to confirm I was following.

"Learn from the past and get clear about your objectives for the future. Then leave the past and the future and *use* the now. The optimal use of your now moments has two elements. The first one is to create. The second one is at least as important. I want to tell you a story.

"A billionaire who has recently died arrives at heaven's gate. An angel opens the door and asks the man for his name, which he provides. The angel checks the list and finds the man's name. 'Welcome, we have been expecting you! Source is awaiting you.' The rich businessman enters heaven. It is a most beautiful place. Although he knows he has an appointment, he takes his time to admire all the beauty around. After the slow walk, finally the angel and the billionaire arrive at a big castle. 'When you go through the front door, you enter a big hallway. Keep walking, and you will find Source on a big throne.' The businessman follows the instruction, and soon enough, he is standing next to the throne. Source speaks: 'Nice to meet you. Has your life on earth been any fun?' Without answering the question, the billionaire talks about his major business successes. Source listens but repeats his question: 'Did you have any fun?' And the man explains the global size and reach of his business. 'Did you have any fun?' Source asks again. Still the man avoids the question, and he tells proudly of all the charity work he has been doing in the last ten years of his life. 'Did you have any fun?' Source asks for a last time. And the man answers, 'I thought that is what heaven is for.' Source looks at the man and says, 'The key objective for life is to have fun. To enjoy. To celebrate. You have clearly misunderstood, my friend.' Source snaps two fingers, and, in a flash, the man returns to earth for a second chance."

"Hahaha, nice story, Ernst. Message clear!"

"Life is our greatest gift, Dax. Life is here to be celebrated. To create is the first element for optimizing your now moments. To enjoy is the second. As we are living our lives, we can get so occupied in the rat race that we forget to enjoy. Enjoyment and celebration are only ever possible in the now. We tend to postpone our joy. I need a diploma first. I need a better job first. I need a relationship first. I need a bigger house first. I need a holiday first. We delay enjoyment. We fail to enjoy as we are living. We strive and strive and strive. And then it is time to leave this earthly plane and we get life's debriefing question. This question is not how much material wealth you have gathered. It is not about your looks and outer appearances. It is not about who you met and who you knew. Life's aftermath question is: did you have any fun?"

"That makes so much sense, Ernst. I am certainly having fun now, being with you and learning from you. My mind just *has* to be here now. But I recognize what you are telling me. My mind frequently wanders in past remorse and future concerns. And I do have the habit of putting off celebration until later. Many times, it does not happen then because there is always another reason for further delay. With such mind, I miss life. With such mind, the day can have been wonderful and full of opportunity, but *my* day can have been terrible."

"Correct, Dax. And if that happens, many times you don't understand why you felt bad on such a beautiful day. The program of our mind can keep us from enjoying all the good moments of our lives. Isn't that sad?"

I was nodding. "You said you had a how-to-live formula, Ernst. Could you share it with me?"

"Of course. If you want to maximize your life, Dax, apply the 4C formula. It puts together the perspective on time that I have been sharing with you. The first C is about *cultivating* the past. Learn from the past; grow through the past. But do not get stuck in the past. Applying the past's lessons in your life now will help you to maximize your life. The second C is about *clarity* for the future. Get clear on who you want to be. What you want to do. What you want to achieve. Knowing what you want will give your life's journey direction and will make it more efficient. The third and the fourth Cs are about *creating* and *celebrating* in the now. Remember, Dax, life only happens in the now. You want to use the now to create your aspired future. And you want to use the now to celebrate life. Never forget this aspect. A life not celebrated is a life not lived!"

"Cultivate the past, get clarity for the future, and create and celebrate in the now," I summarized.

"That's it, Dax. The optimal way to live your chronological life!" Ernst cheerfully raised his arms to make his point.

"Wait, what?" I responded. "Why are you saying your *chronological* life, Ernst? Is that not a pleonasm? Time is always chronological, isn't it?"

Ernst was laughing. "Hahaha, I did that on purpose to trigger your mind. Sounds like I succeeded. It may seem a pleonasm, but it isn't. I said it because I wanted to give you one more lesson about time. We think that time just moves horizontally. From one moment to the next. Chronologically. Masters have studied time throughout the ages and have found that there is a second form of time. Masters call horizontal time, the kind of time we all know, Chronos. It is the past, the now, the future. The second form of time is vertical time. Masters call this Kairos. It is the life in every one of your moments. It is what you do and experience in the moments of your life. Chronos time is limited. We cannot create more Chronos time. The chronological clock will never stop running. But Kairos time is unlimited. We all have the power to create more life in our moments. You expand your life through Kairos."

"That is an interesting idea, Ernst. I think I get it. But can you please explain a bit more? How can I create more life in every moment?"

"Of course, Dax. We are meeting for a purpose. Rama wants you to fully understand how to maximize the time of your life. And the concept of Kairos is an important lesson in this respect. You may have noted that my friends in this amazing living community have a long life experience, right?"

Ernst looked at me with a mischievous look. "You mean they are old?" I responded.

"Senior age does not have to mean you are old, Dax. Age is a number. Young or old is a mindset. What I am saying is that my fellow inhabitants have walked on the beautiful planet Earth for many years. They have experienced life, they have learned from life, and they have reflected on life. I regularly meet with them over coffee, and frequently we talk about each other's life lessons. In these conversations, I ask them about their biggest regrets. What they would do differently if they were still young. There are a few themes, Dax, that come up time and time again. And these themes contain some important life lessons for all of us. Let me first share with you the top three life regrets that elderly people have, and then I will give you the secret of Kairos. You still have some time?"

I nodded. "I do, Ernst. Plenty of time."

"You don't want regrets at the end of your life, Dax. The best way to live is to live fully. When it is time to die, you want to be able to tell yourself that it is all good because you have juiced out life. The first frequently felt regret that my friends share with me is: 'I wish I would have had the courage to live life on my own terms.' They are basically telling me that they would have liked to follow their own dreams for life. They would have liked to live the life they had imagined for themselves. But we are led by our robotic, conditioned mind and forget to connect with our purpose and passion. We forget to make our own choices because we don't put our own life on first spot. You recognize the lessons from Olisa, Sofia, and Raquel, my friend?"

"Yes I do, Ernst. Yes, I do."

"The second thing my friends wished is that they would not have taken life so seriously. They wish they would not have worked so hard. They wish they would have taken more time for themselves, doing what they liked to do. More time to enjoy and laugh. Less time chasing material success that society deems so important. We turn our lives into this serious event, believing that without achievement, we are not worthy. And without recognition from others, we are useless. We march through life like robots following society's rigid instructions. We forget to remember that life is supposed to be a dance, an easy, flowing, enjoyable affair. Taken lightly, not seriously."

"I remember Rama and Sofia talking to me about this, Ernst. Great reminder. Thank you."

"Then big regret number three, Dax. My friends wish that they would have been happier. They wish they would have celebrated life more. We make our happiness dependent on external things. I will be happy when ... When certain conditions are met. We postpone our happiness. We keep waiting, delaying. Until we are old. And then we realize that we have not been happy enough. We have the power to choose happiness at every moment, but we don't. Our robotic mind keeps happiness at a distance. Until it is too late."

"Yes," was the only thing I could utter.

"Yes indeed, Dax. You look around, and you don't note too many happy faces. In a group of young children, yes. But with older people, it is often difficult to find happiness. We need to get rid of this robot, and we need to follow the master's guidance on Kairos time: create more life in your moments. How to do that? It is not too difficult. Actually, it is quite easy. Kairos is about bringing presence to each moment. Making your own choices. It is about consciously spending your precious now moments. Looking for what is good in each moment. Looking for the positive. Looking for the celebration. Looking for things to be grateful for. When you do that, you consciously create moments of joy. You can take time in your hands by creating more Kairos!"

"Thank you, Ernst. Fantastic! I have a new objective for my life: create more Kairos!" I said.

"Great objective to have, Dax. I know all about it. Ever since I have taken my time in my own hands, my life has become so much more beautiful. I was down and out after Tom's death. My life was over, or so I thought. Every moment felt like a drag, useless. Rama resuscitated me with wisdom. Imagine what my life would have been if I had not made the deliberate choice to live. Death happens. There is nothing we can do about it. But we can choose to make the most of every day. I chose life, and Rama helped me to see how I could heal and live life to the fullest. I have turned my mind into a happiness engine, and I have applied the 4Cs ever since. We should all learn to cultivate the past, to get clarity for our future, and then to use the now to create and celebrate. Bring presence to the present, Dax. That is how you can create an infinite amount of joyful Kairos moments! I wish you a great life, my friend. Make sure you celebrate every day!"

Ernst gave me a big hug. "Great to meet you, Dax. Now if you excuse me. I have to freshen up. A barbecue is planned for later this afternoon with thirty of my best friends. Time to take a nap so that I can fully enjoy it."

"Thank you so much, Ernst. You are amazing, an inspiration," I said to him. "I will definitely use my precious time more wisely from now on!"

Ernst smiled. He stood up from the bench and started walking. Just before he reached the entrance, he turned around and shouted, "Enjoy your life, Dax. Here and now!"

Lifetime—Learning Box

Wisdom	My life only happens in the now. My life is a continuous flow of now moments. If I want to make the most of my life, I should make the most of my now moments. Death happens. There is nothing I can do about it, but I can choose to make the most of every day. I can expand my life through Kairos. I have the power to create more life in every moment.
Awareness	Whatever the circumstance, it is possible for you to be happy and peaceful. You can see death as your friend, as your teacher. The lesson that death teaches is to live *now*. When it is time to die, you want to be able to tell yourself that you have no regrets because you have lived life fully. At the end of your life, you will be asked a question. The question is not about your bank account, it is not about your material possessions, it is not about your career, and it is not about your beautiful partner. Life's aftermath question is: did you have fun? All healing starts with a happy mind. Much of your precious time is spent on regretting the past or worrying about the future. This way, you miss life. The purpose of the past is to learn from it and to use its lessons *now* to make your life better. The purpose of the future is to get clarity on your goals.

Story/Tool	The billionaire in heaven.
	The 4C formula to maximize your life; Cultivate the past, get Clarity for the future, Create and Celebrate in the now.
Practice	How do you spend your time? Become more conscious of how you spend your precious now moments.
	Create Kairos moments
	Apply the 4C formula: learn the lessons, get clear, and use the now.

10

Change

You Better Dance

To be smart is to accept change, to be wise is to love change.
—Zen saying

The secret of change is to focus all of your energy
not on fighting the old but on building the new.
—Socrates

Life is a series of natural and spontaneous changes. Don't
resist them; that only creates sorrow. Let reality be reality.
Let things flow naturally forward, in whatever way they like.
—Lao Tzu

Jane's gutfeel about the topic of my next encounter had been right. Life and how to live it. Time and how to optimize it. Ernst had learned about the gift of life the hard way. But he had found and unleashed his inner power to turn his life into a daily celebration. *What a man. Ninety-three years old and still so full of life!* I thought as I was boarding the plane back to Houston. Ernst had given me an understanding and practical guidance that I would definitely use for the benefit of my daily experience of life.

It had been an eventful week in Europe. The comfortable airplane chair was a good place for some reflection. "What did I think of the business meeting?" was the first question I asked myself. I had enjoyed the human connection. But when it came to content, I could not get away from two conclusions that kept appearing in my mind: boring and same old, same old. Had the meeting given me energy? It was a no for me. Had I enjoyed the discussions and the topics? Again, my answer was pretty clear: no. Had I felt inspired to contribute? No. Had it been the best time of my life? No. I was going through some of the passion-finder questions that Sofia had shared. And the only conclusion I could draw was that I was seriously lacking passion for my professional pursuits—a nagging feeling I had observed in myself for a while, but the Istanbul meeting had made things even clearer. Was this how I wanted to spend my precious time going forward? Would this give me the best life in my valuable now moments? My mind moved to my engagement with Ernst, and I was contemplating the same questions. Energy? Yes! Enjoyment? Yes! Inspired? Yes! Best time of my life? Yes! Ernst's life story and lessons had made me feel as if I was on top of the moon. Time had passed in an instant, and I would have liked to continue learning from Ernst for the rest of the day and the days after. I was overthinking the striking difference when suddenly the captain came over the intercom: "Ladies and gentlemen, please fasten your seat belt. We are expecting some heavy turbulence in the next half hour of our flight. Sit tight. Relax. We will soon be in calmer airspace again."

The unexpected interruption from my deep thoughts reminded me of Rama's lesson on uncertainty in life. "The only constant in life is change," he said one day. It is true. Life can be turbulent. Life can be challenging. Life is never certain. Sometimes when you expect it the least, change appears in your life. It is a good thing because it keeps life fresh, new, and unpredictable. But it can also provide tough tests on occasion. I did not really notice the shaking of the plane, as my mind was busy configuring a question for Rama. Ernst had been very eloquent on the importance of the now moment. But what if the now presented you with unexpected change and challenge? How should we deal with that? I made a note of the question with the intent to send it to Rama as soon as I was back home in Houston. The turbulence was soon over.

The rest of the flight was a smooth ride. Jane picked me up at the airport. She was pleased to hear that her prediction about the content of Ernst's lessons had been right. She was not surprised with my personal reflections on purpose and passion. "Dax, you might have kept your eyes closed for a while now, but I have been observing your declining passion for a long time. It is good that Rama is reconnecting you with your inner wants and desires. It is never too late to make a change if that means you will be spending your time and effort on things you truly love," she said lovingly. Jane was spot-on. It felt great to have a partner who had the gut to just tell it like it was.

"Thank you, Jane," I said. "As usual, your gutfeel has been very right!" The Houston highways were treating us well, and within an hour, we were back at our comfortable home. I unpacked, took a shower, and sent a message to Rama.

> Dear Rama,
> Am back in Houston. Ernst is amazing!
> I would love to talk to you about how to best deal with change!
> When is a good time?
> Thank you for your loving guidance,
> Dax

Rama was prompt to respond. Human connection certainly has become so much easier with the introduction of smartphones and all the amazing associated tools. There is much to be said about detrimental impacts of the twenty-four-hour social media revolution, but there is certainly also much good. "Choose your perspective," Wayne would say. Rama and I agreed on a virtual call for two weeks later. Time passed quickly, and soon enough we were connected in our call.

"Glad you liked the stopover in the Netherlands to meet Ernst, Dax. Yes, he is an amazing character. Was deep down when I met him many, many years ago in Amsterdam. Since then, he has grown to be a prime how-to-live example and inspiration. He was dancing on a table at his birthday party? I am not surprised. The man is still full of positive energy and livelihood. Fantastic!" Rama had started off as usual: full of life, full of positivity, full of love, and full of celebration for the success of other people. "You wanted to talk about change, my friend?"

"Yes, Rama, please. I have made Ernst's lessons part of my mindset. It helps to make sure I do have fun every day. Being aware and deliberate about the way I am spending my now moments has already had a positive impact on my days. Not only has my enjoyment grown but also my effectiveness in getting things done. But as I was contemplating my life and these lessons, I started wondering about the impact of change and uncertainty. Yes, I can consciously choose to apply Ernst's 4C model, but what if suddenly change happens? What if change throws my life off track unexpectedly? How do I deal with the challenge of change in my life?"

"Great questions, Dax. Applicable to all of us. Listen. Once there was a flock of sheep walking on the prairie, following the sheep in the front. One sheep tapped another sheep on his woolly shoulder and asked, 'Why do we always follow this stupid leader?' The other sheep said, 'I don't know. They say that he has the map.' Hahaha!" Rama burst out laughing, and so did I. His joy was contagious. "The map, Dax? Nobody has the map. We all go on following other people because we think they know. But they don't. They may in fact be more stupid than you. Life *is* unpredictable. Life *will* present you with change. Always. There *is* no map for life. There is no knowledge that I can give you that makes the unknown go away. Don't rely on knowledge, Dax. It is up to you to build your own experience and to build your own inner guidance so that you can sail comfortably around the cliffs of life. Talking about this, I have a change coming up for you. I have to finish our call here because something else has come in between. But I have a recommendation. You might want to join the webinar of a guy named Malcolm Chan in two weeks. I have heard his story is full of inspiration about dealing with change. Google him, and I am sure you can find how to sign up. Got to go now, Dax. Enjoy!" And that was the end of our call.

Rama always had a practical way of getting his wisdom across. I was surprised to learn that our call was over. I watched my mind as it brought up some robotic ideas why this was not done. But I quickly intervened. I could see how impactful this sudden change was. How it helped me to detect another one of my conditioned thoughts and to deal with it in the moment. I quickly found the webinar of Malcolm Chan on the internet and signed up.

The time difference of fourteen hours meant it was an early webinar for people in the West like me and a late engagement for people in the East, including Malcolm Chan. I woke up early the Saturday of the webinar, excited, curious, ready to be inspired. Just before 6:00 a.m., I switched on my laptop and connected via the link that I had received to find a virtual room full of people. Exactly on the hour, Malcolm Chan joined us all with an energetic "Good evening, good afternoon, good morning. Thank you for being here." I saw a friendly man with a bald head and a vibrant smile. He was wearing what appeared to be an orange cloak. Malcolm continued, "You might notice my attire and think, *Is this guy a monk?* Let me immediately answer that question before we start. Yes, I am, my friends. They call me a Zen monk, although that is just a label and not who I really am. I am what I think I am. It is a great opportunity to share my life experience with you all. I sincerely hope it will be beneficial and give some inspiration for your life." I smiled. The intro sounded good. I was ready to learn.

"I would like to start with telling a story of the early days of my life. I was born the son of the priest of a well-known Zen temple in the southern part of China. There was another temple in the neighborhood, and as I grew up, I learned about the centuries-long rivalry between the two temples. My father was very strict and directive. He forbade all the monks of our temple any interaction with the other monks. There had been no contact for centuries. The priest of the other temple also had a son. He was about my age. My father instructed me not to connect with the boy. 'Never talk to that boy. He is part of a dangerous group of people. Avoid him!' Most likely, the other boy had received similar directions from his father. I was longing to meet the other kid. I grew tired of listening to long sermons and age-old scriptures. I wanted to play, and at our temple, there was nobody. Everybody was engrossed in study and contemplation. Temptation arose in me when my father told me to avoid the boy. That is how temptation arises, my friends. The forbidden fruit is the most tempting fruit. One day, as I was on my way to the local market, I saw the boy on the road. I could not restrain myself. I walked toward him and asked, 'Where are you going?' The boy looked at me with a mysterious look. 'Going? There is nobody going anywhere. I am emptiness. How can I go? I am just a dead leaf that goes with the wind. How stupid are you? You are talking nonsense!' I had heard my father talk about not being and not doing. The Buddha lives like a dead leaf and goes wherever the wind takes it. But to be honest, I had never really understood this. And this boy was pointing out my ignorance. I felt ashamed, embarrassed, humiliated. My father had been right to avoid these people. This boy was playing with me. I had just asked him a simple question, and his answer had shaken me. When I went back to the temple, I told my father. 'I am very sorry. I did not follow your instruction. I was tempted to talk to the son of the other priest, and today I had an opportunity on the way to the market. I asked him, "Where are you going?" and he gave me such a strange answer. "I am emptiness," he was saying and "There is nobody going anywhere."' My father was angry. 'I told you so. These people are strange and dangerous. You should not have engaged with him. But now that you have, you have to prove *our* understanding. Tomorrow, go to the same place. When you meet the boy again, ask him the same question. Then, when he gives you the same answer, say to him, "That is true. You are emptiness, and so am I. But when there is no wind, where will the dead leaf go?" That will embarrass him.

He will not know what to say. So tomorrow, when you meet the boy, defeat him in debate!' I went back the next day, ready to outsmart the other kid. He did show up. And when he was close, I asked him again, 'Where are you going?' The boy looked at me and answered, 'To where my feet are taking me.' I was flabbergasted again. I did not know what to say. Certainly no debate victory. No, I was beaten again. I went back to my dad, who was really upset. 'See? These people are crazy. There is a reason we have not been engaging with them for hundreds of years. But we have to act now. This is not acceptable. Tomorrow, you go and see him again. When he repeats his answer, "To where my feet are taking me," you tell him, "And what if you had no feet?" That will silence him for sure. And you will have won.' The next day, I asked the boy again, 'Where are you going?' And he answered, 'To the market to buy vegetables.'"

"Hahaha!" I could not contain my laughter. And I noted the laughter on the faces of many of the other participants. *Hilarious*, I thought.

"This happened to me. I was nine years old, and I still remember like it was yesterday. Without knowing it at the time, this experience has been one of my biggest lessons in life. It is the lesson I would love to share with you today!"

I was listening.

"We ordinarily function based on the knowledge acquired in the past. The past gives us the false belief that we know. That we know what to expect. That we know how to deal with life. But life goes on changing. Life does not cater to our ideas about it. That is why life can be confusing to us. Because we think we know, but every now and then, we realize we don't. The more knowledgeable we get, the more life will surprise us."

I liked the insight Malcolm was sharing. Life is change. Approaching life based on a past recipe does not set us up for success. *But how then? How do I remain open to whatever life brings and flexible enough to deal with it in the best way possible?* was the question going through my mind.

203

Malcolm continued, "Here is the thing to realize: life is uncertain. Life will never remain the same. We have all experienced this, and we know it. Still, most people find it hard to accept. We desperately want things to be or stay the way we want them to be. Life is never static. Life goes on changing. We better accept this fact of life. If we don't, life will be a struggle. It will be a constant fight against change that we will never win. Once you think you know, life will have moved on. You become blind for what is. If you function out of past experience, you do not see what the case is. You function mechanically, like a robot. The robot will never be up to date because life will always be fresh, anew. Fighting change is a stupid thing to do. It is useless, a waste of your good time and energy."

That made sense. I was thinking of times when I had tried hard to fight changes in my life. Changing schools. Ending friendships. Moving places. New jobs. Innovative technologies. Getting older. Despite my mental resistance, change had happened. I remembered a holiday in Switzerland when I was six years old. We had visited a small, flowing river, and I had attempted to stop the stream by building a stone dam. It had been successful for a few minutes. But then water started zipping through the small holes in the dam. And soon thereafter, the water pressure had grown strong enough to knock over the dam. No change. The river just kept on going.

It was as if Malcolm Chan had picked up my thoughts. After a small pause, he said, "You can't stop the river of life from flowing, my friends. It is not a wise thing to try. It is also not your role. Life just is. You better learn how to flow with life. Who is interested?" Malcolm looked at the screen, where many participants, including me, raised their hands, and then he said, "Let me tell you about the three leaves.

"Imagine you are a leaf. You have just fallen off a tree, and you have landed next to a streaming river. You have been hanging on the same branch of the same tree all your life. And now you are free. You want some adventure. So here you are, standing next to the river. You look around and see a nice spot upstream where you want to go. You dive in the water, and now you are being taken downstream by the flow. That is not where you want to go, so you gather strength and start to swim. You are a strong leaf, so slowly but steadily, you are moving upstream. You are getting closer to your goal. But you are also getting tired. You take a small break. You stop swimming for just a few seconds. And you move downstream. You move away from your goal. Then you swim again and get closer. But every time you relax, you are being removed from your target again. This is how many people live. You see, the river is life. It will flow. People resist the flow. They stubbornly want to go against the flow. And they fight with all their might to reach their upstream goals. Some reach them, yes, but it will take a lot of your energy and effort, and you will have no time to relax and enjoy. You will have to continue swimming."

Malcolm looked at us via the screen, with his calm eyes, as if to ask, "You with me?" I was, and I could make out from the facial expressions of the others that they were. *I recognize what Malcolm is saying,* I thought. *I know this from my own life. Wanting things but having to struggle mightily to get there.*

Malcolm continued. "The poor leaf feels as if there is no support and help on his journey upstream. Fortunately, there are better ways. Let's imagine you are a second leaf, the first leaf's brother. You also fell off the tree, and you are also standing next the river. You have watched your big brother fight and struggle upstream, and you think, *That is not what I want. I don't want to go upstream.* You see, when you are observant, you can learn from everybody and everything around you. So you, the brother leaf, are doing a smart thing. You also think, *The river is too strong for me, so it is no use to set a target downstream.* And then you jump. You go with the flow of the river, but you don't have a goal. You end up in rapids. You bump into rocks on the riverbed. You are being tossed from left to right. You are moving downstream, but you are not going anywhere. And it is a rough ride. You are not enjoying yourself. What are you thinking, my friends?"

A woman raised her hand and said, "Trying to imagine myself in that river, Malcolm, and just going with the flow. Feels a bit better than fighting my way upstream. But I would not want to go randomly through life, being pushed around by the external world."

"Spot-on," Malcolm responded. "The way of this leaf is also not my recommended way. The two brother leaves also had a little sister leaf.

"Imagine now you are this smart little girl leaf. You have been observing your big brothers, and you have absorbed the lessons. It is no use to fight against the natural stream. And it is not smart to not have a destination and therefore be moved around by circumstances and others. So you say to yourself, 'I will go downstream, and I will set a goal. That way, I can use the flow, and I can take deliberate action to navigate myself toward where I want to be!' You jump in. You ride the river. You keep your eyes on your goal. Every time you meet an obstacle, you move around it. And you steer yourself toward the place where you want to be. On the way, you take time to enjoy the ride, and you get better at moving forward. This way, you reach your objective with the minimum amount of effort and the maximum amount of celebration."

That sounds like a good way to live, I reflected.

"This is the wise way to live, my friends. I have named this deliberate and smart way of the girl leaf the DANCE way. It summarizes what it takes to live effectively and efficiently. When you *dance* through life, you are clear. You set a *destination*. Then you *adapt* to and *navigate* around whatever life is throwing at you. There will be obstacles, there will be challenges, there will also be opportunities and support. While you travel your life, you make sure you *celebrate* along the way. Very important. Never postpone your celebration and joy. As you are moving forward, you *evolve*. You develop yourself, and you grow through life. You get better at living the life that you want."

I like it, I thought. *Destination, adaptation, navigation, celebration, evolvement.* Destination precedes achievement. I knew that lesson well by now. Clarity always is the first step. I got this, and I was busy getting clearer about my purpose and pursuits in life. A question was developing in my mind: "How to adapt and navigate through life in the best way possible?" I typed it in the chat.

"Let me talk about adapting and navigating because I see many questions on this in the chat," Malcolm said. "It requires flexibility. When you think you know how life works, you function on automatic pilot. You live life based on your memory of the past. This way, you are no longer flexible. We focus on developing memory, but it does not serve us in life. The older the scripture, the less useful. The older generation gets out of touch with the younger generation because the memory-based software they have installed was suited for the old days. We all need regular upgrades. We all need to keep fresh to whatever life is presenting us with. Having an open mind is the key to remaining flexible. I like the metaphor of a parachute. Who has skydived? Raise your hand." A number of people put up their hand. I did not.

"I have," Malcolm said. "What an experience. Talking about stepping outside of your comfort zone. That is exactly what you have to do when you are up there in a plane and standing next to the open door. When it is time to jump, you experience very mixed thoughts and emotions. Excitement versus resistance. Adventure versus fear. Courage versus ratio. Then you jump. Your lifeline is your parachute. At the right height, you have to pull the red tag. Before you know it, you are swirling across the silent sky and appreciating the magnificent views from above. The parachute has opened! Now imagine what happens if the parachute remains closed. The mind is like a parachute, my friends. When it is open, it will serve you in life. It will literally save you and provide you with a wonderful ride. When the parachute is closed though, it will not help and support. To the contrary. It will make your ride a miserable and catastrophic ride. Living with an open mind is the way to remain flexible. It gives you the ability to adapt to change and to navigate around hindrances and hurdles."

Malcolm paused for a while. I was engrossed in his fascinating story. It felt as if this webinar had been constructed for me. "You probably want to know what it takes to have an open mind?" Malcolm interrupted my thoughts.

I responded in the chat: "Yes please!" I was not the only one ready to learn more.

"An open mind has room available. An open mind is practical. And an open mind is curious. I will explain each characteristic. An open mind has room means there is space for new ideas and new perspectives. I already said that many people believe they know it all. With such a mindset, there is no openness. There is no receptivity for the unknown. It is crazy to think you know it all. It is stupid to get too confident about your knowledge because life simply is too complicated. In Zen, we have a nice saying to illustrate this point: a wise man never knows all; only fools think they know everything. An open mind comes with the realization that you don't know everything. An open mind is a humble mind that leaves scope for surprise and learning."

That makes sense, I thought. *If you are full of yourself and your knowledge, there is no space left for new things and experiences. I can see how one becomes inflexible with such a mindset.*

"Let me move to the practical mind," Malcolm said. "An open mind is not filled with dogmas and doctrines. Just look around. It is amazing how we cling to prescribed ways of living without ever questioning whether the rigid instructions serve us. We get robotized through family, authorities, religion, culture, and education. You know how I call the guidance we get from these five, my friends?"

I didn't.

"A FARCE—family, authorities, religion, culture, education. These institutions leave you with the impression that they know how you should live. They suggest they know better than you. That is nonsense. There is no fixed map for life. Life is fluid. Life is unpredictable. Living according to predefined scriptures will never make you happy, contented, and successful. An open mind is practical and creative. It assesses situations on their unique merits. Then it comes up with case-specific responses that serve and support you.

Don't fill your mind with prescriptions, my friends. Use your practical intelligence to grow your awareness and make your own creative choices. Zen teaches nothing. Zen enables us to wake up and use our own practical awareness to live life in the moment."

These insights were touching and inspiring. Although I was sitting behind my laptop, I felt fully connected to the wisdom Malcolm Chan was sharing. *Physical proximity is not needed to feel truly together,* I thought.

One of the participants in the meantime was frantically waving a hand to indicate he wanted to ask a question. Malcolm noticed. "Do you have a question, sir?" he kindly asked.

The man was unmuted and said, "Yes, I do. Thank you for giving me the opportunity. You just now said that Zen teaches nothing. What about your father? He was your first teacher, right? From your story about the rivalry with the other Zen monastery, it seems that he felt that his ways were better."

"Well spotted," Malcolm said. "The source for rivalry and competition always is the belief that you are right and the other is wrong. I have to say that indeed my father thought that his Zen lineage had a monopoly on the truth. He considered any other monastery with different traditions and habits as false. It is unfortunate that, because of this belief, his life was full of conflict and confrontation. Wherever he observed what he believed to be a falsehood, he would get on the barricades and fight. His life never reached calm waters. Until the very end, it was filled with the urge to convince others of their misinterpretations and wrongdoing. Not very Zen actually."

The gentleman's line was still open. He looked touched. "That is sad to hear, Mister Chan. How come you are different?"

"It is sad indeed, sir. It is not a happy way to live. My father was heavily influenced by his father, who was the priest before him. My grandfather brainwashed my dad into believing that our rites and practices were the only right ones. My father's mindset was shaped by the teachings from his dad and confirmed by the other indoctrinated priests of our religion. He did not know any better. His mind became closed, and he was not open to explore and examine the ideas and convictions that had been handed to him. His robot mind guided his life. And it also guided my life because obviously I was taught the same things when I was young. My mindset pretty much became a carbon copy of my dad's mindset. I was on my way to become just like him. Let me tell you what happened. It was the encounter with the son of the rival priest. A shocking event for me, but it opened my eyes. It made me realize for the first time that life is not predictable. Something in my mind changed that day. My accepting mind became an inquisitive mind. I started examining life. In small steps of course, but since that encounter, I started using my own intelligence. I stopped automatically believing everything that I was told. I started my search for the truth. And on that search, I met a wise teacher called Rama."

My heart leaped. *Rama? My Rama?*

Malcolm continued, "He was visiting our area. I met him on the street. The student Malcolm was ready to meet the teacher Rama. He gave me a ticket for his lecture at the nearby university. I went. I did not tell my dad. That evening, Rama opened my eyes further. He said, 'Find the universal truth. It is the truth that has been shared by sages throughout time, irrespective of where and when they lived. It is the truth that creates freedom. A so-called truth that binds is not the truth. The real truth encourages you to question your upbringing, your learning, your life. It tells you to grow your awareness, to make up your own mind, and to make your own choices. It will never suggest to live according to the terms of others. It will guide you to live a life full of purpose and passion. To pursue your dreams. And it will be clear that happiness and joy are the true objectives of life.' Rama told his audience that day to not get stuck in prescribed ideas. To not unconsciously accept other people's convictions and beliefs. To not believe that others know what is best for your life. To make life worth living by examining it, like the great Greek sage Socrates once said. He encouraged us to find the truth. The real truth that will set you free."

That must have been my Rama, I thought. I was no longer surprised by any so-called miracles like Malcolm meeting Rama that day. By now, I knew they were happening.

Malcolm continued, "This gentleman Rama has been my guide ever since. He has taught me about the true purpose of Zen: to see things as they are and to allow everything to go as it goes. A few years after my training with Rama started, I left the Zen monarchy of my dad. I chose against further conditioning. In Zen, we say let go or be dragged. I chose to let go. Since then, I have followed my own path, guided by various teachers. I have found the truth, and I have come to know that there is no greater pleasure in life than to guide others toward the freedom it has given me."

Various people were now raising their hands. Malcolm chose a woman to ask her question. "What about your dad?" she energetically asked.

"We did not speak for many years. My dad was angry with me but also sad. I did not yet have the calm and stability to face the man I loved but whose path was not my path. It took almost fifteen years for us to reconvene. I went to visit him one day. He was very glad to see me. He welcomed me with his whole heart, and since then, we kept in touch. He wanted his son. He did not want my wisdom. And that is fine. Just before he died, he told me how much he admired me for having chosen my own path. He told me he wished he had done the same, but he had never found the courage. And he told me that he realized that his stubborn mind had given him a lot of anger and grief in his life. I told him that the conditioned mind wants control but that life wants change. He said he would keep it in mind for his next life. That same day, he left our earthly plane with a smile on his face."

People in the webinar looked touched. *Wow,* I thought.

"My dad, my biggest teacher!" Malcom said, suddenly very cheerfully. "There is so much we can all learn from every other person. Sometimes people show us so clearly what we don't want. There is much to learn from that! All right, my friends. Time to continue on the open mind. The third characteristic of an open mind: it has no expectations. When we have a closed mind, we expect other people to be like us. We expect them to think, to behave, to act, to do exactly the way we would. Do you know what this unconscious expectation does? It creates frustration. It creates irritation. It creates disappointment. You know why? Because no other person will ever be or think or behave or act or do precisely like you. The expectation we carry thus is the cause for much negative emotion and conflict in our lives. Zen says getting rid of expectations results in instant inner freedom! And hence the way of Zen is to act without expectation. An open mind carries no expectations. It remains curious and available for the wonders of life. An open mind is happy to be surprised. And believe me, life will always surprise you!"

An open mind has room. An open mind is practical. And an open mind has no expectations, I summarized for myself.

"An open mind is available to the moment. It allows you to make your own assessment of current events and to make your own choices. So when change happens, it is up to you. Don't act based on an outdated script. Be fresh and assess. It is your choice. You are free. Osho has summarized the Zen way beautifully. He has said, 'Zen is a path of liberation. It is freedom from the first step to the last. You are not required to follow any rules. You are required to find out your own rules and your own life in the light of awareness.'"

There was another question. "I love it, Mister Chan, but funny though that you are quoting Osho because he is not a Zen master, is he?"

"That is what people don't always understand, dear lady. We have this tendency to want to label everything and everybody. And we believe that different labels make different people. Christian, Muslim, Buddhist, Zen. It is true that when these labels come with all kinds of dogmas and rigid ideas, they *will* make different people. But the universal wisdom that has been shared by the great masters of all time is one and the same. The truth is only one. So a master like Osho is everything and nothing at the same time. A Zen master but also not a Zen master. He is totally free. His mind is open, and he lives from a place of universal consciousness."

The lady said, "So what you are saying, Mister Chan, is that masters talk one truth. They may have used different words. They may have accommodated their sharing to where and when they were living. But it is the same one truth. The wisdom they have shared has subsequently been translated by ordinary, rational people into rules for life. And these rules have become the rigid instructions that prevent us from living the life that we want. They also make us quite inefficient in dealing with the ever-existing changes that life brings us."

"You got it! But it does not have to be this way. We are all free to choose how we use our mind. All it requires is an awareness that our existing mind is preprogrammed. And it requires a conscious act of keeping our minds open to whatever life brings. It is wise to accept what you cannot change and to take responsibility for what you can change. You cannot change the life that is happening around you. But you *can* change your own mindset. Having a wisdom mindset will be of tremendous help in your life. We can get excited about challenges and obstacles in our life because we feel they hamper us. In Zen, we say, 'Obstacles don't block the path; they are the path.' There is another Zen perspective in this respect. We all think we have so many problems in our life, and we don't like it. We allow problems to burden our life. We allow problems to stop us from living. Zen says, 'Your problem is your biggest opportunity.' It means to say that behind every cloud, there is sunshine. When you deal with your problem, opportunity arises. It is up to all of us, my friends. You can change the way you deal with challenges and changes in your life!"

I could not contain my enthusiasm. Just to myself, I summarized out loud, "Adapt and navigate through life with an open mind and a wisdom perspective!"

"An open mind filled with wisdom will help you to DANCE through life. As you *adapt* and *navigate*, do not forget to *celebrate*. The C in DANCE reminds us to enjoy our journey of life. Life is precious. Life is supposed to be a celebration. In Zen, we say, 'Life should not only be lived. It should be celebrated!' Do you agree? If yes, give me a thumbs-up."

Almost everybody immediately put their thumbs up. Participants had big smiles on their faces. "A day not celebrated is a day not lived" had become one of my favorite mantras. Thanks to the lessons of Rama, I was keeping my mind focused on all the good things in my life. He had once explained to me that what I focus on will grow. I had experienced this principle in all aspects of my life. Since I made celebration my destination, I found so many reasons to celebrate every day, even on days that look gloomy and distressed from the outside.

"We have covered destination, adaptation, navigation, and celebration. This leaves us with the letter E in our DANCE of life. The E stands for *evolve*. If you want to make your DANCE the best dance possible, don't just *go* through life but *grow* through life. Every day, life will present you with opportunities for learning and development. Life sometimes does not work out for you. You might not get the results you want. Do you take this as the definite outcome and give up? Or do you learn from the event and use it to grow? The Zen view on disappointment is this: this is not the way; there is a better way. Or something better is available to you. Be easy about things. It allows you to see the self-improvement opportunity in whatever happens. You can never beat life. But you can beat yourself. Evolving means that you use your experience to become better than you used to be. It means you rise, you expand, you prosper, you advance, you progress through life. As you evolve, beautiful things will unfold for you. Not only in how you feel. But also in what you manifest in your life. When you DANCE through life, you will manifest the life of your dreams. Who has an idea why?"

Hands were raised, including mine, and I heard Malcolm say, "Yes, Dax, tell me why you think that is."

"I guess it has to do with me being the creator of my own life— right, Mister Chan?"

"You most certainly are the author of your own life story, Dax. The secret is that life is an inside job. The masters say, 'As within, so without.' Your life starts with you. Manifestation starts with you. The best way to manage your life is to start within. In Zen, we say, 'Stop changing the world; start changing yourself.' You change yourself through examining your mind and your mindset. When you do that, Dax, you will find much FARCE programming of your mind that does not serve you. You will want to reprogram your mind. It will change your perspective on yourself and your life. And it will make the actions you take to create your life much more effective. When you react to life based on your robotic programming, you are not a deliberate creator. You are just following a script that might or might not have been effective in the past but certainly is no longer up to date now. It will not give you the best possible outcomes. When you train your mind to be open and aware, you will become a responder to life. A response is an action in awareness. A fresh action, not an automated action. Responses are the most effective actions. They will help you to be the conscious sculptor of your own life. Responses allow you to make your life a masterpiece!"

I said, "Thank you, Mister Chan. I have heard it before. Life always starts with me. It is an inside job. And I am really starting to get it. You have a magnificent way of sharing your wisdom with all of us. It makes so much sense. Thank you very much!"

The webinar was coming to an end. I felt full of energy, and from what I observed via the screen, so did Zen monk Malcolm Chan, but it was getting late in the East. He said, "Time for a final question. Who has a burning one?"

I said, "I do!" Somehow my line had not been muted, and hence everybody could hear me, including Malcolm Chan.

He started laughing. "All right, Dax. Last question is yours because you are so passionate!"

"It has been an amazing webinar, Mister Chan. You have truly inspired me and taught me practical insights that will help my life. The question I have is *Will I ever be able to learn it all*? I definitely want to know the truth, but it is so much."

Malcolm Chan started laughing. I did not fully understand why. But then he said, "Dear Dax, finding the truth is not a matter of learning more. It is a matter of *unlearning* more. Examine life and get rid of the FARCE robot. Free your mind. Open your mind. Grow your awareness. Then the truth can be yours! We are all part of the one truth, but we have forgotten because of all the knowledge we have gathered. Take down the veil of your brainwashed mind, and you will *see* again. Do you think that study is the basis for my inspiration to others? It is not. It is an awareness of the truth that we can all have. If only we let go of these so-called great ideas in our minds."

"Thank you, Mister Chan. That is a big relief. It has been my great pleasure to meet you and learn from you. Zen is cool. That I know for sure!"

"Hahaha, yes it is, Dax. Zen is cool indeed but not because somebody tells you it is. Zen is cool because, when applied, a Zen perspective can give you the freedom to take your life in your own hands. It allows you to DANCE through life. When you change your inside, your outside experience of life is going to be so much more beautiful. That is my wish for all of you: to have an inside that makes your life the most delicious dance!" Malcolm Chan smiled. It was time to end the valuable webinar. The Zen monk waved at us with both his hands and folded his hands together. Many of the participants did the same.

"Thank you," I murmured. Two seconds later, the line closed, and Zen monk Malcolm Chan had left. I knew that his wisdom would always stay with me.

Change—Learning Box

Wisdom	I better learn how to flow with life because I cannot stop the river of life from flowing.
	I live with an open mind. This way, I remain flexible.
	My open mind has room. It is practical, and it is curious without expectations.
	I will train my mind to be open and aware to become a responder in life. Responses allow me to turn my life into a masterpiece.
Awareness	Be aware that the only constant in life is change.
	It is never too late to make a change in your life if that means you will be spending your time and effort on things you truly love.
	Life *is* unpredictable. Life *is* uncertain. There *is* no map for life.
	The more you think you know, the more life will surprise you.
	The mind is like a parachute. Functional and helpful when open, detrimental and dangerous when closed.
	Do not believe everything you gather from FARCE (family, authorities, religion, culture, education). Wake up and learn to use your own awareness to live life in the moment.
	The universal truth will set you free. It tells you to grow your awareness, to make up your own mind, and to make your own choices.
	The conditioned mind wants control. Life wants change.
	You will never win your fight with life, so you better develop an open, flexible mind.
	Don't just *go* through life, *grow* through life.

Story/ Tool	The story of Malcolm Chan's childhood. The three leaves. DANCE through life (destination, adaptation, navigation, celebration, evolvement).
Practice	Grow awareness and question the FARCE ideas in your mind. Keep an open mind to whatever happens. See every situation as fresh and full of opportunity, assess it on its own merits, and choose your response deliberately. Apply DANCE: set your goals, be flexible, celebrate, and grow through life.

Contribution

Empty Your Pockets

As you forget self in the service of others, you will find that,
without seeking it, your own cup of happiness will be full.
—Paramahansa Yogananda

The best way to find yourself is to lose
yourself in the service to others.
—Mahatma Gandhi

My mind again had been stretched—stretched to continue the
examination of my FARCE learning and stretched to become more
empty and open. I loved these wisdom stretches. Wisdom always
gave me a feeling of freedom and power. I had very much enjoyed
the webinar format. *Change, yes, but going with the flow of life is a good
thing. The universal truth also inspires via a laptop screen. Truth has
no boundaries,* I reflected. The meeting had been very efficient. No
traveling required. Just pushing some buttons on my laptop.

The weeks after, I watched my thoughts even more carefully than
I had been doing ever since I started my learning with Rama. How
open was my mind? Was there room available? Was it practical? And
what expectations was I carrying? If you investigate your mind in such

a deliberate way, there is a lot you can learn about yourself. Rama had once remarked that when you get to know your mind, you will get to know yourself. Mind training introduces you to yourself. That was definitely my personal experience. I was learning about myself.

My journey with Rama had made me aware of some self-esteem issues and feelings of jealousy in certain situations. I had also found that I was lacking purpose and passion in my life. I did not have laser-sharp clarity on my life direction and aspirations. I had observed that choices in my life had been influenced by wishes and expectations from others. I had learned that my subconscious beliefs about life made it difficult for me to handle criticism and opposition. I had detected that there was a bit of a control freak in me that led to an initial, automatic rejection of change. Step by step, the robot-at-work was becoming clearer. And I was on my way to change the inner programming that did not serve me in the life I wanted. I also found software that supported me. My keenness to learn and grow. My knowing that preparation and action were required to deliver results. My sincere interest in doing new things. My respect and love for other people. I was definitely intending to keep the helpful robotic ideas.

One evening, as Jane and I were sitting outside, we were going over the path that Rama had been laying out for me. Although initially my idea of a robot had been quite different, I had come to fully understand Rama's suggestion that we are all robots. Freedom would require me to get rid of the unhelpful beliefs and convictions that I was carrying in my mind and to replace them with an empowering wisdom mindset. Rama and his friends had given me a chest full of valuable treasures. Intuitively, I felt that the treasury box did not need a lot more filling. It was as if I heard the universe say, "Dax, over to you now!" It made me feel alive and free and powerful, but it also still made me feel anxious. Despite the significant changes in my mindset, I had not yet fully overcome my fear of change. In my heart, I knew that change was coming. But was I ready? My dear Jane suggested for me to talk to Rama and to seek his ever-loving and wise counsel on the blockages in my mind. And so it was that after a beautiful and enjoyable evening with Jane, I ended my day with a message to Rama.

> Dear Rama,
> I would love your guidance on questions in my mind.
> Can we please schedule a virtual call?
> Thank you,
> Dax
> Oh yes, by the way, thanks for your tip to join Malcolm Chan's webinar!
> It was great. He shared with us that he has learned a great deal from you.

Rama for sure had a very busy schedule. He was a much sought-after wisdom coach on a mission to inspire the world to live happily and successfully. Whenever he was not engaging with people, he was writing a new book or developing new inspirational programs. "I want to give the best of me in this precious lifetime," he once said to me. And for Rama, that meant he was making the most of every minute of his life. Still, it felt as if he was always available for me. His foundation of wisdom gave him an inner stability, calm, and focus that made him one of the best organized individuals I knew. "Maximum results with minimum efforts," Rama frequently said. "That is how I want to spend my days!" From my observation, he was extremely efficient and effective. He proved it every time. Already the day after, I received Rama's invite for a call a week later.

My weeks in the office were good. My inner change had brought outer change that made me a more effective professional. I was applying the lessons I was learning in my day-to-day life, and I was happy to see the results. My colleagues were noticing, and they were sharing their observations with me.

"Dax, you have become so focused on getting clarity for our business, both at strategic as well as operational level."

"Dax, you have become a lot calmer. Your impatience has been replaced with a kind persistence."

"Dax, whenever you are out there on stage, you are always able to touch and inspire us. The different perspectives you bring resonate with all of us at a human level."

"Dax, what a great team leader you are. Your people feel empowered and supported at the same time. They have grown their visibility, confidence, and impact."

"Dax, our fearless leader. How do you do that?"

And then there was our business leader who had started calling me the "master of ceremony" of our organization. Whenever we had a business event or a celebration, I would be asked to be on stage for the kickoff because of my ability to bring joy and energy to a room. I had learned that when you bring your own playfulness, vulnerability, and funny self-reflection into a group, it has a contagious effect on the crowd. It helped to open up the people in the room and to get the party going! In so many aspects of my life, I noted the truth in the wisdom guidance "as within, so without." When you change on the inside, your external experience of life will change. It was so visible. Although I knew I was not on my unique personal purpose, I was certainly making sure I enjoyed every day of my office life. "Never forget to celebrate your life" was one of the lessons that I had cemented in my conscious mindset.

It is said that time flies when you are having fun. It is true. My life was fun, and the week in between Rama's message and our call was over before I knew it. It was time to meet. At exactly the agreed time, we were connected via our laptop screens. Rama started, "Good morning, Dax! How are you? How is Jane? I hope you are both enjoying every day!"

He could see from my happy face that the answer was a definite yes! Still, I said, "Yes, Rama, we certainly are. With wisdom as our guide, our lives have only gotten better and better. We feel so blessed to have found this treasure. Wisdom works if you decide to work it. And we do. We work it every day, and we love it!"

Rama looked pleased. "Great to hear, Dax. Give my love to Jane and let's talk."

"Yes, let's talk. I hope no surprises like last time?" I looked at Rama, who gave me a mischievous look. "I have many questions for you, so we will need all the time we have."

"No surprises, Dax. Although you never know for sure. Life can always bring the unexpected change. And surprises can be good, right? Glad you liked Malcolm's webinar!" Rama had a big grin on his face.

"I accept that, Rama, although I sincerely hope that life keeps stable for the next ninety minutes. I have four topics I would like to discuss with you. It would be great if we can do so without being interrupted."

"Of course. Fortunately, life is not continuously throwing change and challenges at us. Planning and preparation for the known actually is a powerful skill to develop as long as you build in sufficient flexibility and open-mindedness. Hahaha! What do you want us to talk about?" Rama asked.

"The first topic I would like to seek your advice on is my progress on updating my inner software. You opened my eyes about me being a robot. And with the inspiration from you and your friends, I have detected a number of bugs in my inner programming that I would like to change. My daily mind-training practice is aimed at setting my mind the way I want, and I am making progress. I can see it in the results I am creating in my external life. Still, I have a number of stubborn beliefs that continue to pop up now and then to drive mechanical behaviors that I don't want. I would love to hear your wise counsel. Am I doing something wrong?"

"Dax, that is a great question. And just as an aside: the last part is symptomatic for most robots. Many people unfortunately suffer from the unhelpful belief that if things don't go their way, they think it is them. They blame themselves. If you don't manage this tendency of your mind, you talk yourself down, and you might give up before you have even really started. You are not doing anything wrong, my friend. In fact, you are doing things very right. You are feeding your mind with the thoughts that you want. That is fantastic. But don't forget that your robotic mind has been set over a long time. You are approximately forty, right? That means that your mindset has a history of forty years. You don't change this overnight. It takes consistent and persistent mind-training action over a period of time. Not the same forty years but a number of years at least. Depends on the person. The reprogramming of your mind is all about changing the software of your subconscious mind where impressions and beliefs gathered over time are stored. You cannot surgically remove these. You cannot uncreate the subconscious ideas that have been created. What you can do is to overwrite them with new ideas. You can superimpose a new way of thinking. The more often you are filling your mind with the new ways, the stronger the new beliefs become and the weaker the old ideas. The old ideas might still come out now and then, as you are experiencing. That is all right. Observe but don't pay attention. Use your conscious mind to remind yourself of the mindset of your choosing. Over time, your automated thought will be the one you want because it will have become so much stronger than the one that was not serving you. You are doing great, Dax, to stick to your practice. You are slowly but steadily creating an invincible wisdom script in your subconscious mind."

"So no reason to doubt myself then, Rama?"

"No reason to doubt yourself, Dax. All reason to congratulate yourself on taking action to train your mind and for having the discipline to stick to it. Change is not an overnight thing. Same for success in life. Sometimes it appears people have changed or have delivered massive success from one day to the other. In reality, the change and success have come about from years of preparation and persistent hard work."

"That helps, Rama. Thank you for giving me the positive perspective, as always. I will continue my practice to train my mind with the mindset of my own choosing. Let's move to my second topic: finding my purpose."

"Great topic. I know we were not able to cover it last time because of some changes. Hahaha. But also because it is you who has to get clear. It is you who needs to find your own unique direction for your life. And previously you were not yet ready. Hence, I skipped the subject. Now is a good time to talk. What about it?"

"My inner search has resulted in clarity on at least one thing, Rama. And that is that I am not on purpose in my current professional endeavors. I like what I do, I enjoy my days in the office, but I know and I feel that I am lacking passion. I got on this professional path pretty much unconsciously. I was following the crowd. I was taking the well-intended advice from others as the talisman for my life. I never really considered my own dreams and aspirations. I am not complaining. This life has given me a lot, and I have had so many enjoyable experiences. But I know it is not what I am meant to be and do with my life. I am not living my unique promise. I am still though not fully clear on my purpose for life. How stupid is this?"

"Let me just stop you there for a moment. I don't want you to be harsh on yourself. Most of us grow up believing that others have this map for life. I told you the anecdote of the sheep. As a consequence, we listen to others, and we follow others. We don't learn to connect with our inner calling. Has there been anybody in your life who introduced you to your promise and purpose when you were a child? Probably not. Only a few of us receive this important guidance at a young age. We all know in our hearts that we are here for a unique purpose, but who teaches us to follow our heart? We are taught to take the same path that everybody else is walking. The education we receive turns us into carbon copies of other people. It does not stimulate us to bring out our unique purpose. The true meaning of education is to bring out the best from within. That is not what our educational system does though. The existing education fills our minds from the outside with ideas of others. It does not make us connect with our inner purpose. You have followed the path that others laid out for you. And you have enjoyed much of it. Great. You know by now, Dax, that you always have a choice to create your own life experience. You can choose what you focus on, whatever the circumstance. You have done well to choose positively in many aspects of your life. It has resulted in a good and positive life for you."

I was absorbed in taking in Rama's perspectives. I always loved the way in which he was able to explain and clarify things in simple and practical ways. He continued.

"You must understand that the vast majority of people never leave the trodden path. They never question their life. They move through life as robots programmed by others. The inner calling will always be there, but we don't learn how to connect with our inside. We only invest in external technology, not in internal technology. So you are privileged. You are only forty, and you are already aware of the fact that you have a life purpose. Not only are you aware, you have started investing in your inner world to find out what it is in order to live your best life. You still have many years to live. The opportunity is yours! You are very blessed, Dax. Please understand this."

"I do, Rama. I most certainly do. I have already seen the huge return for my life from the investments in my inner world. I am appreciating my learning and growth every day. Still, I am not on purpose because I am not clear. My heart and mind are still debating."

"I get what you are saying. And I know that you have not yet fully figured it out, but you are getting closer. Let me give you some guidance that will help to wrestle this monkey to the ground."

"Wrestle which monkey?" I was a bit confused.

"The mind monkey. The mind that is restless and always looking for new things but also problems. The monkey mind will not allow you to come to clarity. You need to calm the monkey and bring yourself to a place of no mind. That is where you will suddenly *see*. That is where you will hear your heart's longing. That is where your unique purpose will be revealed to you. You *can* tame your monkey mind. Rafiki could!"

"Who?"

"Have you not seen the beautiful Disney movie *The Lion King*? Rafiki is the wise master in this movie. He is a monkey, and he has been able to move beyond his mind and see the light. My sense is that Disney chose a monkey master on purpose. To inspire the world that it is possible to calm down the monkey mind. You can also do it." Rama was smiling. And so was I.

"Here is the thing that might be troubling you, Dax. You are probably confusing the what with the how. The quest for clarity is only about the what. What is your unique purpose? What is it that you want to achieve in your life? The mind, though, will almost immediately switch to the how question. When you want clarity, I always say, 'The how is not for now!' The only clarity you want is the *what* clarity. What is it that you would love to do with your life? If you start mixing your what search with the how solutions, you might end up in a vicious circle that does not result in any clarity at all. Every *what* you come up with triggers your mind to start thinking about the how. When you don't immediately figure out the how, you might start wondering about the what. So you adjust the what a bit and you go back to the how. And so on and so forth. This can make you more confused than you were. So just focus on the what."

"I recognize what you are saying. My mind certainly has a tendency to want to understand *how* I can get to the destination. And that is hard to see most of the time, if I am honest."

"Of course it is hard to see, Dax. Who knows the exact path when you start walking into the direction of your dreams? Nobody does. For you, it is important to get clear about your purpose. *How* to get there we will discuss another time."

"Has that also been your experience, Rama? Has your path also become clearer over time?"

"Definitely, Dax. When I gave up the CEO role, I knew *what* I wanted to do, but to be honest, I did not know *how*. That did not stop me from taking the leap. I was convinced that the path would become clearer step by step. My experience has been exactly like that. I started giving inspiration in the environment I knew. Through positive feedback and word of mouth, new opportunities appeared. As I was working with adults and children, I became clearer on the challenges that people were facing. This gave me new ideas for programs and teachings I wanted to share. At a certain moment, I was well-known in India. I appeared on television and in papers, and my heart told me it was time to expand my horizons. That is how I came to Singapore, which is a much better hub to serve Southeast Asia with wisdom. Nowadays, I am frequently traveling to the West and sharing my inspiration there. You never know exactly how your path will go, Dax. But the only way to find out is to start walking."

That made a lot a sense. "And in order to start walking, you need your direction, and you need a stable inside. You need courage, you need self-belief, you need determination and action. Right, Rama?"

"Absolutely, Dax. Every journey requires preparation. I took my training time to prepare for the big change. When I started out, I was fully ready. My mind was clear and well set!"

"Fantastic. So the *what* first. All right, I must be able to do this. Do you have any other practical suggestions that can help me unravel the what?"

"I do. I have a homework task for you. The due date is next time we meet. You will need your heart and your empty mind, and you will need a pen and paper. All right?"

"I got all of that, Rama. The empty mind will be the biggest challenge."

"I want you to write one sentence. That sentence should describe the mission you want to accomplish in the next chapters of your life. One sentence only. That is all the clarity you need. The sentence must be such that if you think about it, it makes you feel great. It gives energy. It moves you to think about delivering it. You can't wait to get going. The right mission makes you emotional. Emotional because you know you have found what you have been looking for your whole life! So the second part of the homework is to sit down and *feel* the mission. If it triggers these types of feelings, you know you've got it. Clear?"

"Very clear, Rama. Homework accepted!"

"There is more I want to share with you on the topic of finding purpose and passion, Dax. I feel that you are ready for this. It is relevant inspiration for finalizing your search. Ever heard of Alexander the Great?"

"Yes, I have. In history class."

"Nice. Well, here is a bit of a history reminder. Alexander the Great was a king of the ancient Greek kingdom of Macedon who lived in the fourth century BC. In his lifetime, he ruled over one of the largest empires in history. He was undefeated in battle and is considered one of the greatest military commanders of all time. Alexander was tutored by the famous Greek sage Aristotle in his youth, which gave him a foundation of wisdom."

"I didn't know he was associated with Aristotle. My history book did not tell."

"Now you know, Dax. But it is not that important. What I want to share with you is the lesson that Alexander wanted to impart when he died. At his impressive funeral procession, the great king was lying on his back with his hands open, pointing toward the sky. With that gesture, he wanted to show his people that he was leaving planet Earth just like he came: empty-handed! Nothing was going with him."

"I like that lesson, Rama. Thank you. Reminds me of one of my favorite teachers, the eloquent late Dr. Wayne Dyer, who used to say that your last suit does not have any pockets. But is it true though? Is there really nothing from life that comes with you when you die?"

"Well there is, and I am about to share it with you. But just to be clear, nothing external will accompany you on your last journey. Not your material possessions, not your bank account, not your relationships, not the roles you have played. You take nothing from this life with the exception of what you have inside."

"Please explain."

"The Buddha was once asked the question, 'What is important in life?' He answered, 'That which you can take with you when you die.' Just like Alexander the Great wanted to teach his people, Buddha wanted to clarify that no external stuff will come with you. He explained that what you take with you is that what you have built inside. It is your experiences. It is your emotions. It is your mindset.

What Buddha wanted people to know is that it is wise to build a life full of happy experiences. To gather many positive emotions and feelings. To develop and grow your wisdom mind. When your inner world of thoughts and emotions comes with you, you better make sure that it is an inner world full of the three most powerful emotions: love, joy, and gratitude. You agree, Dax?"

"That makes sense, Rama. I don't know about death, but I know for a fact that such an inner world feels good while I am alive. It makes my daily experience of life so much better."

"Correct. And there is no reason to spend your precious, conscious mind space on speculating what happens after you die. Buddha did not do that. He just practically said to use your time on earth to build a positive and happy inside. It lifts your life in the here and now. And it is the only thing that comes with you wherever you go from here."

As always, I had been taking in Rama's inspiration with full focus and attention. I observed that the Alexander the Great story and Buddha's lesson on what is important in life resonated with me, but they also confused me. So I said, "Rama, are you suggesting that my purpose should be to build a positive and happy inner world? Is that not a bit too vague?"

"Good question, Dax. We were talking about promise and purpose, and I diverted our conversation to your inside. I can understand why you might be confused. Bear with me. I am not yet done. There are two more things to cover. Firstly, how to build a positive inside?"

I was quick to respond, "By choosing the focus of my mind and developing a mindset with the right ideas and beliefs!"

Rama smiled at me. "True. Life starts with you. I think you've got that by now, my friend. Your mind. Your responsibility. Your promise. Your passion. Your priority. Your perspective. Your life and time. Your dealing with change. You've got all the insights to stop being a robot and to live life on your own terms. There is one final step. And it is time for me to give this one to you. Life starts with you. Absolutely. All the great masters have taught this important lesson. Don't change the world; change yourself first. But life does not *end* with you. We are all just one inhabitant of a world full of other people and living species. We are not alone. So take care of yourself first but know that ultimately life's purpose is about giving to others. It is about you making this world a better place. It is about *contribution*. Your best life results from making a contribution to the lives of others. You with me, Dax?"

"Yes, I am, Rama."

"You contribute by giving. Now here is the crux: you can only give what you have inside. I know that Raquel has already shared this important lesson with you. And I want to stress it again. Let me tell you a beautiful story.

"A highly successful businesswoman decides that it is time to retire. She sells her impressive penthouse in the big city and buys a beautiful property in a little village in the magnificent countryside, surrounded by mountains and lakes. The people in the village are happy with her arrival. She is a wonderful lady and quickly proves herself to be a contributor of joy and happiness to the small community. But not everybody is pleased with her. Her neighbor does not like her. He is very jealous of her wealth and her joyous personality. Soon after she settles in the village, he starts to spoil her life. At night, he enters her large garden and messes up parts of it, making it look like animals did it. To other villagers, he starts to gossip about her, trying to make them believe what a nasty person she is. But nothing changes. The lady remains upbeat and a much-appreciated new arrival in the village. Out of desperation, the neighbor one day collects nasty-smelling trash in a large bucket, climbs over the fence at night, and throws it in front of the house of the lady. In his haste, he forgets to take back the bucket. At dawn, after waking up, the lady spots the dirty sight, and she knows what must have happened. She goes outside after breakfast, cleans the mess diligently, and takes the bucket inside. Her husband asks her, 'What now? What will you do?' She tells him that she will go see the neighbor. She goes with the bucket and rings the bell. When the neighbor looks from behind his curtains, he smiles. *Finally, the lady must have gotten upset.* Feeling pleased with himself, he walks to the front door and opens it. The lady looks at him with a kind face and says, 'I have come to return your bucket,' and she hands it over to him. The bucket is filled with nice-looking apples. The neighbor is surprised. 'What is this?' She answers, 'This is a gift for you.' 'But why?' the neighbor says. 'Well,' says the lady, 'we all gift each other what we have. You left a gift for me last night. That is all right. It is what *you* have got to give. I must return your favor, and I gift you what *I* have got.'

"Here is the lesson, Dax: we all share with the world what we are. We cannot give what we don't have. If you can only give what you have inside, you better make sure that you build a beautiful inner world. That way, you are able to give beauty to the world around you.

"Life's journey always starts with you. It is wise to develop a positive, loving, joyful, truthful, caring, focused, determined, stable, confident inside. When you have grown, the time comes to direct your focus to the world around you. You are ready to make the best possible contributions to others. As you give to others, you are also giving to yourself. As you give value to others, you are growing your inside further. There is such great joy in giving. I have met many people whose sole purpose is contribution to others. You know what they are telling me? They say that the people they help are usually happy and grateful. But they also say that they themselves are the biggest beneficiaries. There truly is much joy in giving. Also for yourself. You are creating experiences that feel good. You are living a life of meaning and service. You are enriching your inner world. And you are gathering a lot of the *stuff* that you can take with you when you die. Beautiful experiences, loving encounters, joyful emotions."

"I think I am getting it, Rama. Let me summarize to check whether my understanding is right. First, I have to manage myself. To build value inside. Then, the best thing to do is to give my value to the world. To contribute to others. Not only will this make my daily experience of life better; it will also help me to grow a beautiful and positive inside, which is, like Buddha said, the truly important thing in life."

"Fantastic summary, Dax!"

"Thank you, Rama. Am I correct to think that everybody has a personal purpose? And that your biggest value to others results from living your unique purpose and passion?"

"Absolutely! We are all unique individuals. We all have our unique talents. We all have our personal preferences and passions. We all have unique skills and traits to give that can be beneficial for others. When you find your purpose and passion, you have found the source for the biggest value contribution you can make to the world. Don't live according to the FARCE script. Live according to your own inner compass.

"There is one more thing that I would like to clarify about making contributions. This is not only about the big gifts, like solving world hunger or finding a cure for a severe illness. It is about the contributions we are making at every moment of our lives. When you meet a beggar on the street, are you giving out kindness or contempt? When you are performing a low-paying job, are you taking pride in delivering the best possible outcome, or are you bored, uninterested, and cutting corners? When you comment on events in the world, are you focusing on the positive or are you engrossed in the negative? Every moment, you can choose to contribute something good to the world. It is your choice. Nobody can take that away from you. But you will have to overcome your robot mind if you want to consciously contribute. Your collected software is usually no guarantee for giving your best.

"Contribution, Dax. *That* is the final goal for life. Connect with your promise, find your purpose and passion, write it down in your mission statement, and go out to share and to give. That is how you can make the biggest contribution to the world."

"Wow, Rama, you have answered my second question in an elaborate and unexpected way. Once more, you have given my mind a lot of inspiring food for thought. I now understand that my whole inner development journey is not about me. It is meant to set me up to be able to give my best to others. Thinking about doing that makes me feel good, instantaneously. The human trinity at work," I said cheerfully.

"Good we covered your second question. Up to you now to do your homework on finalizing your life's mission and to get ready to make your biggest contributions! I look forward to hearing the result. You said you had four topics you wanted to cover?"

"I did. And this is a good bridge to my last two questions. I have to admit that I have felt anxious lately. Anxious because I had this feeling that this amazing journey from being a robot to being free will soon be coming to an end. I have learned so much. Or should I say, with reference to Malcolm Chan, I have unlearned so much? My question is this: is my learning from you and your inspiring friends coming to a close here? I feel sad thinking about this. Also, I have come to the conclusion in my mind that it is time for some significant changes in my life. It is time to jump. To live according to my promise. I sincerely believe I have built a stable and confident inner foundation that will help me to find the courage and the persistence to change. Still, the prospect of making a big shift in my life triggers concern and doubt in my mind. Can I do it? How to make it work? What if I don't succeed? These types of questions are troubling my mind, Rama. I would love to hear your perspective on my uneasy thoughts."

Rama had been listening with an ever-calm, loving, and reassuring expression on his face. Already I felt better, without him saying a word. I had come to learn that just the presence of a guru could make you feel lighter and more positive. The word *guru* originates from the ancient language Sanskrit. The word means "dispeller of darkness," or in other words, a guru brings light. Light that we sometimes need in the uncertain moments of our lives. My life in no way was dark. To the contrary, my life had been good and had only gotten better under the wisdom guidance of my guru. But it did not mean that there were no dark moments in my mind. The negative wolf from the Native American story did sometimes show up and brought the kind of apprehension that I was feeling. I knew Rama would be able to show me the light, and I felt grateful to be in touch with him.

"Dax, my friend. It is very good you are allowing your thoughts of concern. And it is even better you openly share them with others. We have a robotic tendency to resist disturbing thoughts. We don't want to connect with our dark thoughts, and we pretend they are not there. That is *not* how you remove your thoughts of fear and apprehension. Imagine a room that has been dark for many years. Curtains and shutters have been down all that time. The door has not been opened. How long does it take to bring the light?"

Funny, I thought. *I was just thinking about the meaning of the word guru, and now Rama is talking about a dark room and bringing some light.* I answered, "I guess if you open the curtains and lift the shutters or flip the light switch, you can bring instant light."

"Correct, Dax. And the same applies to darkness in our mind. When we bring a perspective of light, we can remove the burden of negative thought in the moment. It is wise to always realize that your thoughts create your reality. You have learned this lesson, and you are experiencing this truth every day. So when you choose thoughts of light, your reality will change immediately. Thoughts of light are thoughts that make you feel good. They give hope and inspiration. Can you follow?"

Yes I could.

"You are asking whether your learning journey is over? I have a simple answer for you: life never stops teaching. Mastery has no finish line! So if you want to stay young, if you want to stay up to date, you better never stop learning. The whole purpose of your journey has been to make you aware of your robot mind. If you would have asked me the same question when we first met, I might have said yes to your question. An unaware and automated mind does not learn anymore. It thinks it knows it all. It is closed for growth and development. When you open your mind and create space, you will become curious and humble again. You will find that there are teachers all around. And you will taste the joy of lifelong learning and growing. Learning should commence at birth and cease only at death. Mahatma Gandhi left us with a wise piece of advice, 'Live as if you would die tomorrow and learn as if you will live forever!' That says it all. Your learning journey is not over at all! You are pretty much only starting." Rama was laughing out loud as he said that. "Happy?"

I was smiling. "Yes, I am very happy with that, Rama. And how do I find all these teachers?"

"By just keeping your eyes and other senses open! Learn from dogs how to always be happy. Learn from the sun about selfless giving. Learn from the tree about growing roots. Learn from children how to forgive. Learn from the cockroach how to be resilient. Have a willingness to learn, be in touch with your surroundings, and you will find lessons everywhere. You think you can do that?"

"I think I can!" I responded. "Your light reminds me of a recent walk in the forest that Jane and I took. We saw an anthill and decided to observe the ants from a distance for a while. Ants work tenaciously, and they work well together. I did not see the ants as my teachers when we were there. But with a learning perspective, I can see that we can learn from them about persistence, discipline, and teamwork. I like it."

"Good example! Believe me, if you watch with awareness, you will find that you can learn from everybody and everything. In view of time though, let's talk about your fear of the big changes you are considering for your life. Masters tell us that we are born with only two fears: the fear of falling from heights and the fear of loud noises. All other fears are self-created by our mind. The robot mind is full of fear. Fear of rejection, fear of failure, fear of public speaking, fear of doing something new. There is a long list of man-created fears that occupy and burden our mind every day. Fears have a negative impact on our life. They keep us small. They keep us in our comfort zone. They keep us from living our promise. They keep us from following our purpose and passion. Fears are not real. They are an illusion of the mind. There are only two things you can do with your fears. You can allow your fear to paralyze you and not make a move. Or you can feel your fear and take action anyway. This requires courage. It requires you to follow your heart and to go beyond your doubting and fearful mind. If you want to live life to the max, Dax, you *will* have to face your fears. It is good to be aware that there is light behind the fear. Your best life lies outside of your comfort zone. And there is more light: only if you close a door, there is space for others to open. In other words, closing a chapter in your life is not the end. It is the beginning of a whole new and exciting chapter."

"Rama, do you mean to say that I will never find my best life if I leave the door closed?"

"That is exactly what I am saying. If you know that you are not living your dharma, the only way to live up to your unique promise is to close the current door and open a whole raft of new doors. *You* will have to do it. We all have responsibility for our *own* life. It is up to you to find the courage and to jump. Look at it this way: which regret do you think is bigger when you look back on your life, regret about the things you have done or regret about the things you wanted to do but you didn't?"

"It must be the latter."

"Yes, it is. The master's way of living is to juice out life. To live in such a way that when it is time to say farewell, you know in your heart that you have given your life your all. To have no regrets. To empty your pockets. To be good to go when your time has come."

"You leave me no choice, Rama."

"You always have a choice, my friend. I told you long ago that your power to choose can never be taken away from you. I give you inspiration. I give you light. But ultimately, it is always *your* choice. You can choose passively and make no choice. That is the option most people robotically apply. Or you can choose actively and make deliberate choices for your life. The way of wisdom. It is always up to you!"

"But what if I don't succeed?"

"What is success? When the robot thinks about success, it only thinks about material success. Wealth is great, don't misunderstand me. But what are material riches without happiness and joy? It is wise to get the order right. Happiness first, and the rest will follow. If you trod the path of your purpose and passion, you will give your biggest value to the world. Your contribution to others brings you joy. The value others experience from your giving brings you happiness. And there is more. The universal law of karma tells us that what you give is what you will get. When you give value, you will get value back. When you give your best value, you will get the best value back. Don't allow yourself to be misguided by your fearful mind, Dax. Truly successful people do what they love. They are happy and joyful. And they create abundance in their lives. That is your destiny when you follow your heart. Your role is to do your very best. There are so many other factors that influence the results you will get. Do not worry about these. The advice I would like to give you is do your best and leave the rest. The universe is a benevolent place. It will reward you for the contributions you are making."

Rama looked at his watch. I looked at Rama. It is said that deep down we all know why we are here. But we forget because we allow the robot to take over. We cannot see our truth because it is hidden behind all the wrong ideas that we gather over a lifetime. It is hidden in the dark. I knew by now that wisdom was the light required to reconnect with our uniqueness and our personal dharma. Rama had lit a number of candles in my mind again. I knew that this light would help make my life bigger, better, brighter, and braver.

"Thank you, Rama. You have helped me to see clearer again. It is up to me now. Time to make some real choices. Choices that will allow me to be the best I can be."

"Yes, Dax. Live your life based on *your* choices, not the choices of your robotic mind. You are ready. I know it. Life's purpose is contribution, my friend. Time to step up your life and offer the world the best value that you can give."

Rama looked at me in a calm and loving manner. I looked at him. I felt good. I felt ready.

"Let us stop here for today, Dax. But not before I give you your first detective assignment."

"My what?"

"Your robot detective assignment. You frequently meet beggars in Houston, right?"

"Yes, I do."

"Here is your task. Have a real conversation with one of them. Listen to the person. Ask the person questions and learn about his or her mindset. Detect what might be the robotic, blocking thoughts that keep the beggar's life small. Find out what stops the person from living the best life possible. I would love to hear your findings. OK?"

"OK, Rama. I think I already know who I will connect with. Yes, I am ready to do this."

"Great, Dax. Time for me to go play now with the children of one of the local orphanages. I go there every week. Being with these kids is magical. The world thinks that I am doing these children a favor with my voluntary contribution. I see it differently. These kids are doing *me* a favor by showing me their shining true selves every time we meet. I am looking forward to it. Curious to learn what this afternoon will bring."

"Enjoy, Rama, and thank you for your wise inspiration."

"Oh yes, Dax—before I forget. Are you up for climbing Blackcomb Mountain in the Canadian Rockies with me three months from now? Think about it and drop me a note! Got to go now. Bye!"

Rama left our meeting, and I was on my own. *Detective assignment? Mountain climbing? What a way to end a great conversation!*

Contribution—Learning Box

Wisdom	I am getting rid of the unhelpful beliefs and convictions in my mind, and I replace them with empowering wisdom ideas. Through mind training, step by step, I am creating an invincible wisdom script in my subconscious mind. I need to find my own unique direction and purpose for my life (not somebody else's). I am here to contribute. When I find my purpose and passion, I have found the source for the biggest value I can contribute to the world. I know that my best life lies outside of my comfort zone. I do my best, and I leave the rest.
Awareness	Wisdom works for you if you work wisdom. You *can* change your mind. It takes consistent and persistent mind-training action over a period of time. You *can* superimpose a new way of thinking. Make sure you invest in your inner world. Do not only invest in external stuff. The quest for clarity in your life is only about the what. Do not confuse your what with uncertainty or doubts about the how. Once you start walking into the direction of your dreams, you do not know the exact path. That is perfectly fine. You will find your path when you start walking. You take nothing from this life except what you have on the inside. Life starts with you, but life does not end with you. Ultimately, life's purpose is contribution. Life never stops teaching. If you want to stay up to date, you better never stop learning. If you want to live life to the max, you *will* have to face your fears.

Story/ Tool	Alexander the Great's funeral procession. The lady and the bucket of apples.
Practice	Describe the *what* for your life in one sentence. Whenever you feel in darkness, bring light (maybe via a guru or a coach).

12

The Human (Freedom)

Kill the Cow (or Bear)

Is freedom anything else than the right
to live as we wish? Nothing else.
—Epictetus

Life without liberty is like a body without spirit.
—Kahlil Gibran

"Life's purpose is contribution." Rama had reminded me of this important lesson. Upon reflection the days after, I realized that I had known this all along. I also recognized that the truths about life, that we all intuitively know, can get hidden underneath our acquired robotic thoughts. Before Rama had become my guru, mentor, and coach, I had been learning from other masters of life. And I had continued doing so. True masters not only impact the world during their lifetime; their wisdom legacy extends well beyond their living years. Although most of my teachers were deceased, they were still very much alive. The eternal guidance they had left behind in spoken and written words would always retain its power to inspire. True masters all spoke one truth. They would tune their message to the time and circumstances of their presence. Ultimately, their teachings were all one and the same. None of them would ever claim to be the inventor of the wisdom they were sharing. The true master would humbly explain that she was just a divine channel for sharing the universal truth. I always found that the message of one master resonated with the messages of other masters.

I had felt the resonance when Rama had pointed out that contribution is the true purpose of life. It made me remember the words of a wise swami from India: "When you master yourself, you come to understand that you are here to serve and benefit others." Swami had explained that no matter who we are in our lives, we are all still human. "Behave like a human, which ensures you don't forget other people," swami had said. And, "Your humanness will keep you from building a wall between yourself and others." Without a wall, contribution to others is only natural. I intended to make contribution part of my mission for life.

Jane was laughing when I told her about my detective assignment and the casual mountain climb invite. "Sounds like Rama thinks you are ready to be tested," she commented. "The climbing is a good surprise. Always be a yes-man, Dax!" After a few days, I sent Rama the following message.

> Dear Rama,
> I would love to climb Blackcomb Mountain with you.
> Thank you for the invite.
> I look forward to hearing more!
> Sending you my love and gratitude,
> Dax
> By the way, am preparing for my detective job!

On a Saturday morning, I paid a visit to Tony at his regular street spot. He was the first person who came to mind when Rama had given me my detective assignment. Jane and I had met Tony many times, and we had had the occasional friendly chat. Never though had I taken the time and made the effort to hear and inquire about his life story. I realized I should have done it before, but finally now I would show some real human interest. I brought us Starbucks coffees. Tony was eager to share. His life story came out as a well-rehearsed script. Given up by his young, single mum. Grown up with foster parents and in children's homes. Never felt any love from anybody—except from one kind, elderly gentlemen who had been his guardian angel since Tony was eight until the man passed away six years ago. Surprisingly good-performing student at schools. University honors degree. Independent. Focus on earning money to be in control. Had been very successful. Made millions and spent big. Had been in touch with crime but was never tempted to join. Teenage love of his life, or so he had thought. Never married but were together for twenty years. Then she had left him, taking all his money. Had to leave his home. Broke. Living on the streets now for the past four years. Only one friend left in life, his dog.

"Life sucks, Dax," Tony said. "Can't trust anybody. Especially not this b*tch that took all I had. People only care for themselves. That's why I love dogs. Always loving and trustworthy. All these so-called caretakers who were supposed to raise and support ..." Tony sighed. "They have ruined my life. No idea why I am here. Nothing left for me ..."

I did not have to do much inquiry. Tony shared his whole story in great detail. He spoke his mind. I felt empathy for him. And my mind detective was at work. I recognized many robotic thinking patterns that, I knew by now, had not been of service to Tony's life. As you think, so your life shall be. I could see the reconciliation between Tony's mindset and his life. Tony thanked me for listening to him. "It is nice when people show some human heart toward me, Dax. I have always tried to do the same."

I really wanted to help this man, but I had no idea where to start. "Thank you, Tony. We'll keep in touch," was all that I could bring out at the end of our two-hour conversation.

I shared my spiritual detective observations with Rama in an email the day after.

Dear Rama,

I took action on the assignment you gave me. Yesterday, I met Tony for two hours.

Here are my detective findings:

1. I clearly saw the ancient wisdom "as you think, so your life shall be" at work. Tony told me that the only man he ever trusted said to him when he was eight, "If you grow up like you did, Tony, the rest of your life is screwed." Tony has turned this into the leading belief for his life. He said to me, pointing at his life on the street, "This is what happens when you have a childhood like mine."

2. Tony blames the whole world for his situation: his mum, the government agencies, the people where he lived, his former girlfriend. He feels like a victim. He finds it difficult to take responsibility for his own life.

3. At a young age, Tony decided to have money as his leading indicator for his life. He hated pretty much every day of his professional life. It brought him a lot of wealth, but it did not bring him joy and contentment. Not living his promise. No purpose, no passion. The lack of passion and the constant struggle have given him many physical problems.

4. At a certain moment, Tony thought he had found happiness based on his material wealth, his relationship with his girlfriend, and his dog. When two of these external pillars disappeared, he fell into a dark hole. Now that he can no longer take care of his dog, his happiness based on externals is totally gone. He has no inner foundation to be happy and resilient.

There is more, Rama, but these are my four key observations.

I found so much resonance with all your lessons. That is great, but at the same time I feel bad for Tony. I really want to help this man. But to be honest, I do not know where to start because he is totally stuck in his own ways.

Sending you my love and gratitude,
Dax

For my own life, it was time to create full clarity on my dharma. No more doubts. No more questions from the robot. I knew the clear purpose was available but not in my robot mind. My mind was getting less automated, but there were still trails of old habitual thoughts. Beliefs and ideas that would argue with my heart's longing. I knew that if I wanted clarity on my unique purpose, I had to go beyond my rational mind. To the place of silence where things get clear. The only way to get there is through meditation. I resolved to sit down to meditate for thirty minutes every day. And I did something else. I decided to apply the age-old wisdom of "seek and ye shall find." I consciously kept my mind and senses open for any universal guidance that might appear in my life. It is said that if the universe knocks three times on your door, you better open it. I believe, in the weeks after, I received three guiding messages from the universe to support my pursuit for clarity.

The first message came after a big celebration in the office, during which I once more acted as the master of ceremony. Many people gave me as feedback: "Dax, you have an amazing talent to inspire people. Your selfless ways and your stories simply touch us. You should do more of this!"

Inspire people? Yes, that is what I love to do! I thought.

The second message arrived in the form of Rama's brief response to my mail:

> Well done, Dax. You are a great spiritual detective!
> If only the world would learn about the power of the
> mind, the power of taking responsibility, and the power
> of living with wisdom. Where to start with Tony or
> with anybody? Change starts for everybody with a
> true willingness to change. Only if Tony truly has had
> enough, he will become receptive for the guidance
> toward a better life. Much love, Rama

The thought of helping people to live their best life gave me goose bumps and lots of energy.

The third message was one for Jane and me together. We were pregnant! Our dream was coming true. We knew we wanted to be the best parents we could be to our child. To inspire our child in the spirit of Gandhi's famous *be the change you wish to see* lesson—my favorite line for leadership in both my professional and my personal life. If I wanted to lead by example as a future dad, I had to make sure I was true to my dharma.

It all started making sense. The universe was helping. Also, my daily silent meditation was effective. I had not landed my clarity fully yet, but it was coming together, and whatever it exactly was, it felt good. I was certain I would be ready to share with Rama during the upcoming mountain climb.

Rama, in the meantime, had advised me of the exact dates and location for the trip. It would be starting in Whistler, a little town in British Columbia, Canada, not too far away from the beautiful city of Vancouver. On the web, I found that the place is surrounded by stunning nature and attracts many tourists throughout the year. We would be there in summertime. I had started my preparation for the trip. This included some physical exercise and sorting out the clothing I would need. Some gear I would have to rent while there. I had also made my travel arrangements. A direct flight from Houston would take me to Vancouver. From there, I would drive a rental car to Whistler. My excitement about the trip was growing.

With two weeks to go, I received a message from Rama.

Dear Dax,
Ready to climb Blackcomb Mountain?
We will not climb alone! My good friend Sydney will
be our guide.
I am sure she is also very interested to hear your one-
line life mission.
Trust it is all coming together.
See you soon.
With love,
Rama

That answered the question that had been going through my mind: was Rama also a mountain guide? No, he was not. He also knew when to benefit from a coach or guide. And I was not surprised he had a good friend in Canada who would shepherd us on this trip.

The day of my flight to Vancouver arrived. Jane took me to the airport, where she wished me a wonderful trip. She gave me a big hug and whispered in my ear, "Enjoy, Dax. This could well be the trip of a lifetime for you. Not only will you climb the mountain and be surrounded by the most beautiful nature; it could also be the start for the next chapters of your life. Say hi from me to Rama and have fun!"

The flight was smooth. The rental car was ready, and by four in the afternoon, I arrived at the charming lodge in Whistler that Rama had reserved for us. The three of us were scheduled to meet for dinner that evening.

After check-in, I used the rest of the afternoon for a stroll through charming Whistler, a beautiful holiday village with tourist accommodations, restaurants, outdoor stores, and souvenir shops everywhere. It was quiet. Winter, when the population grows from around ten thousand in summer to forty thousand people, is the main season for this little town. The sun was shining. Mountain ranges were visible all around. I saw an eagle flying high up in the air. "Magical," I murmured to myself. And I wondered which of the many mountains was Blackcomb. At 6:15 p.m., I was back at our lodge, well in time to freshen up for dinner at 7:00 p.m.

I walked into the restaurant exactly on time. It was not hard to find my company. The place was small, and Rama was cheerfully chatting with a lady at one of the tables. When he spotted me, he got up, walked over, and gave me a big hug. "Dax, so nice to meet again in person. Welcome to Whistler! Isn't this a great place?" Without waiting for my response, he continued, "Let me introduce you to my dear friend Sydney." The lady had also gotten up and was smiling at the sight of our friendly embrace.

"Hi. I am Sydney."

I looked at her. She was not too tall or muscular but made an energetic impression. She was shining and had the kindest expression on her face. Casually dressed, she radiated joy and happiness. "Hi, Sydney. I am Dax. So nice to meet you, and thank you for taking us up the mountain this week!"

Rama gestured for us to sit down at our table. He said, "I am hungry. It has been a long day for me. Some food will give me energy and also a good base for a proper night of sleep." We ordered food and drinks, and we entered into a most entertaining conversation.

Sydney was a local from Vancouver. She was the CEO of the Canadian branch of an international energy company. I learned that her biggest passion in her corporate role was to inspire her people to bring out their best and to build winning teams. Her biggest passion in life was the mountains. She was outdoors in the Canadian Rockies whenever she had time available. And she was a trained and seasoned mountain guide who loved to show other people the beauty of nature. So, yes, she was very much looking forward to taking Rama and me up Blackcomb Mountain. I asked Sydney my standard question whenever I met one of Rama's friends: "Where did you meet each other and when?" I learned that the two of them had known each other for more than twenty years. After her love for mountaineering had bloomed, it had become Sydney's dream to visit the Himalayas, the roof of the world.

"I made the trip, Dax, in my early thirties. We were in India, China, Nepal, Bhutan. We walked various areas of the magnificent Himalayas. We visited a number of cities, including Srinagar in the north of India. The Srinagar city program contained a lecture with the topic 'Living at the Top of Your World.' I thought it was about the life of hermits living in the Himalayas, and I was intrigued, so I went. But it wasn't. It was Rama who inspired us to live up to our promise, the only way to be at the top of our world. I fell in love with the wisdom inspiration he shared there and then. We have been in touch ever since, and frequently we have talked about climbing a mountain together. It will finally happen this week." Sydney looked lovingly at Rama. "I am so happy you are here, Rama. And, Dax, great you are joining us. You are both up for a beautiful journey! But now it is time to discuss our next two days!" She suddenly changed the topic and put the focus on our upcoming tour.

"Tomorrow we will embark on our trip. We will take two days to climb up to Blackcomb peak. This allows us to take sufficient rest and to adjust to the altitude. Also, we have plenty of time to enjoy the magnificent views that are going to be available to us. We are guests of one of the most beautiful places in the world, if you ask me." She smiled. "After breakfast tomorrow morning, we will go get our climbing gear and food supplies in the village. We want to be well prepared. We will enjoy a carb-rich lunch here in Whistler, and then we will make the first part of our journey. Day-one destination is a lovely lodge at just over six thousand feet. We don't need our climbing gear tomorrow. We can walk up. There are nice walking trails. The challenge will be the four-thousand-foot height difference that we will need to cover. And the occasional black bear of course that we might encounter." Sydney was laughing.

"Black bears?" I asked.

"Yeah. What do you think, Dax? We will be in the wild. This is bear country. But don't worry. Just read the instruction manual in your hotel room, and you will know exactly what to do when you find a bear on your way." She looked at me and then casually continued,

251

"We will have a great dinner at the lodge, and we will spend the night there. On day two, we need to climb another elevation change of two thousand feet to reach the top of Blackcomb. This will be a very different journey, as we are going to traverse the Blackcomb glacier on the way up and make our final ascent via the steep west side of the mountain. We will leave at 8:15 a.m., and we will definitely need our climbing gear. When we reach the top, we will spend a good amount of time to admire the stunning views and to hear your story, Dax!" She looked at me in a playful manner. "We will descend via the other side of Blackcomb to get back to our lodge for a well-deserved lunch. Then we will continue to move down to arrive back in Whistler in the afternoon. Questions?"

I shook my head. Rama radiated enthusiasm, like a young child ready to explore. "No questions, Sydney. I can't wait. Finally we will be hiking in the mountains together. Do you know you are a great guide? You direct us based on your own experience, leading by example. And you are very clear in laying out the path that Dax and I, as your students, should walk in order to succeed. These are the two characteristics of a great mentor and coach. I know the two days are going to be spectacular!"

We had finished our delicious desserts, and it was time to retire to our rooms for a good night of sleep. Sydney gave Rama a big hug. Then she looked at me as if to ask, "You want one?" I opened my arms to receive a wonderful embrace.

"See you tomorrow morning at breakfast," we said almost simultaneously, and we retreated to our lodge rooms.

It had been a good evening. I felt full of joy and anticipation, but something was roaming my mind: black bears. When I was back in my room, I searched for the bear instruction manual that Sydney had mentioned. I found it. It said: "Make noise as you walk. Bears often leave an area when they are aware of human presence. When you still encounter a bear in the wild, do not approach the bear. Do not run away. Do not provoke the bear. Stay calm. When the bear approaches, make yourself as big as possible, for example by stretching your arms while holding your backpack. The bear might walk away. However, if the bear attacks, lie down on your stomach and protect your head." I was taking in the guidance and imagining the situation as described. "A bear on my back? And then what?" Fortunately, the manual also knew how to deal with this unfortunate situation: "When the bear is still on your back after fifteen minutes, consider fighting back!" And that was it. I started to laugh. "Consider fighting back?" My imagination ran wild. I saw myself turning around, looking at the bear, and telling him, "You have been on my back too long. Now you will have it!" Then I would wrestle the bear down, and the animal would decide to run away. At a sufficient distance, the bear would turn and shout, "Sorry!" I found the instruction so hilarious that I decided to send a picture of it to Jane just to make sure she also knew how to deal with a bear in case she encountered one in downtown Houston. I brushed my teeth and went to bed with a big smile on my face.

We all arrived at our breakfast table well rested, full of energy, and ready for the adventure. As per the guidance of Sydney, we spent the morning getting our rental climbing equipment to walk the glacier. Crampons, which are steel spikes to protect us from slipping. Climbing helmets. Ropes, harnesses, and crevasse rescue equipment to protect against crevasse falls. I bought myself a new pair of semiprofessional hiking boots. Sydney had seen my old boots and suggested that I needed firmer support for my ankles in the terrain we were going to be in. She helped me to choose the new shoes. Also based on her advice, Rama and I both got ourselves some warm underwear, a Gore-Tex Whistler jacket, and professional hand protection. She was determined to keep us warm and safe. Finally we bought nutrition supplies at the local grocery. Rama and I did not need to think. We acted in line with the professional guidance of our coach, Sydney. Rama said, "If you have the right coach, trust her to give you the right advice, and just follow her!" And so we did. It was time for lunch, and we decided on a delicious, nourishing, and energizing pasta. We were all set to go!

When we started our walk, Sydney turned to me and said, "Dax, as we embark on our journey to the top of the mountain, there is a story I would like to tell you. Rama told me you love stories!"

I looked at Rama, who was nodding his head. "I'd love to hear the story, Sydney," I responded.

"All right, here it goes.

"A man had recently moved to a beautiful little village close to the foot of an impressive mountain. From his bedroom window, he saw the mountain every day. The man had started wondering how the climb would be and what it would look like at the top of the mountain. It became his dream to climb up to the top. One day, he set out to go up the mountain. He walked to its foot and met the first traveler who had just been at the top. The man asked, 'How has your journey been, and what is the view at the top?' The traveler shared his journey and his experience at the peak. The man listened and considered that such a journey would be too exhausting for him. He found a second traveler who had just come down from the mountain and asked her, 'How has your journey been, and what is the view at the top?' The traveler talked about a different path to climb and gave her perspective on the view. With this information, the man started wondering about the route to take, so he did not yet embark on his journey. He found twenty-five more recent travelers and asked each one of them, 'How has your journey been, and what is the view at the top?' All of them shared their travel experience and what they had seen at the top. At the end of the day, the man made up his mind. *Now that all these people have shared their path with me and also what they saw at the top, I don't need to climb anymore.* And he went home without ascending the mountain."

Sydney became silent. She looked at Rama, who said, "You still remember that story that I told in Srinagar after all these years?"

She nodded. "Yes, I do, Rama. I pretty much remember everything you shared about being at the top of my world that day."

She then addressed me. "You see, Dax, we all have been given this precious gift called life. We all have the possibility to reach the top of the mountain that we choose to climb. Metaphorically speaking. In other words, we all have the potential to live the life that we want and be the best that we can be. But it is *your* journey. *You* will have to walk it. You can certainly benefit from the information and experience of others. But if you don't make your own journey, you will never reach *your* top. Any idea what it takes to get there?"

I had a vague idea, but I shook my head. I wanted to hear more from Sydney.

"*You* have to choose the mountain you want to climb. Not your parents. Not your family and friends. Not your teachers and coaches. It is your life, so it must be *your* mountain. Then, *you* will have to make the journey. It will come with risks. It will come with challenges. It will come with tests. *You* will have to be determined. *You* will have to persevere. *You* will have to learn and grow and change if the journey is not getting you where you want to be. And when you reach the top, *you* have to take time to admire the view. Take time to celebrate. To be grateful. To look around and keep your mind open. It might give you clarity for the next mountain you want to climb on your journey called life."

"Love it, Sydney. Thanks. You are talking about all people's individual lives, right?" I asked.

"Yes, I am, Dax. I most certainly am. When you live the life of your own choosing, it will be your best life possible. When you travel the journey of your dreams, it will move you to the top of *your* world!"

Rama had also been listening. He was smiling. "Well done, Sydney. Do you also still remember the advice that Buddha gave to one of his students when he was asked how to reach your goals?"

"Absolutely, Rama. It was very early in the morning when Buddha and his student embarked on their journey to climb a mountain. The student got anxious when he saw a huge mountain in the far distance with very steep slopes. 'How?' the student asked his teacher. And Buddha answered, 'Keep your eyes on the destination. Then take one step at the time. Do it happily, keep going, and in time, all things will be accomplished.'"

"I like it," I said. "That is both wise and practical counsel on how to achieve in life."

Sydney smiled at me and continued, "Let's check on whether we are putting Buddha's wise guidance into practice. Are we clear on the destination?" Yes, we were. "Are we taking one step at a time?" Yes, we were. "Are we doing it happily?" I confirmed, and Sydney was quick to add, "Yes, we are, but we can do better. We are going to be silent for the next half hour to enjoy the sensational nature around us with full awareness. No distractions."

"Silent?" I immediately said. "But what about the bears?"

Sydney laughed. "I can hear you have read the bear instruction manual, Dax. Well done. But don't worry. The sound of us walking will still be more than enough to scare away the bears. Also, our peace and quiet will have a calming effect on the animals. They will feel our love for nature and will know that we are not here to hurt them. We are safe. All right, Dax?"

I was cool. How could I not be in the presence of a master and a seasoned mountain guide?

Sydney went back to Buddha's advice. "One more question before our silence: do you think we will accomplish our mission if we are persistent?"

I looked up and could see Blackcomb peak in the far distance. I looked at Sydney and Rama and said, "Definitely, yes. I am sold. Buddha's guidance works!" We started laughing, and then all three of us became silent.

We were walking through a densely populated forest. Pine trees. Cedar trees. Hemlock trees. Next to the well-maintained hiking path we were on, we saw mosses, lichens, and a multitude of smaller plants. Green. Fresh. Energizing. Bears were nowhere to be seen except in my mind. I just *had to* think about them after reading the instruction manual. "Consider fighting back ..." We spotted some other animals. Squirrels and chipmunks playing in the trees. Hares running away in the distance. We saw birds flying high up in the air. *Some of them must be prey birds*, I thought, but I could not make them out. It was warm, though I could feel the air getting cooler as we climbed the mountain. Small, flowing streams carrying melted ice and rainwater kept the mountain well irrigated. Sydney was walking in the front at a casual speed. Occasionally, she stopped to point out a plant or an animal she wanted us to see, without speaking. We were all silently enjoying the beauties of nature. The path swirled through the forest. We were making steady progress.

As we rose up the mountain, the forest became less dense to indicate we were approaching the tree line, the elevation level where trees just can't grow. After half an hour, Sydney suddenly spoke again. "How about that?"

Rama had a blissful smile on his face to indicate his enjoyment. I also felt great. "With full attention, my experience of life always gets so much better," I said. "I am just loving this walk in nature."

"Glad you like it, Dax. When you want to maximize your experience of life, it is good to be truly present. To be here in the now. To not allow distractions that take you to other places. Walking through nature in silence helps to connect with all your senses, which makes your experience more magical," Sydney explained as a true master. "By the way, we will soon leave the forest and move into the rocky mountain terrain. We might see some hoary marmots that gave Whistler its name."

"How so?" I asked.

"Because of the shrill whistle sound these rock-dwelling rodents make. When settlers came and heard it, they started calling this area Whistler."

The mountain terrain soon presented itself. Rougher. With rocks everywhere. Grass vegetation. Wildflowers. Sydney introduced us to the beautiful purply-red fireweed. To the red columbine, a flower thought to resemble birds sitting around a dish. And the tiger lily. Rama was smiling when looking at this lily. I knew it was related to his favorite flower. Sydney also pointed out the various stunning views we now had from the wider area. We took our time to watch nature in its full glory.

After three hours of hiking, we had arrived at the beautifully located lodge for our overnight stay. There were views all around. And Blackcomb peak was towering high up at the back of the building. It was very clear now where we were going to be the next day. But first it was time to take a rest, relax, and celebrate our successful day-one hike. Rama, Sydney and I retreated to our rooms to freshen up. At 5:00 p.m., we gathered at the terrace of our spectacular shelter. We enjoyed the gorgeous location, the infrequent sound of animals, one another's company, and some good drinks and food. At 9:00 p.m., Sydney stood up. She looked at us and said, "Rama and Dax, this was day one of our trip. I trust you have enjoyed it." She smiled. "Time for a good night of sleep. Breakfast at seven because we will start our glacier climb at eight fifteen sharp. Good night, my friends. I am grateful for your company." We ended the day with big hugs.

The two biggest risks when walking in the mountains are changing weather conditions and nutrition shortage. Our expert guide, Sydney, made sure we mitigated both risks in the best way possible. She had checked the weather and made sure that it would be on our side on the day of our climb. At breakfast, she advised us on what food to prepare for the day ahead in addition to the supplies we had brought from Whistler. As we were about to set off, she helped us to pack our climbing gear. At 8:15 a.m. sharp, we started our ascent of Blackcomb peak.

It is said that beauty makes one quiet. With spectacular nature all around, we did not feel like talking. Silently, we walked the trail through the rocky landscape covered with the wide variety of wildflowers. It did not take us long to reach the Blackcomb glacier that we would be traversing on our journey to the top. It was time to put on the rented crampons and climbing helmets. Sydney helped us with our harnesses, and finally she connected the three of us with a rope. "Are you ready?" she asked. Yes, we were. "Let's go then!" Sydney shouted enthusiastically, and she started walking.

Rama followed, and I closed the line of three. The crampons worked. I felt rocksteady walking the glacier ice. Sydney made sure we were safe. She walked slowly with a careful watch on the uneven terrain. Frequently she used the wooden stick she had brought to scan the surface for holes as she was navigating us over the ice. Now and then, she stopped to point out crevasses and to tell us about the history and the formation of the glacier. We were reaching the almost vertical part of the glacier, an impressive ice wall that was shining as it reflected the early-morning sun rays. Sydney had already told us that we would not be traveling this wall. Ice climbing was for another time. Instead, we turned left to leave the glacier and to continue our climb to the peak via the west side of the mountain. When we left the icy terrain, we entered a steep, rock-covered path with a deep fall on both sides. We took off the crampons, and Sydney released us from our harnesses and the rope connection. "Watch your every step," she said to Rama and me. "The climb to the top is an uneven, rocky road. Make sure you put your foot down firmly before you take your next step. Watch my movement and follow me. We still have to cover more than a thousand feet elevation change, so we will take our time. Just like Buddha, we will take one step at the time and make sure we enjoy the ride." She had a big smile on her face.

The climb was strenuous, exciting, and memorable. Rama and I followed Sydney's lead, and we continued our stillness. The surroundings were touching all our senses. There was no urge to speak. We were taking in the experience of a lifetime. It took us an hour, and suddenly we had arrived. We were at Blackcomb peak.

Nature's highlights don't come announced. They happen. Sydney did not have to tell Rama and me that we had reached the top. We knew. Sydney's guidance and our persistence had made us reach the destination of our journey. We felt great. We put our arms in the air and started cheering. On top of the world! Then we became silent again. Present in the now. We were taking in the exhilarating surroundings, and we were feeling the joy flowing through us. We hugged. We celebrated. It was quiet. Peaceful. Bliss.

Sydney and Rama looked at each other, and they were nodding their heads. They turned to me and were watching me with an intense and expecting gaze. I knew what they meant. I had promised to share my life's purpose with Rama and Sydney at the top of Blackcomb. It was time to reveal my dharma. Many thoughts crossed my mind. My wisdom journey under the loving guidance of Rama. My inner search. My much-improved life. My love, Jane. My clarity. And also the story that Sydney had told the day before. If you want to reach the top of your own life, you will have to make the journey yourself. I smiled. I looked at the two of them, and without hesitation, I spoke my purpose. "I want to give the world the power of the mind!"

Rama and Sydney took a moment to take it in. Then they started clapping and yelling. "Fantastic, Dax," Rama said. "This is a big moment. You have discovered your dharma. It is very clear. The one sentence says it all. I am so happy for you. And I know one thing: you *will* give the world the power of the mind. Your life story, your learning, your experience are all the right ingredients to inspire many people toward a life of happiness and success. Congratulations! You have taken the essential step toward reaching the top of *your* world!"

High up in the sky, eagles were flying. Rama pointed them out and said, "Dax, do you remember the eagle that grew up as a duck?"

"I do, Rama. You shared the story many years ago. What about the eagle?"

"Well, my friend, I never told you the end of the story. You want to hear?" I nodded. Rama said, "When the wise old eagle from the high skies reminds the eagle duck that he is an eagle, he does not believe it. He answers: 'What do you mean? I am a duck!' That is how I previously ended. This is how the story continues.

"The wise eagle tries to convince the eagle duck, but whatever she says, she cannot convince him. Then she asks the eagle duck to get out of the water and to stand next to her. When the eagle duck obliges, the wise old eagle says, 'Look in the water and tell me what you see.' The eagle duck looks in the water, looks at the wise old eagle, and looks in the water again. Now the eagle duck starts to believe. The old eagle says, 'You are an eagle. You only just forgot!' Finally, the eagle duck realizes who he is—a mighty eagle destined to roam the skies."

Sydney jumped in. "I love that story, Rama. I still remember when you shared it with me."

"It is indeed a story to remember, Sydney. It applies to all of us. Here is the thing, Dax. You were never born a robot. You were born a human, utterly free, but along your journey, you have forgotten. You accept and adopt the mindset of other people. Step by step, you get programmed according to other people's beliefs, ideas, and convictions about yourself and your life. Much of the software you gather is not in line with your own wishes and dreams for your life. And much of the software does not support you to live your best life. But you are not aware. Most people are not awake. Those who live by their robotic mind are all asleep. They are eagles who believe they are ducks. They are humans who live like robots. They are not free. You have been an eager student of wisdom. You have woken up. If you embrace the lessons you have learned on your journey, you will be transformed from robot to human. You will be the robot who became a human again. Your awareness will expand the territories of your conditioned mind. And your life will grow to your best life possible. Short of regret. Full of celebration."

"The robot who became a human," I mused.

"The human who is on purpose and lives life to the max," Sydney added.

"Yes, Dax. We have reached the top of Blackcomb. Now it is time for you to go and reach the top of your life. As a robot, you will never get there. As a free human, you will. Remember your promise. Follow your passion. Take responsibility. Leverage the power of your mind. Choose your perspective. Believe. Take care of yourself first. Befriend change. Use your time wisely. This way, you are ready to make your most valuable contribution to the world. Go out into the world and fly. Fly high like an eagle. Be the inspiration you are destined to be, Dax. Improve the lives of millions of people!"

We were still at the top of the mountain. I felt good. I couldn't get away from the thought that Rama had planned this trip to the peak as the last part of my learning journey all along. It made things very clear.

You need a destination for your life. If you want to reach it, it is up to you. A guide can help you, but if you want to experience the top, you will have to walk yourself. Along the way, many things will happen. Your mindset defines whether they make you or break you. If you are flexible and if you persist, in time you can reach the goals you have set.

Sydney had also been listening to the wise council of Rama. I could note from her demeanor that she had enjoyed every minute of it, just like me. She looked at her watch. "Gentlemen, it is time to start our descent."

I felt grateful. "Thank you, Rama. Thank you, Sydney. I am ready for the remainder of this mountain journey. And I am ready to reach new heights in the next chapters of my life journey!"

Sydney guided us down from the top via the other side of Blackcomb. Soon we were back in the rocky terrain of Blackcomb, and at 12:45 p.m., we sat down for a well-deserved lunch at the lodge. Just before we embarked on the final stage of our walk, I said, "Rama, you advised me to first get clear on my purpose. On the *what*. You said, 'Do not let your *what* get confused by thinking about the *how*.' The *what* is clear now, and we still have our walk down the mountain back to Whistler. I would love to hear from you *how* I am going to turn my purpose into a reality."

Rama smiled. "Great question, Dax. Great timing." We had paid the bill and started walking again. "Listen, my friend," Rama said as we were entering the forest. "I have a beautiful story to share to answer your question.

"A master is traveling with a student through a large forest. It is time to look for a place to rest. They come to an open area where they spot a little dwelling. They knock on the door, and a man opens it. The master asks, 'Can we spend the night here?' The man welcomes them in his modest home. They meet the family: the wife and five children. They all live in one small area. The man apologizes for their poverty. But the master is grateful, and he asks about the family. They have lived there for ten years. They grow some crop for their livelihood. Sometimes they have some extra produce, which they sell in the nearby village. The only valuable thing they have is their cow. 'A cow?' the master enquires. And the man explains how important the cow is. She gives milk. She helps with chores around the house. She carries crop to the local market. She plays with the children. 'Where is your cow?' the master asks. The man points to the big shed behind their small home. 'We let her have the big space because she is so important for us.' It is time to rest. The man offers them a sleeping place in the big cow barn. 'The only place we have.' The master thanks the family and tells them that he and his student will have to leave early in the morning.

"They wake up and leave before sunrise. Soon after they have left, the master stops and tells his student to wait. The master walks back to the big shed. Suddenly he reappears, running. 'Quick, we need to get out of here as fast as possible,' he tells the student. They run for a while until the master stops. 'What happened, Master? Why did we have to run?' the student asks. 'I will tell you if you promise to never share this with anybody,' the master says. The student promises. The master says, 'I went back to kill the cow.' The student is in shock. 'Leave it,' the master says. 'We will not talk about this anymore.'

"Many years later, the master and the student pass through the same forest. The student remembers, and he suggests to go somewhere else. 'What if the family still lives here?' The master does not pay attention. They reach the area where they stayed before. Instead of the small dwelling, they now see a huge, four-story mansion. The master knocks on the door. A man appears. He looks and says, 'You visited us many years ago, right?' The master says, 'Yes, we did. How have you and the family been?' The man explains that the morning the master left, misfortune struck. Their cow had suddenly died. 'Wow,' says the master. 'What happened next?' The man says that initially he and his wife had been in complete despair. How to live without the cow? But then they realized that somehow they had to find new ways. 'We grew our crop and ate less for a while. We made some extra money from selling the extra crop. Within a year, we had saved enough to rent a little piece of extra land to grow more crop. We went back to our normal food rationing, but still we had more crop to sell. We invested our savings in renting more land. We continued doing so. After four years, we started buying our own land. After five years, we realized a two-story mansion. Since then, we have added two stories that we have been renting out to travelers. We now hire local villagers to work our land. Our children are studying at the best schools.' The man is visibly happy.

"The master congratulates the man. 'Very well done, my friend. I am happy for you. You have made your life bigger, better, and brighter.' Then he takes his student aside and says, 'The cow was keeping this family small. But they did not know. That is why I killed her. Everybody has a cow. It is wise to find out what cow is keeping you from living your best life and then to kill it!'"

I looked at Rama and said jokingly. "Do you think they also have cows in this forest? Or only bears?"

Rama was laughing. "Your cow or your bear. Doesn't matter what we call it, Dax. As long as you find out what is keeping you small in your life. What is keeping you from living your unique promise."

"I get it, Rama. The story makes sense. In my heart, I have been knowing all along what my cow is. Time to kill it. Time to be free. Time to pursue my purpose and passion."

"You bet, Dax. I know you know what your cow is. *You* will have to kill it. I cannot do that for you. That is step one of the how. There is a second step, and Sydney shared it already with you yesterday. Do you remember the wise counsel of Buddha on how to reach your goals?"

"I do, Rama. Buddha said, 'Keep your eyes on your destination, take one step at the time, do it happily, be persistent, and in time, all things will be accomplished.'"

"That's it, Dax. Throughout the ages, masters have given mankind the same advice: live life to the max. It requires that you replace your robotic software with the programming of your own choosing. It requires you to become human again. Then, great things will happen. David Henry Thoreau said it so eloquently: 'If one advances confidently in the direction of his dreams, and endeavors to live the life which he has imagined, he will meet with a success unexpected in common hours.' Material success is available to you. But more importantly, when you live your purpose and passion, you will have inner success. You will be happy, contented, and joyful. Your life will be the best possible experience."

"It sounds like your experience of life, Rama," I said.

"It sure is, Dax. I was a robot. Under the loving guidance of my teachers, I became aware, and I started making my own choices. I had to kill a big cow. What do you think would have happened if I had not quit my CEO role? For sure my life would have developed differently. I would not have created the opportunity to inspire and guide thousands of people toward their best lives. And what do you think would have happened if I had not had the right mindset as I was treading the path of my dharma? We all climb our own mountain step by step, and things do not always work out the way we would like. With the right mindset, you will feel empowered to stay the course, to deal with setbacks, to learn from obstacles, to grow and evolve, so that one day you will reach your top. And from there, you will see the next mountain to climb to make your life go higher and higher. This has been my experience, Dax. And it has been the experience of all the people who have been living up to their true human potential."

We were getting to the forest boundary. I could see Whistler village ahead of us. The trip was almost over. Rama must have caught the thoughts going through my mind because he said, "This trip is almost over. The next chapter of the journey of your life is only to start, Dax. It is up to you to take full control over it. It is time for you to live your unconditioned life. To live in the spirit of your name."

"What do you mean, Rama? What about my name?"

"Well, my friend, your name is a great reminder of how to live your life. Dax actually means leader. Did you know?"

"Really, Rama? No, I did not know."

"Now you know, Dax. You have acquired everything you need to be the *leader* of your own best life. Apply the lessons, become free from the robot mind, and *be* the human you are destined to be!"

The Human (Freedom)—Learning Box

Wisdom	It is *my* life. It is *my* journey. *I* will have to climb the mountain. When I travel the journey of my dreams, I am on my way to reaching the top of *my* world. I remember my promise and purpose. I follow my passion. I take responsibility. I leverage the power of my mind. I choose my perspective. I take care of myself first. I grow an unshakeable belief in myself. I befriend change. I use my time wisely. I contribute my best self to the world.
Awareness	When you master yourself, you come to understand that you are here to serve and benefit others. Your humanness will keep you from building a wall between yourself and others. The best coach leads by the example of his own life and has the ability to give you clear instructions on how to succeed. If you have found the right coach, trust her to give the right advice and follow her guidance. To accomplish anything in your life, keep your eyes on the destination, take one step at the time, do it happily, persevere, and in time, you will succeed. As you live by your robotic mind, you are asleep. You are the eagle who believes he is a duck. Your cow is keeping you small in life. It keeps you from living your best life. Find your cow and kill it.

Story/Tool	The man who wanted to climb the mountain. The cow.
Practice	Meditate; still your mind. Find your cow.

Acknowledgments

My mom and dad, you are my heroes! Thank you for being the loving channel to entertain my life's longing. Thank you for the roots and wings you gave me that have always allowed me to be myself.

My dear Cate, you teach me through your life. Thank you for your ever-existing love, support, and encouragement. You have made me aware of the power of awareness. You have shown me the way through your own search for life's answers. You were the one who found Vikas. I love you.

My guru, mentor, and coach Vikas Malkani. Thank you for your light, love, and guidance toward liberty. You have made wisdom real in my life. You say, "Wisdom wins!" and you have made me see and experience how. I am eternally grateful.

My other masters and teachers: Paramahansa Yogananda, Swami Rama, Osho, Dr. Wayne Dyer, Deepak Chopra, Paulo Coelho, Robin Sharma, Napoleon Hill, Mitch Albom, Abraham-Hicks, J. Donald Walters (Kriyananda), Sogyal Rinpoche, Mahatma Gandhi, Nelson Mandela. Your inspiration has changed my life. I appreciate you tremendously.

My friends at Balboa Press. You have helped me to live my dream of publishing this book. Because of your professionalism, perseverance, and kindness, the dream has become an amazing dream. Thank you for all your advice and support.

My clients and students. Your positive experiences and your thankful feedback show me the power of wisdom inspiration and application every day. Thank you for giving me the opportunity to inspire you to live better and enjoy more.

Life. Thank you for the precious gift of life you gave me. Thank you for just always being yourself. Thank you for being the ever-existing evidence of the wisdom truths. You are my greatest teacher.

About the Author

Anton Broers *was* in a career.

He was a senior leader in multinational oil and gas company, Shell, who lived and worked on three continents in a corporate career spanning twenty-five years.

He *was and is* a student of life. While living in Singapore, he sought a unique teacher and found Vikas Malkani, the number one wisdom coach in the world. Under Vikas's enlightening guidance, Anton started integrating wisdom into his life. It improved and transformed his life. It made him find his dharma, his unique life's purpose. An inner longing to serve and share arose in his heart. It changed his life.

Anton *is* on a mission.

It is his mission to let the world know that *if you train your mind, you can design your life.* It is his pursuit to teach people practical wisdom and tools that allow them to live their best lives.

In 2020, he founded Mind ur Life in the Netherlands, together with his wife, Cate. With Mind ur Life, he trains and coaches people in mind mastery and the power of wisdom and he has reached clients on all continents of the world. Through his company, he offers:

1. Life-changing *individual coaching* for adults, children, leaders, and professionals.

2. Performance and happiness enhancing *corporate training*, both virtual and live.
3. Inspirational and transformational *key notes and presentations*.

This book is one of his childhood dreams come true. It is intended to support his mission and work and to reach and inspire many readers across the world.

If you were to meet Anton and ask him about his favorite word, his answer would be "Joy!" And he would explain, "Life is a gift. We are here to en*joy* our lives. When you develop a mindset of wisdom, you will start to see how."

He would love to work with you to make your life or business more en*joy*able, happy and successful!

To contact Anton for wisdom-inspired training or coaching or speaking arrangements or media appearances, please visit www.mindurlife.com or send him an email at anton@mindurlife.nl.

Printed in the United States
by Baker & Taylor Publisher Services

Printed in the United States
by Baker & Taylor Publisher Services